Thomas F. Torrance
and the Church Fathers

Thomas F. Torrance and the Church Fathers

A Reformed, Evangelical, and Ecumenical
Reconstruction of the Patristic Tradition

JASON ROBERT RADCLIFF

Foreword by
THOMAS A. NOBLE

☙PICKWICK *Publications* · Eugene, Oregon

THOMAS F. TORRANCE AND THE CHURCH FATHERS
A Reformed, Evangelical, and Ecumenical Reconstruction
of the Patristic Tradition

Pickwick Publications
An Imprint of Wipf and Stock Publishers
199 W. 8th Ave., Suite 3
Eugene, OR 97401

www.wipfandstock.com

ISBN 13: 978-1-62564-603-3

Cataloguing-in-Publication Data

Radcliff, Jason Robert.

   A Reformed, evangelical, and ecumenical reconstruction / Jason Robert Radcliff, with a foreword by T. A. Noble

   xx + 228 p. ; 23 cm. Includes bibliographical references and indices.

   ISBN 13: 978-1-62564-603-3

   1. Torrance, Thomas F. (Thomas Forsyth), 1913–2007. 2. Theology, Doctrinal—History—20th century. 3. Fathers of the church. I. Noble, Thomas A. II. Title.

BT40 R122 2014

Manufactured in the U.S.A.   11/04/2014

This book is dedicated to the monks of St. Gregory Palamas Greek Orthodox Monastery in Hayesville, Ohio. Thank you for graciously welcoming a Presbyterian into your midst and introducing me to the lives and teachings of The Fathers.

Contents

Foreword

T. F. Torrance's lectures were exhilarating. In the early seventies, he, as Professor of Christian Dogmatics, and his colleague, John McIntyre, the Professor of Divinity, lectured to the General Theology class, the first-year class for B.D. students at New College, Edinburgh. McIntyre's lectures on theological epistemology were incisive and witty: Torrance's were expansive and exhilarating. That was true, at least for those of us who were already graduates, but B.D. studies had been opened to students without a first degree, and they must have found it daunting! Athanasius and Einstein, the Cappadocians and Polanyi, patristics and nuclear physics all featured in a series of breathtaking lectures on the Apostles' Creed.

At this point, Torrance's main publication was *Theological Science*, a truly stretching examination of theological method, arguing for its scientific status. The case was argued from a deep knowledge of philosophy of science, and although the first-year lectures were on the Creed, method and content were not divorced. Torrance would enter in his teaching gown (as most still did in the seventies) and appeared to lecture extemporaneously, transfixing us with his penetrating gaze over his half-moon spectacles. Questions and discussion were soon provoked, and since the class included graduates from the Faculties of both Arts and Sciences, the conversation was rich and thought-provoking. Discussion bridged the division between what C. P. Snow had called "the two cultures."

Forty years later, the theological world at large is only beginning to appreciate the abiding strength of Torrance's thinking. He was not the kind of fashionable theologian of the day who leapt on the latest bandwagons and sold pop-theology, much of which is now outmoded. His comprehensive grasp of historical theology enabled him to put the current fashions and moods in perspective and to dismiss what he called mere "paper theology." The historical perspective made him aware of the deeper cultural movements. While the now-fashionable word "postmodernity" was not then in common use, Torrance's grasp of the cultural and epistemological implications of Einstein's thought in physics, made him aware that the Newtonian era of the Enlightenment was over. In alliance with the Hungarian chemist and philosopher of science Michael Polanyi, he dismissed the myth that the physical sciences were totally "objective" while theology was merely "subjective."

But it was only after his so-called "retirement" that most of Torrance's major theological works were written, and it is only in the last twenty years that a fuller appreciation of his theology has begun to emerge. Several writers, including Elmer Colyer, Alister McGrath, and Paul Molnar, have written introductions to his thought as a whole, and a series of monographs has appeared on different aspects of his thinking—his links with Polanyi, his doctrine of Christ, his Trinitarian soteriology, his view of *theosis*, and so on. It was also only after his retirement that he wrote most extensively on the Trinitarian theology of The Fathers. In this book, Dr. Jason Radcliff focuses on his patristics, his account of the *Consensus Patrum*. This is most obvious in his major book, *The Trinitarian Faith*, marking the 1600th anniversary of the Council of Constantinople of AD 381.

It was always evident to his students that Torrance's greatest loyalty was to Athanasius. He did in fact have differences with his other two main mentors, Calvin and Barth (although, out of immense respect perhaps, these were not made evident), but it is doubtful whether he had any disagreement at all with Athanasius! The *homoousion* of the Nicene Creed, which Athanasius defended *contra mundum*, was the "lynchpin" of the Christian faith without which the gospel collapsed into incoherence. Irenaeus and Hilary were also to be studied, and (with some reservations) the Cappadocians, but at the heart of the *Consensus Patrum* was the "axis" from Athanasius to Cyril of Alexandria.

Dr. Radcliff places Torrance's enthusiasm for The Fathers in the context of other attempts to recover patristic theology—from Newman and Harnack through Eastern Orthodox scholars to the evangelical theologies of retrieval in the late twentieth century. What distinguishes Torrance, however, from some who abandoned their own evangelical traditions for Orthodoxy or Catholicism, is that he presented a "Reformed, evangelical, and ecumenical reconstruction of the church fathers." The word, "reconstruction," is significant, for Torrance is not merely a historian or patrologist. Some have criticized him for reading his own theology into The Fathers, but Radcliff argues that we have to understand what he is doing. He is not an antiquarian. Rather he takes The Fathers as authoritative thought-partners for today.

That has its dangers of course, and Radcliff accepts that in Torrance's hands Athanasius can begin to sound rather like Barth! But overall,

Torrance's presentation of the *Consensus Patrum* is an enriching one for today's church. For the sake of mission today (and Torrance, as the son of evangelical missionaries, was always concerned with mission), the riches of patristic theology must be mined. In today's multi-cultural world, the foundational work of The Fathers in their multi-cultural world on Christology and Trinity are needed to give an essential foundation to the focus on salvation in the evangelical traditions stemming from the Reformation. The way forward is "towards an evangelical patristic theology" and this book, adding a new and essential dimension to the ongoing study of Torrance's thought, helps us to deepen our understanding of what that should look like.

Thomas A. Noble,
Professor of Theology,
Nazarene Theological Seminary, Kansas City;
Senior Research Fellow,
Nazarene Theological College, Manchester

Acknowledgments

I am profoundly thankful for the support and encouragement of many throughout the process of completing this book and the PhD dissertation which served as its basis. I am exceedingly grateful to my doctoral supervisor at the University of Edinburgh, David Fergusson. His selfless devotion to his students is an inspiration and his gentle, pious, and careful guidance throughout my studies was indispensable. I would also like to thank Donald Fairbairn for offering insight on patristic scholarship via correspondence and George Dragas for introducing me to the theology of T. F. Torrance, through his own exciting Christ-centered approach to the church fathers in his patristics courses. I also thank the many members of the Torrance family for their kindness towards me during my time in Edinburgh completing my doctorate. I am particularly grateful to Robert Walker, David W. Torrance, and David J. Torrance for their friendship and deep insight into Christ and his Gospel. Thanks as well to my PhD examiners, Sara Parvis and Tom Noble for their careful reading of an early version of this book and for helpful feedback in the form of a *viva voce* and subsequent correspondence and also to my editors at Wipf & Stock, Justin Haskill and Robin Parry, for helpful editorial comments and suggestions.

The prayers and encouragement of many have sustained me throughout the process of writing this book. I am thankful for the prayers of my grandparents, Bob and Barbara Radcliff and Nancy and Clifford St Clair, as well as my wider family and friends in America, Scotland, and England, particularly my father, Robert, who read through the whole of this book and offered helpful feedback, my mother, Donna, and my siblings, Corey, Doug, and Megan.

Most of all, I am thankful beyond expression for my wife, Alexandra; her grace, love, support, encouragement, and care has sustained me throughout the process of completing this book in infinite ways. I am particularly grateful for such a beautiful editor and conversation partner on the topic of Torrance, The Fathers, and theology.

Abbreviations

Introduction

Thomas F. Torrance

and the *Consensus Patrum*

[T. F. Torrance is] a theologian who is at the same time Orthodox, Catholic and Reformed because he seeks to build up his theology on the one, historical common ground of all three traditions and because he is prepared at the same time to confess in full modesty and sincerity their historical particularities and fortify himself only with their positive forces. Is this not what ought to be commended today across the boundaries of the Christian traditions when Patriarch and Pope and Reformed theologian have been united in reminding the world about the Gift of God's boundless Love, Grace and Truth in and through Christ and His Church?

George Dion. Dragas, "The Significance for the Church of Professor Torrance's Election As Moderator of the General Assembly of the Church of Scotland," 226.

INTRODUCTION

The twentieth century has seen a movement *ad fontes* of the church fathers[1] unprecedented other than, perhaps, the time of the Reformation itself. Eastern Orthodox and Roman Catholic theologians have always used The Fathers, the Reformers used The Fathers, however there was a large gap during a time of the diverging traditions of liberalism and fundamentalism

---

1. Throughout this book the term "Fathers" is used to denote patristic figures in general, "Greek Fathers" is used to denote patristic figures writing in Greek and "Latin Fathers" is used to denote patristic figures writing in Latin.

when Protestants did not allow the consensual patristic tradition, or the *Consensus Patrum* ("Consensus of The Fathers"),[2] to inform their theology.[3] The Reformation included a "return to the sources" in regards to both the Bible and the church fathers as the Reformers sought to prove that they were in line not only with New Testament Christianity but also the theology of the early church, albeit with an emphasis on the Western Augustinian tradition. The early twentieth century found evangelical[4] Protestants largely

2. See Torrance, *The Christian Frame of Mind*, 5. "Consensus Patrum" is a Latin phrase used by Catholic and Orthodox theologians to denote the consensual patristic tradition. It is not a phrase that Torrance himself uses very often, more regularly using phrases such as "the classical tradition" and "consensus." See Torrance, *Trinitarian Faith*, 2ff. Torrance also refers to "the Athanasius-Cyril axis of classical theology." See Torrance, *Theology in Reconciliation*, 14. The concept of the "Consensus Patrum" is usually traced back to Vincent of Lérins' famous call to hold to "that which has been believed everywhere, always, and by all." See Vincent of Lérins, *Commonitorium, 2.6.* In this book phrases such as "patristic tradition," "patristic consensus," "consensus of The Fathers," and the Latin phrase "Consensus Patrum" will all be used to denote the concept of a consensual patristic tradition.

3. See the following chapter of this book for elaboration upon this claim.

4. The term "evangelical" is used in in a two ways in this book to mean: (1) evangelical in the wide sense of "committed to the Gospel of grace" and (2) conservative evangelical, sometimes in the fundamentalist/legalist sense. In doing so, the usage of the term in this book follows Torrance's own use of it. See e.g. Torrance, "Karl Barth and the Latin Heresy," for both uses in one article. See p. 464, 478 for use #1 and p. 472, 477, 479, 480, 481, 482 for use #2. Torrance's employment of the term in the former sense appears to derive from the traditional use of the term within Protestant circles as denoting the churches arising out of the Protestant Reformation in general (and also, more specifically, delineating them from the liberal churches) but Torrance constructively applies this sense of the term much wider in seeing a greater evangelical tradition extending back through to the patristic era and forward into the contemporary era through Barth (see further chapter 4 of this book). Torrance employs the term positively in this sense. The latter sense of the term is typically coupled with words such as "fundamentalist" or "legalist" and, as such, Torrance appears to be thinking of conservative evangelicals. Typically, Torrance's employment of the term in this sense refers particularly to conservative evangelicals in the Westminster tradition of Calvinism following in the tradition of Charles Hodge and B. B. Warfield. It is difficult to pinpoint exactly whom Torrance had mind in his own time, but generally, this negative use of the term denotes those who use Protestant confessions in a literal and static sense ("fundamentally" and "legalistically") filtering the Gospel through the confessions whereas the positive use of the term refers to those who remain committed to the Gospel of God's gracious self-giving in Christ and read everything else (the Bible, creeds, confessions, etc.,) in light of Christ. Torrance never puts it as such, but it is probably fair to say the positive use of the term refers to conservative evangelicals appreciative of Karl Barth and the negative use of the term refers to those in the evangelical tradition of Torrance's time who were suspicious of Barthian theology during its entrance into the English-speaking world. Cf. Noble, *Tyndale House and Fellowship*, 71–78 and Bebbington, *Evangelicalism in Modern Britain*, 254f. See also Noble's excellent summary of Torrance's relationship to these two traditions within British evangelicalism in Noble, "T. F. Torrance on the Centenary of

ignorant of their patristic heritage on account of, on the one hand, The Fathers being given equal importance to Scripture in medieval Catholicism and, on the other hand, the bypassing of The Fathers in liberal Protestantism. The resulting paucity of knowledge in this regard has meant that many Protestants who later "discover" The Fathers conclude that there is a necessity to convert to Roman Catholicism[5] or Eastern Orthodoxy.[6] Moreover, many of those who have returned to The Fathers but remained Protestant have failed to offer any clearly defined Reformed and evangelical hermeneutic to guide patristic interpretation that allows for a truly evangelical reading that is also historically faithful to The Fathers.[7]

Fr. George Dragas, Professor of Patrology at Holy Cross Greek Orthodox School of Theology, has been known to tell his students the story of his first interaction with his beloved professor, Thomas F. Torrance.[8] When young Fr. George first sat down with "Professor Tom" in his office at New College, Edinburgh, the budding student's eyes were drawn to two items in the scholar's study: An icon of St. Athanasius and a painting of John Calvin. Upon Fr. George's inquiry about the items, Professor Torrance told Fr. George, "*Always follow the example of St. Athanasius.*"[9] When Fr. George asked about the other figure, Torrance responded, "Well, you should read him." This colorful anecdote illustrates Torrance's unique approach to Reformed and patristic theology and, in many ways, encapsulates the essence of this book.

Torrance constructs (or to use his own recurring term, "reconstructs")[10] his patristic consensus around catholic (or ecumenical) themes and figures.[11] Torrance is unique for his time in that as a Protestant, evangelical, and Reformed theologian he uses the church fathers as an authoritative voice speaking within the theological tradition into his own theological system. However, Torrance's uniqueness goes even deeper inasmuch as, being a western Protestant theologian, his patristic reconstruction consists primarily of the Greek Fathers of the Christian East. He provides a fresh

His Birth" 11–17. In this book, as in Torrance, the term is used in both ways and context clarifies which sense is in use.

5. Howard, *Evangelical Is Not Enough.*

6. Gillquist, *Becoming Orthodox.*

7. Perhaps the two most famous: Oden, *The Rebirth of Orthodoxy*; Webber, *Ancient-Future Faith.*

8. See Dragas, "Interview Regarding T. F. Torrance," 32 for written account of this story.

9. According to Dragas, Torrance called Athanasius "*the theologian.*" See ibid.

10. Torrance, *Theology in Reconstruction.*

11. See Torrance, *The Trinitarian Faith* for the full flowering of Torrance's reconstruction. However, it exists throughout all of his published and unpublished material.

voice into the theological conversation of his time by means of his approach to dogmatic and historical theology as a Reformed theologian with strong catholic leanings, intentionally situating himself and his reading within the universal church. Torrance's reading of The Fathers is unique amongst other interpreters because as both evangelical and Reformed, he combines them with theological themes and figures from his own tradition. Torrance has a unique conception of the consensual patristic tradition, which is centered upon Christology and informed by grace, consisting of primarily Athanasius and Cyril of Alexandria, along with figures such as Irenaeus of Lyons, Didymus the Blind, Epiphanius of Salamis, John Calvin, Karl Barth, and H. R. Mackintosh. For Torrance this *Consensus Patrum* is contained within the core message of The Fathers, namely, the Nicene ὁμοούσιον ("one essence") with the Father and the epistemological and soteriological implications therein, which he understands to be best encapsulated by Athanasius and Cyril of Alexandria.

Torrance's patristic consensus is a creative attempt to produce a Reformed and evangelical version of the *Consensus Patrum* which involves significant changes to both the standard interpretations of The Fathers and Torrance's own Reformed and evangelical tradition. The Torrancian *Consensus Patrum* has many constructive achievements that have been overlooked by his contemporaries and later commentators on account of his being evaluated simply as an historian of Christian thought or a Reformed dogmatic theologian. When Torrance is viewed rather as a Reformed and evangelical theologian constructing a uniquely Reformed and evangelical version of the *Consensus Patrum,* as he is in this book, Torrance's many contributions emerge more clearly.

SCOPE OF THE BOOK

This book explores Torrance's version of the *Consensus Patrum*. It traces the patristic scholarship of Torrance and his appropriation of it into his own evangelical and Reformed tradition by means of his construction of the Torrancian patristic consensus. Moreover, this book offers an exploration of where Torrance's project fits within the map of theological and patrological scholarship. The questions this book seeks to answer are: (1) What is the nature of Torrance's patristic scholarship, (2) is his project a successful constructive-theological endeavor, and (3) in what ways should contemporary theological scholarship carry Torrance's project forward?

This book argues that Torrance constructs his *Consensus Patrum* around key theological themes and figures. The primary theme is the Nicene doctrine of ὁμοούσιον τῷ Πατρί ("of one essence with the Father") and the primary figure is Athanasius of Alexandria. Additionally, other patristic themes and figures, inasmuch as they are situated in relation to Athanasius' basic theological ὁμοούσιον-centered commitments, fit within the patristic consensus.

Torrance's reconstruction of the patristic tradition contains much from which theologians, particular evangelical, can learn. A full study and assessment of it, in addition to a proposed "next step," therefore, has much to offer the church and the academy. From an historical viewpoint the results will show how a systematic theologian used patristic sources. From an ecclesiastical viewpoint it will supply the Reformed evangelical community with, at the very least, an example of a theologian who effectively appropriates The Fathers in such a way that preserves faithfulness to The Fathers and commitment to the Reformed evangelical tradition. It will also contribute to the growing discussion amongst Protestants, especially evangelical, who are returning to The Fathers and hopefully provide further impetus for ecumenical discussion on the basis of a shared theological tradition. Thus, it is important both to look at Torrance, a major Protestant theologian who uses The Fathers, and work from Torrance towards an evangelical hermeneutic of interpreting The Fathers; indeed, an "evangelical patristic theology."

OUTLINE OF THE BOOK

After (1) exploring the pre-Torrancian history of the *Consensus Patrum* and (2) situating Torrance in his more immediate context, this book is organized by (3) major catholic (ecumenical) themes and (4) major catholic (ecumenical) figures in the Torrancian *Consensus Patrum* as organized primarily by Torrance in his magisterial text, *The Trinitarian Faith* (but also elsewhere) and (5) by exploring Torrance's ecumenical relevance, especially as seen in the Reformed-Orthodox Dialogue within which he played a major role. In the conclusion, a proposed way forward, an "evangelical patristic theology," is offered.

The chapters of the book are organized accordingly. Chapter 1 is an historical introduction to the concept of the *Consensus Patrum*. This chapter examines the manner in which all traditions approaching the patristic tradition have a lens through which they view The Fathers. This chapter offers an historical narrative of the prevailing approaches to The Fathers by Roman Catholics, Eastern Orthodox, and Protestants. Chapter 2 places Torrance in his immediate context, namely, evangelical "discoveries" and "recoveries" of The Fathers, and begins to highlight Torrance's uniqueness. Chapters 3 and 4 offer an exploration of the catholic themes and figures of Torrance's

version of the patristic tradition. These chapters examine the way in which
Torrance's approach to The Fathers is both faithful to the patristic tradition and to his own Reformed evangelical commitments and also involves
significant changes to both standard readings of The Fathers and his own
tradition. Chapter 5 explores Torrance's ecumenical relevance. This chapter
argues that Torrance's appropriation of The Fathers into his Reformed and
evangelical tradition is an achievement of his broad catholic (ecumenical)
ecclesiology, which allows him to remain faithfully within his own tradition
while appropriating truly Greek patristic themes and figures, allowing the
two to dynamically inform and reform one another. The concluding chapter
explores a critical appropriation of the Torrancian *Consensus Patrum* and
offers the next steps towards an "evangelical patristic theology."

The argument throughout the book is that Torrance offers a viable Reformed evangelical reconstruction of The Fathers which has yet to be fully
appreciated by patristics scholars and theologians. This is argued by means
of exploration of the Torrancian *consensus* consisting of catholic themes and
figures (primarily the ὁμοούσιον and Athanasius). The argument is that Torrance's project has much merit and relevance and an "evangelical patristic
theology" should critically adopt the Torrancian *Consensus Patrum* and
move forward on the path paved by Torrance, assuming many elements of
Torrance's reading while revisiting portions thereof.

CONCLUSION

Torrance's reconstruction of the *Consensus Patrum* is a bounteous well from
which much can be drawn. Prior to exploring its nature and merit, it is
necessary to first explore the history of the *consensus* in Roman Catholic,
Eastern Orthodox, and Protestant theology in order to begin to view Torrance's project in its historical and theological context. Therefore, it is with
an historical overview of the *Consensus Patrum* with which this book begins.

CHAPTER 1

The *Consensus Patrum*

AN HISTORICAL OVERVIEW

*In the catholic church itself, all possible care must be taken, that we
hold that faith which has been believed everywhere, always, by all.
For that is truly and properly universal, which, as the name itself
and the reason of the thing declare, comprehends all universally.*

Vincent of Lérins, *Commonitory*, 2.6.

INTRODUCTION

Theologians throughout the centuries have long considered the notion of
the existence of some sort of consensual tradition existing amongst the
church fathers. From the earliest centuries, The Fathers themselves sought
to prove that their theological views were in line with antiquity.[1] Tertullian pointed to the Rule of Faith.[2] Basil the Great referred to an "unwritten
tradition."[3] Athanasius of Alexandria defended the doctrine of the Trinity
as "preserved by The Fathers."[4] Eventually, the church began to formulate

1. For example, when they tried to prove the connection between Plato and Moses
in order to prove the antiquity of their theology. See Justin Martyr, *1 Apology*, 59.

2. Tertullian, *Against Marcion*, 4.2.1.

3. Basil of Caesarea, *On the Holy Spirit*, 27.

4. Athanasius, *Letters on the Holy Spirit*, 1.28.

creeds to encapsulate their view.[5] Then, in their polemics, The Fathers began to compile *florigelium* in their works, in order to portray their viewpoint as in line with the *Consensus Patrum*.[6] Finally, upon the dawn of the Reformation in the Western church, the Reformers sought to prove that they were in line with The Fathers and that the medieval Catholics were not.[7]

By the time of the Reformation Roman Catholics, Eastern Orthodox, and Protestants each viewed themselves as the community truly faithful to the classic patristic tradition. Accordingly, each group viewed The Fathers through the lens that they were the faithful continuation of the early church and read the patristic tradition in light of their current ecclesiastical situation, viewing their community as the faithful continuation of ancient Christianity. The Eastern churches tended to read the *Consensus Patrum* through the developments in Byzantine theology (especially Gregory Palamas). The Western churches, both Protestant and Roman Catholic, tended to emphasize Augustinian theological themes. Whereas the Protestant communities have continued emphasizing Augustine, the Roman Catholics filter Augustine through Aquinas.

This approach continued in Protestantism following the Reformation until nineteenth-century Protestant liberal theology.[8] Following the time of Protestant liberalism, Protestants, whether liberal or evangelical, tended towards the view propagated by liberalism: that Protestantism bypassed the patristic era and returned to true, biblical Christianity. The ensuing neglect

5. As Williams puts it: "While the ancient Christians always regarded the past with esteem, one can point to an increasing number of instances in the late fifth and sixth centuries when writers thought of the earlier fathers as privileged witnesses to Christian truth." See Williams, *Evangelicals and Tradition*, 50.

6. These were lists of patristic sayings in support of their viewpoint. See Louth, *St John Damascene*, 14f. Louth notes that they first were used leading up to the Council of Chalcedon. Eventually, *florigelium* were used by The Fathers in polemics in instances such as the *filioque* debate.

7. See Lane, *John Calvin*, 3; Oort, "John Calvin" 697–99. Indeed, as one scholar aptly puts it: "In the controversies that followed the Reformation, Catholic and Protestant scholasticism took on a more polemical edge, coloring their development of theology's rational conclusions by their needs to defend respective ecclesial positions. Catholic theology stressed the structures and role of church authority, and the legitimacy of practices and beliefs lacking obvious roots in scripture; Protestant scholasticism stressed the primacy of the Word of God in church organization and worship, and distanced itself from any aspects of Catholic teaching lacking biblical warrant." See Flynn and Murray, *Ressourcement*, 335.

8. Though, as Fairbairn argues, even the liberals (e.g,. Harnack) had a lens through which they read The Fathers. See Fairbairn, "Patristic Soteriology," 290–93. As shall be explored below, the liberal approach often assumed the lens that the Protestant church faithfully and rightly *bypassed* the patristic era returning to a better, more biblical Christianity.

of not only patristic scholarship but also allowing The Fathers to undergird dogmatic theology was a denial of the way of the Reformers and it opened the door towards twentieth-century Protestant "retrievals" of The Fathers.[9] Torrance, a Protestant in the Reformed and evangelical tradition, has much to offer as an excellent example of a largely successful retrieval.

This chapter will explore the different approaches to the *Consensus Patrum* within historical Roman Catholicism, Eastern Orthodoxy, and Protestantism by looking at the vision of various figures and their ideas in order to put Torrance's project in its historical and ecclesiastical context. The most detailed analysis will be upon Protestantism because Torrance emerged out of this group and, indeed, was most faithful to the Protestant, especially Reformed and evangelical, approach to The Fathers. This chapter will argue that each group had its own lens through which they viewed The Fathers. The conclusion will be that Torrance's notion of the *consensus* and the lens through which he views it emerges out of his own Protestant tradition, sharing many core traits and convictions with it, although there are substantial points of contact between Torrance and other figures as well.

THE *CONSENSUS PATRUM* IN ROMAN CATHOLICISM

There have been a variety of components contributing to Roman Catholic readings of the *consensus*. However, three fundamentals have dominated their reading throughout history: (1) their conception of the *consensus* as quantitative, (2) their tendency to interpret The Fathers through Augustine and, eventually, Thomas Aquinas, and (3) their conception of the *consensus* as developing.

In the theology of Counter-Reformation, Roman Catholicism turned to the famous adage of Vincent of Lérins that:

> In the catholic church itself, all possible care must be taken, that we hold that faith which has been believed everywhere (*ubique*), always (*semper*), by all (*ab omnibus*). For that is truly (*vere*) and properly (*proprieque*) universal (*catholicum*), which, as the name itself and the reason of the thing declare, comprehends all universally. This rule we shall observe if we follow universality, antiquity, consent. We shall follow universality if we confess that one faith to be true, which the whole church throughout the world confesses; antiquity, if we in no wise depart from those interpretations which it is manifest were notoriously held by

9. "Theologies of retrieval" is John Webster's term. See Webster, "Theologies of Retrieval," 584–99.

our holy ancestors and fathers; consent, in like manner, if in antiquity itself we adhere to the consentient definitions and determinations of all, or at the least of almost all priests and doctors.[10]

For the Roman Catholics, the key to Vincent's credo is in the statement's first sentence, "everywhere, always, and by all." To Roman Catholics of the Counter-Reformation this implied a numerical *consensus*. Roman Catholics of this era maintained that individually The Fathers could err but taken as a whole they were authoritative and even infallible.[11] Thus, unanimity was greatly stressed.[12] Indeed, only the teaching of The Fathers as a whole was considered to be authoritative.[13]

Francis Turretin, hailing from the Reformed tradition, provides a witness to this numerical emphasis historically. Turretin lists three opinions that the Roman Catholics of his time held concerning the authority of The Fathers: (1) their writings are equal to Scripture both individually and collectively, (2) their writings are merely human, and (3) individually The Fathers are fallible but collectively they are infallible.[14] Furthermore, according to Turretin, the council of Trent asserts "the traditions of The Fathers pertaining both to faith and practice must be received with equal affection of piety with the Old and New Testaments."[15] Turretin sees the majority of the Catholics of his time contending that the collective teaching of The Fathers was as authoritative as the Scriptures. Thus, at least according to certain of their opponents, in their Counter-Reformation polemics the Catholics held the collective tradition in equal authority to the Scriptures.[16]

The second element of the Roman Catholic reading of the *Consensus Patrum* is their emphasis on Augustine. Western theologians from at least the medieval period onward emphasized Augustine and Augustinian theological themes. Peter Lombard is an illustrative example. As Bougerol

---

10. Vincent of Lérins, *Commonitory*, 2.6. PL 50.0640.

11. Quantin, "The Fathers in Seventeenth Century," 960.

12. Ibid., 960–67.

13. According to Geoffrey Bromiley this often amounted to "patristic prooftexting" e.g., in Peter Lombard. See Bromiley, "Promise of Patristic Studies," 129.

14. Turretin, *Institutes of Elenctic Theology*, II.21.3.

15. Ibid., II.21.3.

16. This was not simply a polemical attack by Turretin. Thomas Aquinas held to this view and placed the writings of The Fathers on the side of the Bible in terms of authority. See Elders, "Thomas Aquinas," 339–40 citing Aquinas, *Quodlib.* XII, art. 26 (q.17, art. Un.): *Dicendum quoad ab eodem Spiritu Scripturae sunt expositae et editae* ("the writing [of The Fathers] and the Scripture were written and explained by the same Spirit ").

puts it, for Lombard, "Augustine by far outclasses any other 'authorities.'"[17] This was no less the case for Thomas Aquinas.[18] Indeed, according to Elders' helpful chart, Aquinas cited Augustine far more than any other theological figure.[19] Thus, for medieval Catholic theologians, Augustine and Augustinian theology dominated.

Eventually, this emphasis on Augustine developed into an emphasis on Augustine filtered through Thomas Aquinas. By the turn of the twentieth century, Roman Catholic theology was steeped in Thomistic thought. In his book on twentieth-century Catholic theologians, Fergus Kerr humorously paints a picture of the context leading up to the theologians in the Nouvelle Théologie school of Catholicism and the Second Vatican Council: a boring recitation of neothomist theology.[20] However, when the Nouvelle Théologie theologians entered the scene, they began to protest this bland form of neoscholastic Thomist theology. Yves Congar[21] and Henri de Lubac[22] jump-started this movement and it was carried on by figures such as Hans Urs von Balthasar.[23]

These Catholic theologians attempted, by means of a departure from bland neoscholasticism/neothomism and return to the broader *consensus*, to read Aquinas as a part of the whole tradition rather than a-contextually

---

17. Bougerol, "The Church Fathers," 115.

18. Elders, "Thomas Aquinas," 338. Aquinas no doubt read and appropriated the Greek Fathers as well, particularly Pseudo-Dionysius. See 344–47. Here he perhaps paved the way for the return to the mysticism of Origen by twentieth-century Catholic theologians. See below. However, Aquinas cited Pseudo-Dionysius significantly less than Augustine.

19. Ibid., 346–47.

20. Kerr, *Twentieth-Century Catholic Theologians,* 1–6.

21. According to Kerr, Congar believed neoscholasticism was not a preservation of the ancient tradition, as it claimed to be. Accordingly, Congar held that, "the reform or renewal of the Catholic Church . . . was to be on the basis of a retrieval of the fullness of the Catholic tradition that he believed had been lost as Catholics reacted against Protestantism in the so-called Counter-Reformation, and against the ancient churches of the East when they rejected papal authority as conceived and practiced in the early Middle Ages." See ibid., 37–38. Accordingly, the movement was inherently ecumenical in nature.

22. According to Webster, de Lubac et al. traced the fall of Catholic theology to Duns Scotus and Ockham. See Webster, "Theologies of Retrieval," 588. Webster also notes that Radical Orthodoxy has picked up this stream of retrieval.

23. Kerr, *Twentieth-Century Catholic Theologians,* 122–25. Though there were undoubtedly differences between each of these figures. See Flynn and Murray, *Ressourcement,* 279–88 for an excellent discussion of the differences between de Lubac and Balthasar, that latter of whom these authors say was more in line with neothomism than the former.

and a-historically.[24] Accordingly, in their polemics the theologians of the Nouvelle Théologie school worked to portray neoscholasticism as a departure from the classic tradition of The Fathers and present the Nouvelle Théologie movement as truly faithful to The Fathers, and therefore, providing the faithful interpretation of Thomas Aquinas.[25] Interestingly, in their reinterpretation of Aquinas, they returned to Origen.[26] Their attempt to read Aquinas and scholastic theology in light of the broader theological tradition was, nevertheless, an emphasis on Aquinas. Therefore, this "new" theology, while ecumenically relevant in many ways,[27] is typically Western in its focus upon Augustine and typically Roman Catholic in its centeredness upon Aquinas.

The third element of the Roman Catholic approach is their emphasis on doctrine as developing. John Henry Newman[28] has played a major role in developing the Roman Catholic tradition's approach to the *Consensus Patrum* in this regard.[29] Newman contended doctrine continually "deepens" and "develops"[30] throughout the history of the church.[31] He saw the "development of doctrine" as the way in which doctrine is brought into "consistency and form."[32] Newman held that one could not understand the

---

24. Kerr, *Twentieth-Century Catholic Theologians*, 32–33. Here Kerr discusses Marie-Dominique Chenu; though, the recovery and re-reading of Aquinas was the main element of the other figures as well.

25. Kerr, *Twentieth-Century Catholic Theologians*, 85–86.

26. Kerr states: "The most surprising development in twentieth-century Catholic theology—for neoscholastic theologians and especially for Thomists—was the retrieval of Origen." Kerr traces this to Jean Danièlou and Olivier Rousseau. See ibid., 80. Notably, even Karl Rahner's first text was on Origen (101).

27. The relation of, for example, Karl Rahner to T. F. Torrance will be discussed later in this book.

28. See King, *Newman and the Alexandrian Fathers* for an excellent tracing of Newman's view of the Greek Fathers.

29. See Newman, *The Arians of the Fourth Century*; Newman, *Lectures on the Prophetical Office*; Newman, *An Essay on the Development of Christian Doctrine*; Newman, *An Essay in Aid of a Grammar* for Newman's discussions of the tradition of The Fathers.

30. Newman certainly developed in his view of the tradition of The Fathers. During this early stage, Newman saw the Anglican tradition as "via media" and a faithful continuation of the early church. See Daley, "The Church Fathers," 29. Early on Newman had a more static notion of tradition. Later, after concluding doctrine "develops," Newman saw the Roman Catholic Church as the faithful continuation of the early church.

31. Newman, *An Essay on the Development of Christian Doctrine*, 21–22. Though this view was already developed to some extent by the Catholic faculty at Tübingen. See Biemer, *Newman on Tradition*, 1.

32. Newman, *An Essay on the Development of Christian Doctrine*, 28.

early Fathers without the later Fathers and from here began to understand doctrine as having developed throughout the patristic era and beyond.[33]

Newman seemed to imagine that this view could imply a variety of outcomes with which he did not agree. Therefore, Newman laid out what he saw as the characteristics of faithful development: preservation of the type, shared principles, the same organization, anticipation in the beginning of the subsequent phases, later protection and subservience of the earlier, and the power of assimilation.[34] Without these characteristics the development could in no way be considered faithful. Rather, Newman saw any divergences as heretical development.

Despite seeing the Anglican tradition as a "via media" between Roman Catholicism and Protestantism in his earlier theology,[35] Newman's eventual conclusion[36] was that "modern Catholicism is nothing else but simply the legitimate growth and complement that is the natural and necessary development of the doctrine of the early church."[37] For him, though contemporary Roman Catholic doctrines could not be found in patristic theology explicitly, they were legitimate developments of the teaching of The Fathers. He included numerous examples of this in his *Essay on the Development of Doctrine*, which was, in many ways, a justification of his conversion to Roman Catholicism.[38] This is why for Newman, "to be deep in history is to cease to be a Protestant"[39] and "were Athanasius to come to life he would undoubtedly recognize the Catholic Church as his own communion."[40] In his mind, Protestant doctrine was not a faithful development of the theology of the early church, as was Roman Catholic teaching.

THE CONSENSUS PATRUM IN EASTERN ORTHODOXY

Turning now to Eastern Orthodoxy, there are a variety of elements which have influenced the Eastern Orthodox view of the *Consensus Patrum.*

---

33. King, *Newman and the Alexandrian Fathers*, 51–52.

34. Newman, *An Essay on the Development of Christian Doctrine*, 124.

35. Though he put Anglicanism closer to Roman Catholicism than Protestantism. See Chadwick, *Tradition and Exploration*, 160–61.

36. Of course, this is summing up Newman's fascinating biography into far too small a space.

37. Newman, *An Essay on the Development of Christian Doctrine*, 123.

38. See McCarren, "Development of Doctrine," 118. Though the view was present in a nascent form in Newman's earlier works (119).

39. Newman, *An Essay on the Development of Christian Doctrine*, 6.

40. Ibid., 71.

Central, however, are the two key elements that (1) the *consensus* is inherently synthetic and (2) ultimately, the Byzantine tradition is central, particularly as read through the neopalamite tradition of Lossky.

Georges Florovsky, the Orthodox theologian who propagated a call for an Eastern Orthodox "return to The Fathers," has had much to say concerning the *consensus*.[41] Primarily, he contended that the "Vincentian canon" was inadequate. This means that Vincent of Lérins' call to hold what has been believed "everywhere, always, and by all" cannot be understood numerically nor empirically. As Florovsky puts it:

> Decisive value resides in inner catholicity, not in empirical universality. The opinions of The Fathers are accepted, not as formal subjection to outward authority, but because of the inner evidence of their catholic truth. The whole body of the Church has the right of verifying, or, to be more exact, the right, and not only the right but the duty of certifying.[42]

This means that the *consensus* for Florovsky is not a numerical mean nor even empirically verifiable at all. Rather, the authentic *consensus* is that which reflects the mind of the church, the "ἐκκλησιαστικον φρόνημα."[43] Florovsky saw this as the way in which The Fathers themselves understood tradition. In his words, "the appeal to Tradition was actually an appeal to the mind of the Church."[44] Thus, in the thought of The Fathers, Florovsky argues, tradition is primarily a hermeneutical principle and method.[45]

Therefore, for Florovsky, the *consensus* is synthetic in nature.[46] Herein, he called for theologians to follow the "neopatristic synthesis." Florovsky contends that "following the Holy Fathers" could not refer to some sort of abstract Tradition. Rather, it must be an appeal to Holy Witnesses and examples.[47] Thus, he viewed Athanasius, for example, within the synthesis of the other Fathers. As such, Gregory Palamas is within the line of patristic tradition via connections with the Cappadocians and Maximus the Confessor.[48]

---

41. See further Sauve, "Georges V. Florovsky."

42. Florovsky, *Bible, Church, Tradition*, 51–54.

43. Ibid., 103.

44. Ibid., 83.

45. Ibid., 79.

46. Ibid., 106. Florovsky calls it a "living tradition" because, ultimately, he argues, Tradition is "the abiding presence of the Holy Spirit in the Church."

47. Ibid., 106.

48. See ibid., 113–20.

Florovsky held that the goal of theology is the acquirement of the mind of The Fathers.[49] Florovsky's neopatristic synthesis is a combination of the entire tradition of The Fathers and indeed an appeal to their "mind." Florovsky believed it would be wrong to refer to any sort of static or abstract *consensus.* He saw this in the Roman Catholics who end the *consensus* with the Scholastics, the Protestants who end it with the fifth century, and even the Orthodox who end it with the Seventh Ecumenical Council.[50] Contrary to these three views, Florovsky argued that the Holy Spirit is still working and therefore the *consensus* continues into contemporary times.[51] Herein, he critiqued modern theologians for leaving out the Byzantine period of theological development.[52]

John Meyendorff, the famed patristics scholar and Orthodox theologian, carried this forward. Meyendorff contended that because the same Spirit inspired the Scriptures who inspired the saints, they are to be read together.[53] Thus, the Gospel must always be interpreted within the framework of the "apostolic tradition" or "the wider, living, and uninterrupted continuity of the apostolic church."[54]

A statement concerning his method, though lengthy, deserves to be quoted in full:

> In any systematic presentation of Byzantine theology, there is
> . . . a danger of forcing it into the mold of rational categories for-
> eign to its very nature. This is precisely what occurred in many
> textbooks of dogmatic theology which appeared in the Ortho-
> dox East after the eighteenth century, which claimed to remain
> faithful to the theology of the Byzantine Fathers. They have
> been ably characterized by Georges Florovsky as expressions
> of a "Western captivity" of the Orthodox mind. For, it is not
> enough to quote an abundance of proof-texts from patristic or
> Byzantine authors: true consistency requires a unity of method
> and congeniality of approach.[55]

---

49. Ibid,. 107–9. Florovsky argues that the key is to not quote The Fathers but rather to acquire their mind and follow them because the tradition of The Fathers is inherently *kerygmatic* and centered on piety.

50. Ibid., 110.

51. Ibid., 111.

52. Ibid., 112.

53. Meyendorff, *Byzantine Theology*, 22.

54. Ibid., 8.

55. Ibid., 128.

Thus, Meyendorff, and Florovsky with him, wanted to reform the way in which Byzantine theology was studied in general and patristic studies in particular. Instead of reading it through a Western, often scholastic lens, they propose reading The Fathers on their own terms.

Ultimately, however, the Orthodox read the *consensus* through the lens of "neopalamism."[56] Simply put, in an attempt to preserve God's ultimate transcendence, this view contends that God limits interaction with the world to God's uncreated (and impersonal) energies.[57] This view is perhaps rooted, at least in part, in Lossky's unique notion of the development of doctrine.[58]

There are definite differences between Florovsky, Meyendorff, and the neopalamites, but they and others attempting retrievals of the earlier Fathers assumed elements of neopalamism and read the earlier Fathers through a neopalamite reading of Gregory Palamas and the later Byzantine Fathers. Essentially, the neopalamite reading views the early Fathers through this certain reading of Gregory Palamas. Florovsky, for example, saw significant similarities between Athanasius and Gregory Palamas.[59] Additionally, Meyendorff held that Athanasius believed in a sharp distinction between essence and energy in God. In Meyendorff's words:

> The notion of creation, as expressed by Athanasius, leads to a distinction in God between his transcendent essence and his properties such as "power" or "goodness," which expresses his existence and action *ad extra*, not his essence.[60]

Meyendorff explicated the opinion that what would later be called "Palamism" was in fact precisely the theology Athanasius espoused concerning the distinction between γεννάω (*begetting*) and γενάω (*creating*).[61] Meyen-

---

56. Or, in the words of Zizioulas, "neopalamite spectacles" See Zizioulas, *Communion and Otherness*, 139. In this instance, Zizioulas criticizes those who attack Gregory Palamas and read him through Lossky. Nevertheless, embedded within this was no doubt a critique of Lossky and the neopalamites themselves. This is not to accuse Florovsky and Meyendorff of neopalamism. Rather, it is simply a statement that elements of the neopalamite assumptions existed in their theology, namely, reading the early Fathers through a certain reading of the later Fathers (especially Palamas).

57. See Lossky, *The Mystical Theology of the Eastern Church*, 213 for a classic neopalamite rendering of this idea.

58. See Sauve, "Georges V. Florovsky," 102–8.

59. See Meyendorff, *Byzantine Theology*, 130–32 and Florovsky, *Creation and Redemption*, 43–78. This chapter in Florovsky's book is an otherwise excellent chapter; however, he attempts to portray Athanasius as basically a Palamite.

60. Meyendorff, *Byzantine Theology*, 130.

61. Ibid., 131–32.

dorff saw this distinction as being especially important in the context of deification.[62] Thus, Palamas' formulation of what Meyendorff held to be an Athanasian distinction of the three elements of God: essence, energy, and the three hypostases,[63] and, herein, the allocation of God's interaction with the world to his energies (and, by implication, the preservation of God's essence and hypostases from interaction with the world).

THE *CONSENSUS PATRUM* IN EARLY PROTESTANTISM

Turning now to Protestantism, Protestant theologians and churchmen have studied The Fathers from the very beginning of the movement. The Reformation took place during the Renaissance surge of *ad fontes* or "return to the sources." Following this, the Reformers returned not only to the Bible in its original languages but also to its patristic interpreters and commentators.[64] Emerging from the Western tradition, Protestants such as Calvin and Luther unsurprisingly focused on Augustine and Augustinian theology, seeing him as the theologian *par excellence* of the *Consensus Patrum* and, accordingly, had a western lens through which they viewed The Fathers. Protestants also held to an concept of an ecclesiastical golden age" and conceived of themselves as inheriting the tradition of the early Fathers. Three key elements drove the early Protestant approach to The Fathers: (1) They are not authoritative, (2) Protestantism is in line with The Fathers (rather than Catholicism), (3) an ecclesiastical "golden-age" existed after which time the church began her decline, (4) Augustine is central.

---

62. Ibid., 186.

63. Ibid., citing PG, 151.1173B. See also Meyendorff, *Byzantine Theology,* 187 for further elaboration on the Palamite viewpoint of a threefold distinction between energy, hypostases, and essence.

64. The Reformers, however, did not have the full palate of patristic sources available to them. Indeed, there were only particular texts and particular editions of The Fathers in circulation during the time of the Reformation. Widely available to the Reformers were the following Latin compilations and editions: *Harmony of Discordant Canons* (later called *The Decree of Gratian*) which focused upon the first four councils, *The Glossa Ordinaria* which offered commentary on the Gospels, Gregory the Great's *Epistle 25* which emphasized the first four councils as canonical, and Vincent of Lérins' *Commonitorium* (see Williams, *Evangelicals and Tradition*, 75–78). Williams also notes that these collections were generally based on Latin compilations. Additionally, there were editions of Irenaeus (see Backus, *Historical Method*, 134–37) and Tertullian (see Backus, *Historical Method*, 158ff) and the Reformers heavily relied upon Latin editions of the Greek Fathers such as Athanasius and Basil for defense of the doctrine of the Trinity (see Backus, *Historical Method*, 174). Also, there were a variety of guides on how to read The Fathers in circulation (see Backus, *Historical Method*, 196–252).

The Reformer Martin Luther in many ways paved the way for the mindset Protestants later would bring to patristic interpretation. For Luther, The Fathers were to be read solely as theological conversation partners. At times Luther listened to The Fathers because he generally considered them to be good scholars.[65] Yet, they held no more authority than Luther's own contemporaries and were simply, in the helpful words of Schulze, "theological controversialists."[66] For example, Luther saw the doctrine of justification by faith as core and critiqued The Fathers for not being as explicit about this as he would have liked.[67] Indeed, for Luther The Fathers could be corrected and parts of their theology could be entirely erroneous. Herein, as Schulze puts it, "[Luther] rendered an inestimable scholarly service to the church, to theology, and to historiography: He freed The Fathers from tradition. At long last it was possible for them to be mistaken."[68] For Luther no Father was considered better or more authoritative than any other. Indeed, every Father could be mistaken and must be read simply as fellow theological scholars; each could be wrong and probably was at certain points. Only the Scriptures were to be held as authoritative. As such, Luther set the stage for later Protestant approaches to The Fathers, both evangelical and liberal.

For the Reformer John Calvin The Fathers should be viewed as slightly more authoritative than Luther, though still able to be erroneous. Indeed, for this Reformer The Fathers ought to be read as more than simply fellow scholars or readers of Scripture. Key for Calvin was portraying the Protestant Reformation as returning to the ancient Christianity of The Fathers. Still, according to Anthony Lane, for Calvin Scripture is primarily authoritative and The Fathers were considered to be lesser authorities.[69] Indeed, only Scripture is normative and the theological teaching of The Fathers must always be judged in the light of Scripture.[70] Therefore, when doing theology Calvin was always prepared, if necessary, to stand alone against the *consensus* of The Fathers but he never stood against Scripture.[71] Scripture was the only normative text for Calvin. Where The Fathers disagreed with Scripture it was the latter who trumped the former. Yet, he did view at least some of The Fathers as authoritative interpreters of Scripture.[72]

65. Schulze, "Martin Luther and the Church Fathers," 613.

66. Ibid., 615.

67. Ibid., 609–13. Perhaps paving the way for the liberal critique of The Fathers.

68. Ibid., 625.

69. Lane, *John Calvin*, 29.

70. Ibid., 35.

71. Ibid., 36.

72. Ibid., 29.

Central for Calvin was that the Reformation, rather than Catholicism, was in line with the tradition of The Fathers.[73] Calvin used The Fathers polemically to support his Reformed tradition, but he also, as Lane states, "genuinely believed them to support his cause."[74] Calvin saw The Fathers as ancient witnesses to the truth of Reformed theology and examples of theologians sharing the same convictions as he and his fellow Reformers. Herein, "Calvin's use of The Fathers was a masterly attempt to relate Protestantism to historic Christianity and show how the Roman error had arisen."[75] Thus, for Calvin, The Fathers were examples of early explicators of specific Reformed doctrines.

The polemical edge of Calvin's use of The Fathers is more fully seen in his prefatory address to King Francis in his *Institutes*. Here, Calvin depicts where he sees himself and his fellow Reformers standing, namely, in line with tradition and antiquity; it is the Roman Catholics who had departed.[76] In his words, "it is a calumny to represent us as opposed to The Fathers."[77] Calvin believes that "there is much that is admirable and wise in those Fathers."[78] Yet, Calvin makes clear in the *Prefatory Address* that he considers the teaching of The Fathers helpful in places and extremely unhelpful in places. For him, it is essential to use their teachings only inasmuch as they are in agreement with Scripture.

Furthermore, for the Calvin and the Protestant Reformers the church had a "golden age."[79] Calvin greatly respected the first four ecumenical coun-

---

73. According to Lane, Calvin's use of The Fathers was primarily polemical. See Lane, *John Calvin*, 3 for the second thesis of Calvin's use of The Fathers. See also Oort, "John Calvin," 697–99.

74. Lane, *John Calvin*, 27–28.

75. Ibid., 54. However, as Lane helpfully points out, Calvin held a more static conception of doctrine whereas modern theological and patristic scholarship has shown that there are deeply rooted differences between the Reformers and The Fathers.

76. Ibid., 33.

77. Calvin, *Institutes of the Christian Religion*, prefatory address.

78. Ibid.

79. For Calvin and the Reformed, there were certain Fathers that were more right and therefore to be used more authoritatively. Calvin's view of The Fathers consists of some figures who were "in" and some who were "out." He certainly had a few favorites such as John Chrysostom and Cyril of Alexandra who he saw as the best explicators of biblical theology and commentators on the Bible. See Backus, *Historical Method*, 101ff; Oort, "John Calvin," 693. Indeed, Calvin cited Chrysostom often in regards to Biblical exegesis. In addition, Calvin had great respect for the Cappadocian Fathers, especially Gregory Nazianzen of whose Triadology he was particularly fond. See Calvin, *Institutes*, I.13.17 citing Gregory Nazianzen *Sermon on Sacred Baptism*. Calvin also deeply respected Hilary of Poitiers (see Oort, "John Calvin," 688) and cited Irenaeus of Lyons often (see Oort, "John Calvin," 685–86).

cils[80] and he contended that there was a purer age of the church, namely the early centuries of Christianity.[81] For Calvin there was no specific date when the church "fell" from this purer age. Rather, Calvin understood there to have been a more gradual decline.[82] Here began a "pattern of decay" in the Protestant genealogy of church history.[83]

For Calvin and the Reformed, Augustine was central. Though definitely breaking with many elements of the Western Christianity of his time, Calvin continued in the tradition of viewing Augustine, at least implicitly, as the theologian *par excellence.* As Oort puts it, "without doubt [Augustine] was not only the most cited, but also the most appreciated church father for Calvin."[84] Furthermore, Backus argues that there were ways, such as ecclesiology, wherein Augustine influenced the Reformed and Calvinists in an unacknowledged, but definitely present, fashion.[85] This emphasis on Augustine and Augustinian theological themes carried into later Protestant theology as well.[86]

However, Calvin and the other Reformers did not rely solely upon Augustine. Indeed, they turned to a plethora of sources from both the Greek East and Latin West.[87] As van Oort notes, Calvin was particularly reliant upon Hilary of Poitiers for his doctrine of the Trinity.[88] Additionally, Calvin was very fond of the Greek Fathers such as the Cappadocian Fathers and Cyril of Alexandria.[89]

THE CONSENSUS PATRUM IN LATER PROTESTANTISM

After the time of the Reformation there were a variety of approaches to the *consensus* in the west; the common denominator, however, was a use of Augustine and Augustinian theological themes. Later theologians standing

80. Lane, *John Calvin*, 39–40.

81. Ibid., 40–41.

82. Ibid., 46.

83. A term taken from Georges Florovsky. See Florovsky, *Bible, Church, Tradition*, 110. Florovsky critiques Protestants as a whole for holding to this genealogy of church history. While this critique is no doubt valid as a general statement and can be seen in figures like Calvin, it is also a bit of a generalization.

84. Oort, "John Calvin," 689.

85. Backus, *Historical Method*, 52.

86. Bromiley, "Promise of Patristic Studies," 128.

87. See Backus, *Historical Method*, 61.

88. Oort, "John Calvin," 688.

89. See ibid., 685–99 for a comprehensive overview of Calvin's reading of many Greek Fathers.

within the Protestant tradition continued within this mindset and continued to read and study The Fathers from this perspective. However, they differed in many ways from their Roman Catholic predecessors. Some theologians vehemently disagreed with any type of numerical notion of the *Consensus Patrum* considering it to be Roman Catholic. Yet, they typically had a place for the theology of The Fathers[90] and regarded The Fathers as reliable and authoritative theological sources and interpreters of Scripture.[91]

Once Protestantism had become more established in the west, their reading of The Fathers became more set and organized. Reformed theologians of later Calvinist theology attempted to provide a *via media* between the error of the Roman Catholic notion of the *consensus* and the Anti-Trinitarians who denied the patristic formulations of Trinity and Christology.[92] Turretin, for example, points out that the Papists of his time held that "The Fathers are to be considered judges capable of deciding controversies of faith by their infallible authority" but the Reformed contend that "The Fathers are to be considered witnesses giving testimony of the consent of the ancient church and the opinion of the church in their own age."[93] These Catholics argued that the collective teaching of The Fathers was to be considered authoritative and infallible. Turretin and the others wanted to preserve the Reformed doctrine of *Sola Scriptura* against the Catholics who conceived of The Fathers as infallible. In response, Turretin argued that, contrary to the Catholic viewpoint, it is actually impossible to reach a numerical *consensus*.[94] Furthermore, The Fathers (individually and collectively) were not prophets or apostles who had the gift of infallibility.[95] They are no more than witnesses to the truth of Scripture. Turretin argued that The Fathers should only be viewed as witnesses to the truth. In viewing The Fathers as such Turretin stood in a long line of Protestant tradition in reading The Fathers.[96]

Yet for these later Protestants, The Fathers were more than simply fellow theologians as they were for Luther, and more than early proponents of Reformed theology as they were for the Reformed; they were *testes veritatis*

90. For example, Polanus, Webb, and Turretin. See Meijering, "The Fathers in Calvinist Orthodoxy," 867–68.

91. For example, the seventeenth-century Anglicans. See Quantin, "The Fathers in Seventeenth Century Anglican Theology," 990.

92. Meijering, "The Fathers in Calvinist Orthodoxy," 867–68. The examples of Polanus, Wolleb, and Turretin are provided.

93. See Turretin, *Institutes of Elentic Theology*, II.21.6.

94. Ibid., II. 21.16.

95. Ibid., II.21.10.

96. Meijering, "The Fathers in Calvinist Orthodoxy," 868.

(witnesses to the truth").[97] For Turretin, Christians are to follow and listen to The Fathers, yet not place them on the same level as the Scriptures. Turretin held that The Fathers closest to the apostles are the purest.[98] Indeed, many of the Reformed saw themselves as following these Fathers' methods in many ways, for example in using non-Biblical terminology in order to clarify Biblical concepts.[99] Turretin believed that The Fathers must not be given too much praise but also they must not be robbed of their due praise.[100]

Much like Calvin, the later Reformed often saw The Fathers as early spokesmen of Protestant doctrines.[101] Indeed, many later Reformed saw them as strong advocates of Reformed theology and the emphasis on grace. Thus, by the time of the solidification of Reformed and evangelical theology in the west, The Fathers were viewed as witnesses to the fact that the Protestant Reformation was a return to the ancient Christian tradition.

Philip Schaff carried this viewpoint forward and developed it substantially.[102] In his genealogy of church history, Schaff roots the Protestant churches solidly in the Western medieval tradition.[103] In his genealogy of church history, Schaff distinguishes between Catholicism and Romanism. An extensive, but extremely illustrative quote, portrays Schaff's view:

> We must distinguish between Catholicism and Romanism. The former embraces the ancient Oriental church, the mediaeval church, and we may say, in a wider sense, all the modern evangelical churches. Romanism is the Latin church turned against the Reformation, consolidated by the Council of Trent and completed by the Vatican Council of 1870 with its dogma of papal absolutism and papal infallibility. Medieval Catholicism

97. Ibid., 868.

98. Turretin, *Institutes of Elentic Theology*, II.21.12. Turretin states: "Although some extend their age down to the tenth century, we do not think it ought to be carried down further than the sixth. For it is certain that purity of doctrine and worship became greatly corrupted after the sixth-hundredth year (in which the antichrist raised his head)—error and superstitions increasing by the just judgment of God." Thus, the Protestant "golden age" concept was carried on by Turretin. See Turretin, *Institutes of Elentic Theology*, II.21.3.

99. Meijering, "The Fathers in Calvinist Orthodoxy," 872. Though it is too much to say with Meijering that the Protestant Scholastic approach was closer to The Fathers than the earlier Reformed. See 884–85.

100. Turretin, *Institutes of Elentic Theology*, II.21.17.

101. Meijering, "The Fathers in Calvinist Orthodoxy," 865.

102. Bromiley, "Promise of Patristic Studies," 128.

103. Schaff, *History of the Church*, 1–4. Additionally, Schaff compared the importance of the Reformation to the importance of the first century and the split between East and West on the *filioque*.

is evangelical, looking to the Reformation; modern Romanism is anti-evangelical, condemning the Reformation, yet holding with unyielding tenacity the ecumenical doctrines once sanctioned, and doing this all the more by virtue of its claim to infallibility.[104]

Thus, in his view of the historical development of the church, Schaff drew a sharp distinction between "Catholicism" and "Romanism." He saw the Reformed and evangelical churches as catholic and the churches under Rome as "Romanists." Furthermore, Schaff saw Romanism as medieval Catholicism taken to its extreme form.[105]

Schaff hoped for an age of ecumenical rapprochement called "evangelical catholicism," which he saw as in line with the ancient church.[106] Herein, Schaff strongly rejected Protestant "sectarianism" which he believed was the perennial temptation and struggle of Protestantism.[107] Schaff unpacks this viewpoint in his text, *The Principle of Protestantism.*[108] In order to reach this age of ecumenical rapprochement, Schaff proposed a charitable study of church history.[109]

In the eyes of the Reformers and later Protestants, the Protestant Reformation was, therefore, a return to the witness of the classical Church Fathers. For the first generation Reformers like Calvin and also the later Protestants like Turretin, there existed some sort of ecclesiastical "golden age" following which the church fell away into varying levels of heresy and the cry of the day for the Reformers was not only to return to Scripture but to faithfulness to this ecclesiastical "golden age."[110] Granted, the Reformers were limited in The Fathers which they had available owing to available

104. Ibid., 4. The language has been slightly updated.

105. Ibid., 5.

106. Shriver, *Philip Schaff,* 112.

107. Ibid., 22.

108. Ibid., 22–23. Notably, Charles Hodge reviewed this work positively (ibid., 23).

109. Ibid., 96.

110. Kenneth Stewart states: "The current resurgence of interest in early Christianity is *not* a swing of the pendulum towards something neglected for the five centuries of Protestantism's existence. It is in fact a return to emphases *regularly* present in historic Protestantism." See Stewart, "Evangelicalism and Patristic Christianity," 309. In his article Stewart traces Protestant evangelical use of The Fathers from the sixteenth to the twentieth century. See p. 309–19. Though Stewart convincingly argues for the essential connection between patristic theology and the Reformers and points to examples of evangelical usage of The Fathers since the Reformation he fails to successfully portray returning to The Fathers as indeed a part of what it meant to be evangelical following the Reformation. Indeed, a Biblicist approach developed that was essentially the opposite. See below.

editions and were more informed by Western Fathers such as Augustine; however, they indeed returned to the classical Greek Fathers as well, seeing the patristic tradition as evidence that the Protestant community was a continuation of the ancient church. However, this approach would soon change.

THE LIBERAL AND BIBLICIST APPROACHES OF NINETEENTH AND TWENTIETH-CENTURY PROTESTANTISM

Though the Reformers returned to The Fathers they failed to outline any sort of objective guideline for appropriation of The Fathers and Protestant evangelicals have subsequently avoided The Fathers due, further, to both medieval Catholicism and modern liberalism.[111] Accordingly, in the words of Geoffrey Bromiley, "patristics is one of the most neglected areas in evangelical theology."[112] Despite the fact that the Protestant Reformation was nothing less than an attempt at a return to The Fathers and the patristic "golden age" as the Reformers saw it, following the first generation Reformers and their immediate followers, the Protestant appropriation of the Greek Fathers turned into one of two approaches. Protestants either viewed the Greek Fathers via the liberal Protestant lens of separating the "kernel" from the "chaff" or via the fundamentalist and Biblicist interpretation of the Reformation principle of *Sola Scriptura*, essentially ignoring the theological tradition from which they arose.[113] These opposing approaches paved the way for evangelicals to "discover" the Greek Fathers during and following Torrance's time (the subject of the following chapter of this book).

In many ways, Rudolf Bultmann encapsulates the liberal Protestant theological methodology towards both the Bible and The Fathers. Herein he provides an example of the methodology of the liberal Protestant approach to written theological sources. Bultmann did not look at The Fathers

---

111. Though, as Bromiley helpfully puts it "one should not overdraw the picture." He notes Philip Schaff's patristic scholarship as well as the more general appreciation of Augustine in Reformed theology, both of which this chapter has discussed. See Bromiley, "Promise of Patristic Studies," 128.

112. Ibid., 125.

113. Though as Stewart aptly puts it: "Extremely liberal segments of Protestant Christianity in the twentieth century—those which allowed to be called into question the virginal conception of Jesus, his physical resurrection three days after death and his personal return at the end of this age—cannot be thought to have taken very seriously the early ecumenical councils or the theological consensus of early Christianity." See Stewart, "Evangelicalism and Patristic Christianity," 308.

as directly as theologians such as Adolf von Harnack did, yet he did have, more broadly, a reading of the theological tradition. For Bultmann, the key to theological interpretation is "de-mythologizing."

De-mythologizing is the process of looking for the existential message of the Gospel within the worldview in which it was embedded. According to David Fergusson, "it seeks to bring out the real intention of myth. . ."[114] Fergusson lucidly examines how this worked itself out in Bultmann by a comparison of Barth to Bultmann. According to Fergusson, for Barth the life, death and resurrection of Christ is intrinsically significant; for Bultmann it is only significant as it was existentially encountered in the present."[115]

Adolf von Harnack,[116] the famed historian of dogma is perhaps the clearest example of the liberal Protestant approach to the Greek Fathers in particular.[117] Harnack was faithful to the general liberal methodology as exemplified in Bultmann and, following this methodology, he had a certain approach to The Fathers, especially the Greek Fathers. Harnack saw certain Fathers as more "in" than others. Furthermore, for him, a core to theological history exists containing key theological assertions. Harnack saw the job of the theologian and historian of dogma to be to extract this "kernel" from the "chaff."

For Harnack, doctrine developed both positively and negatively. Arianism and Papism, for example, were negative developments. They emerged and were erroneous and need to be removed by the theologian. For him, much of doctrine and historical Christianity is the "Hellenization of the Gospel" and the application of Greek thought to Biblical concepts.[118] The key in dogmatics is thus to always search deeply for "Jesus Christ and his Gospel"[119] and to distinguish the "kernel and husk."[120] Indeed, while the language and even thought of the Gospel was done in the cultural framework of its time, the kernel could be preserved owing to its permanent validity.[121]

---

114. Fergusson, *Bultmann*, 108.

115. Ibid., 118–19. This is why Bultmann agreed with Barth's dialectical project in *Romans*. However, for Bultmann the dialectic was only significant as it was experienced in the life of the believer (ibid., 22).

116. See Harnack, *History of Dogma* for his magisterial work.

117. Though, as Bromiley notes, liberalism has unquestionably "produced some of the finest patristic work of the modern period." Yet, liberal presuppositions are "readily enough perceived." See Bromiley, "Promise of Patristic Studies," 128.

118. See Harnack, *What Is Christianity?*, 207–9, for example.

119. Ibid., 10.

120. Ibid., 12.

121. Ibid., 12–14.

Thus, theology is searching for the "Gospel in the Gospel" and looking for the core "Christian idea."[122]

Perhaps ironically, Harnack had a particular fondness for Athanasius of Alexandria.[123] For Harnack, Athanasius was in many ways a theologian from which his own German liberal tradition emerged. He contended that Athanasius saved the church and preserved the core of the Gospel: "fellowship of God with man" for in Harnack's words, "the entire Faith, everything in defense of which Athanasius staked his life, is described in one sentence: *God himself has entered into humanity*."[124] This core teaching was, to use Bultmann's language, the "existential truth" embedded in the Christian myth and other external and mythological developments were simply the "Hellenization" of the Gospel.

A number of other theologians approached The Fathers via this lens. R. P. C. Hanson, the famed patristics scholar wrote a number of texts in this vein.[125] Hanson held to the "development of doctrine." He saw orthodoxy as a process of trial and error. Indeed for him orthodoxy was "found" not "maintained."[126] He states, "the story is the story of how orthodoxy was reached, found, not of how it was maintained."[127] Charles Kanengiesser is also in the liberal tradition of reading the patristic tradition. He believed that Athanasius was an example of a theologian who should be followed in style and method today but not necessarily in substance. For Kannengiesser the principles and beliefs of the early church must not be followed today—thus theologians cannot use The Fathers like Newman did—rather knowledge of the early church can help the church today in moving forward away from the backward views held during the patristic era. Maurice Wiles viewed orthodoxy in much the same way as Hanson, seeing saw as a development and something which was "made."[128] For example, Wiles' text

---

122. Ibid., 14–15.

123. Harnack, as John Behr helpfully puts it, "admired Athanasius, for while he might have 'erased every trait of the historical Jesus of Nazareth' (whatever that meant to Harnack), Athanasius nevertheless 'saved the character of Christianity as a religion of the living fellowship with God.'" Behr, *The Nicene Faith: Part I*, 165 citing Harnack, *History of Dogma*, 4:45. See also 4:26 where Harnack elaborates upon his view that Athanasius' theology was rooted in soteriology, a soteriology of union between God and man.

124. Harnack, *History of Dogma*, 26, italics original.

125. Hanson, *The Search for the Christian Doctrine of God*.

126. Ibid., 848.

127. Ibid., 870.

128. See Wiles, *The Making of Christian Doctrine*.

Archetypal Heresy: Arianism through the Centuries[129] argues that Arianism as traditionally presented was in fact a polemical invention of Athanasius.

For the liberal tradition the church fathers in general and the Greek Fathers in particular were subject to the critique of Hellenization and mythologizing. However, there were figures (such as Athanasius for Harnack) who preserved the kernel of the "Christian idea" in their theology and who, after a process of de-mythologizing and removing the chaff, could be retrieved. Ultimately, figures like Harnack from the liberal tradition indeed have provided much to be appreciated from a historical perspective but also have caused serious theological problems inasmuch as they simply read their own liberal and existentialist "de-Hellenizing" tradition back into The Fathers.[130]

On the opposite end of the spectrum, and most likely a Protestant Reformation "throwing of the baby out with the bath water" in response to either medieval Roman Catholicism[131] or nineteenth and twentieth-century liberal Protestantism, was the Biblicist and fundamentalist avoidance of any aspect of tradition. Holmes paints this mindset as holding the commitment that:

> God has given us his truth in the Bible, our job is to live it and proclaim it, what other people may or may not have thought about it in the past is of no interest to us, that they were generally wrong is evident from the poor state of the 'traditional' churches.[132]

These Protestants (often evangelicals) have bought into Georges Florovsky's "pattern of decay" reading of the patristic era discussed earlier in this chapter. As Bromiley helpfully puts it:

> As they seem to see it, the patristic age brought a rapid declension from apostolic Christianity. From at least the early second century, doctrines and practices developed that swept the church into a movement which culminated in the Middle Ages and which still continues in Roman Catholicism, Eastern Orthodoxy, and the Coptic Church. The Reformation represented a return to biblical Christianity but, in the eyes of some, even this was an imperfect return both theologically and practically. Hence the patristic appeal of the Reformers might be construed

129. Wiles, *Archetypal Heresy*.

130. Sara Parvis argues much of patristic scholarship from this time is "ineluctably Hegelian." See Parvis, *Marcellus of Ancyra*, 3.

131. Perhaps the focus on the numerical *Consensus Patrum*.

132. Holmes, *Listening to the Past*, x.

as a point of weakness rather than of strength . . . Granted this
type of interpretation, there is obviously little to be learned from
The Fathers.[133]

This viewpoint is the traditional Protestant and Reformed view of an "ecclesiastical golden age" intensified to its extreme in response to medieval
Roman Catholicism and Protestant liberalism. So, by the time of the mid-
twentieth century, evangelical Protestants were, in large part, ignorant of
the tradition of The Fathers. As such, the time was ripe for a "return" to and
"discovery" of the patristic tradition amongst evangelical Protestants, which
shall be explored in the next chapter of this book.

CONCLUSION

This chapter has explored how there have been diverse views of the *Consensus Patrum*, not only among Protestants, Catholics, and Orthodox but
also (and perhaps even more so) among the early Protestants themselves.
This chapter argued that the Eastern Orthodox traditionally view the patristic tradition synthetically and through the lens of Gregory Palamas (often
as he is interpreted in the neopalamite school). This chapter also argued
that the common factor among Western theologians turning to the *consensus* is that Augustine is core and Augustinian themes are central (for the
Catholics, Augustine read through Aquinas). However, by the time of the
mid-twentieth century, the majority of evangelical Protestants avoided The
Fathers. Indeed, it seemed that The Fathers and the *Consensus Patrum* were
the inheritance of Roman Catholics, Eastern Orthodox and (in a very critical way) the liberal tradition. Thus, immediately prior to Torrance's time,
his own evangelical and Reformed tradition was dominated by two opposite
viewpoints, namely, a liberal denial of the importance of The Fathers or the
Biblicist avoidance of The Fathers.

There are numerous parallel elements as well as divergences between
Torrance's notion of the *Consensus Patrum* and the view of the patristic tradition of the Roman Catholic, Eastern Orthodox, and Protestant traditions
discussed in this chapter. As will be discussed in the subsequent chapters of
this book, Torrance's notion of the *consensus* is Christologically-centered
and rooted in the Nicene doctrine of ὁμοούσιον τῷ Πατρί and the epistemological and soteriological implications that surround them, as Torrance
sees them. This conception is traditionally Protestant in many ways, for
example following the Reformed emphasis on the doctrines of Trinity and

---

133. Bromiley, "Promise of Patristic Studies," 127.

Christology (as seen in Calvin) and having select key figures rather than the Orthodox synthetic approach and the Catholic numerical view. Yet Torrance also shares elements in common with the Roman Catholics and the Eastern Orthodox, as shall be seen, particularly Florovsky's call to return to the "mind" of The Fathers and the emphasis on piety. In many ways, the Torrancian *Consensus Patrum* is, in a sense, a Reformed evangelical version of Newman's "development of doctrine." As such, Torrance's vision of the *consensus* is unique in relation to others' notions of the *consensus* including his own Reformed tradition.

Torrance's conception of the *consensus* is not numerical in any way. For him, the *consensus* cannot be measured in an empirical sense at all. Rather, as noted in the introduction of this book, for him the *consensus* means "classical theology" and chapters 3 and 4 of this book will show how it is more of a shared mindset and conviction, centered upon the fulcrum of the ὁμοούσιον. However, Torrance's view has certain similarities to the Catholic view of the development of doctrine. Torrance does not explore the notion as such explicitly anywhere. Yet, for him different eras of the history of theology provided different areas of theological development. For example, as shall be seen in chapter 4 of this book, Torrance sees The Fathers as contributing an emphasis on the being of God in his acts, and Reformers, the acts of God in his being, and Karl Barth bringing the two together. Furthermore, Torrance, in many ways, sees Athanasius and Karl Barth as mutually informing one another owing to their shared theological conviction surrounding the being of God and the acts of God. Therefore, though Athanasius may not have used Barthian language, Torrance feels comfortable putting Barthian-type words in his mouth. No doubt, this is not exactly the same as Newman's development of doctrine, but there is substantial overlap.

Torrance's notion of the *consensus* is most similar to the traditional Protestant conception. The first aspect of notability is that his overall vision is basically the same. Torrance does not explicitly define any era of orthodoxy or intentionally identify a "golden era," but Athanasius and Cyril of Alexandria are clear favorites. Therefore, in practice Torrance sees a golden era of patristic theology, namely, from Irenaeus to Cyril of Alexandria. Second, Torrance's genealogy of church history has significant similarity to that of Philip Schaff inasmuch as they both view an evangelical stream faithful to the Gospel running through church history. The following chapters of this book will unpack these elements in full.

In conclusion, Torrance's vision of the *Consensus Patrum* shares many traits with other views. Yet, it is also unique. Mainly, Torrance's uniqueness lies in his rooting the *consensus* in the ὁμοούσιον and Athanasius, and more generally, catholic themes and figures. Torrance's vision is a unique synthesis of Reformed and patristic orthodoxy, centered on the person of Christ. Herein, he provides a way forward for ecumenical rapprochement between different Christian denominations also rooted in the theology of The Fathers.

Torrance did not exist in a cultural vacuum. By the time of the mid-twentieth century the two opposing approaches to tradition (liberal and fundamentalist) set the parameters for potential readings of the tradition of The Fathers. This polarized situation typically left evangelicals in complete ignorance of the patristic tradition and set the stage for evangelicals to "discover" The Fathers. On account of this, the twentieth century has witnessed a movement of *ressourcement* among Protestant evangelicals. Nevertheless, the outcome of this discovery of The Fathers has been varying amongst evangelicals. The next chapter of this book will examine the twentieth century return to the patristic tradition by evangelicals, arguing for Torrance's uniqueness and setting the stage for a full study and assessment of Torrance's own version of the *Consensus Patrum*.

Chapter 2

Protestant Evangelical "Discoveries" of The Fathers

After centuries of separation, the orthodox way is at long last dis-covering its evangelical partners. For too long, evangelicals have remained distanced from many of the classic themes of orthodoxy . . . But why just now this rediscovery of classic Christian wisdom occurring among evangelicals? What is drawing evangelicals to-ward ancient Christian writers and their way of reading scripture? What accounts for this rapid and basic reversal of mood among the inheritors of the traditions of Protestant revivalism?

Thomas Oden, *The Rebirth of Orthodoxy*, 65.

INTRODUCTION

The previous chapter offered an historical overview of the *Consensus Patrum* in Roman Catholicism, Eastern Orthodoxy, and Protestantism. The chapter argued that by the twentieth century evangelical Protestantism found itself on a precipice faced with the polarized options of Biblicist ignorance or lib-eral avoidance of the tradition of The Fathers. Chronologically, this chapter picks up where the previous chapter left off and offers a close-up examina-tion of mid-twentieth century evangelicalism's relationship to the church fathers; by this time evangelical Protestantism was ripe for a "discovery" of The Fathers.

In his article *Theologies of Retrieval*[1] John Webster argues that there is a movement of *ressourcement* in contemporary theology wherein theologians are returning to classical theological sources by which to inform the present theological condition. For Webster, theologies of retrieval, though differing from one another in many ways, especially regarding a "genealogy of modernity," all share the view that modern and contemporary Christian theology has wrongly separated theology both from its object and the classical theologians of the past who were considerably more theologically objective.[2] Accordingly, theologies of retrieval attempt to return theological reflection to its objective and realist focus by means of using classical theologians from the past who were more objectively focused.[3] Therefore, theologians of retrieval work to safeguard theology from "the constraints of circumstance" and refocus theology on "the object of Christian doctrine, God."[4]

Webster has a number of critiques of theologies of retrieval.[5] One such critique concerns how theologians of retrieval choose their sources. As he points out throughout his article, the plethora of different theologians of retrieval have diverse "sources of choice." Seemingly if all theologians of retrieval are as objective and realist as Webster surmises there should not be as much discrepancy among them regarding sources. This chapter will argue that all theologies of retrieval are not, in fact, as entirely objectively focused as Webster's article would suggest. Furthermore, not all theologians of retrieval effectively remain faithful to their own tradition while retrieving The Fathers. The argument shall emerge that Torrance's Christologically objective and evangelically informed method of retrieval centered upon the ὁμοούσιον and informed by a personal notion of grace (which the remaining chapters of this book shall focus upon) is an example for Protestant and evangelical theologians wishing to return to and appropriate the Greek Fathers in an objective manner while remaining faithful to their own tradition.

THE CONTEXT

The ecclesiastical and cultural climate of the mid-twentieth century was ripe for a return to The Fathers. Last chapter argued that although, in the eyes of the Reformers at least, the Protestant Reformation was a return to The

---

1. Webster, "Theologies of Retrieval," 583–99. Though, Webster admits, "'theologies of retrieval' . . . is simply a convenience in absence of a better designation . . . " (584).

2. Ibid., 584.

3. Ibid., 590.

4. Ibid., 594.

5. Ibid., 596–97.

Fathers and to the faith and practice of the early Christian church, the Reformers failed to provide a consensual and detailed objective guide for appropriation of The Fathers other than, perhaps, reading them in submission to the Scriptures. However, during the past thirty to fifty years (and even more recently as "Generation X" Christians have grown into adulthood) the prevailing paradigm has shifted from modernism to postmodernism and evangelical Christians have been returning to classical Christianity in hordes.[6] Indeed, one reporter, Tom Breen, reports that about one-third of all Orthodox priests in the U.S. and about 43% of Orthodox seminarians are converts.[7]

Last chapter argued that immediately preceding these movements of retrieval, liberal de-Hellenization and Biblicist avoidance of The Fathers was the approach of much of twentieth-century Protestant theology and, accordingly, The Fathers were basically ignored. It is out of the latter group of Christians that the contemporary return to and retrieval of classical patristic theology has emerged. While this version of Protestant Christianity does not always exist in textbook theology[8] it is best represented in the writings of those figures so dissatisfied with their own tradition that they converted to another.[9] Indeed, this approach has not existed so much in writing as in practice of popular evangelical piety. The fundamentalist approach to The Fathers is generally found within those groups that have an extremely narrow interpretation of the Reformation principle of *Sola Scriptura*. Regardless, over the past half century to century (if not longer) evangelicals have generally avoided the church fathers, at least in practice if not formally.[10]

6. See Carroll, *The New Faithful*. Carroll documents this return across denominational boundaries. Though this trend really began a century earlier with John Henry Newman as was hinted at in the previous chapter of this book and will be explored more fully below.

7. See Breen, "More Americans."

8. Because with the exception of highly fundamentalist theologians most scholars still looked to The Fathers such as Augustine.

9. In the words of Stewart: "We must be frank in admitting that such writers have reached their conclusions on the basis of perceptions gleaned within the strands of Evangelicalism in which they were nurtured." See Stewart, "Evangelicalism and Patristic Christianity," 308. He later puts it: "The neglect of the early Church and its teaching is a relatively modern phenomenon, afflicting both conservative and liberal Protestantism for a period of some decades early in the twentieth century, and waning since the 1950s" (320). The point being that ignorance of classical Christianity is not a Protestant principle; indeed the opposite is the case. The Protestant Reformation was a return to classical Christianity. The ignorance of tradition has only occurred in twentieth-century Protestantism and is entirely un-Protestant.

10. Holmes notes that Protestantism has seen itself in line with tradition throughout its history and though there was a short denial of this during the enlightenment,

There have been a plethora of examples of Protestants who have converted to Roman Catholicism or to Eastern Orthodoxy after their "discovery" of the Greek Fathers including Jaroslav Pelikan who became Eastern Orthodox after a life as a Lutheran historian of dogma,[11] Peter Gillquist who along with a large group from the evangelical parachurch organization Campus Crusade for Christ became Antiochene Orthodox,[12] and, of course, John Henry Newman who became Roman Catholic.[13] These groups fairly consistently depict their tradition, at least in practice if not formally, as ignoring all aspects of Christian tradition, especially Eastern. What opened the eyes of these Protestants? What allowed them to "discover" classical Christianity?

Theologians have noted that during the past thirty years or so the church has experienced what sociologists have termed the cultural shift from the "modern"[14] to the "postmodern"[15] mindset. Accordingly, the door has been opened towards a return to the classical Christian tradition. The modern to postmodern paradigm shift has brought about a change in Christianity in a multiplicity of regards and many evangelical theologians have noted the influence of this shift upon the church.[16] However, relevant

---

Protestantism resumed the earlier mindset in nineteenth century with, for example, Schleiermacher, even while totally changing tradition, seeing himself in line with it. See Holmes, *Listening to the Past*, 2. Though, as this chapter pointed out earlier, the Protestant liberal tradition clearly saw itself in line with tradition in a much different way than the Reformers, namely, looking to some figures (e.g., Athanasius for Harnack) who preserved the "core" of the Gospel in a Christianity that had largely been "Hellenized."

11. See Stewart, "Evangelicalism and Patristic Christianity," 307. This is indeed a generalization for, of course, Pelikan cannot be said to have "discovered" The Fathers as he was a very influential historian of dogma.

12. See Gillquist, *Becoming Orthodox* and Gillquist, *Coming Home*.

13. Newman, *Apologia Pro Vita Sua*.

14. Generally considered to be dualist, rationalist, individualist, and objective.

15. Generally considered to be holistic, sensual, communal, and subjective/relativist.

16. Scot McKnight states: "Living as a Christian in a postmodern context means different things to different people. Some . . . will minister *to* postmoderns, others *with* postmoderns, and still others *as* postmoderns. David Wells at Gordon-Conwell Theological Seminary falls into the *to* category, seeing postmoderns as trapped in moral relativism and epistemological bankruptcy out of which they must be rescued. Others minister *with* postmoderns. That is, they live with, work with, and converse with postmoderns, accepting their postmodernity as a fact of life in our world. Such Christians view postmodernity as a present condition into which we are called to proclaim and live out the gospel" (McKnight, "Five Streams of the Emerging Church").

to this book, the paradigm broke the evangelical church out of a-historical individualism.[17]

Robert Webber has commented on the postmodern opening of the door. He argues that the mindset and cultural milieu of postmodernism is similar to that of the early Christian Fathers and thus has traced a significant number of postmodern Christians returning to classical Christianity.[18] According to Webber, Christians in the postmodern world with postmodern yearnings and a postmodern mindset find the classical Fathers of Christianity attractive owing to a shared mindset, shared surrounding culture, and the sense of historical authority. Webber traced and predicted further retrievals of the classical Christian tradition and figures by the postmodern Christian generation.[19]

The latter half of the twentieth century and beginning of the twenty-first century has seen a paradigm shift from modernism to postmodernism which opened the door for evangelicals to return to classical Christianity. Accordingly, during this time there has been a resurgence of patristic studies among evangelicals. Indeed, there has been a move towards *ressourcement* within evangelicalism, in which Torrance has played and continues to play an influential role. This may be a sign of something big. As Webber puts it, "throughout history a revived interest in the insights of the early church has usually been accompanied by significant renewal in the church."[20] Thus, it

17. Though this is generally true across national and cultural borders, it should be noted that evangelicalism's a-historical individualism is, in many ways, more of a North American phenomenon. As Alistair McGrath points out, evangelicalism in Britain has a stronger common mindset of "family history" because of the fact that evangelicalism has usually existed within the mainline churches (as opposed to parachurch organizations, smaller denominations, and non-denominational churches as in North America). Thus, British evangelicalism sees itself going back to the 18th century revivals and even the patristic era. Owing to this difference, the North American Christians have witnessed a trend towards mass conversion to, for example, Eastern Orthodoxy, because of their sense of history. This is not as common in Britain. See McGrath, "Trinitarian Theology," 52. Notably, McGrath goes on to argue that the common strand to all of Christian tradition is the doctrine of the Trinity; he proposed a return to this classic doctrine as a way forward to Christian ecumenism based on common tradition (see ibid., 55–60).

18. Webber, *Ancient-Future Faith*, 21–22, 27. Webber notes the switch from dualism to holism and rationalism to mystery in addition to ambiguity, community, interrelationship of all things, symbolism, and emphasis on the visual (35). He says: "Classical Christianity speaks to a holistic and integrated view of life," which, Webber contends, is what the postmodern generation loves (27).

19. This is not to equate postmodernism with *ressourcement*. Rather, postmodernism opened the door for *ressourcement* by breaking Western Christianity out of a prevailing individualist a-historical mindset.

20. Webber, *Ancient-Future Faith*, 34.

seems highly probable that the current trend towards the classical Church Fathers signifies Christianity is currently on the brink of important revival, making Torrance highly relevant as a figure to be uplifted as an example.

Currently, evangelicals are returning to classical Christianity in great masses.[21] In her recent journalistic study, Colleen Carroll has documented this current trend towards traditional Christianity. By means of interviews, surveys, and significant study, Caroll has chronicled that currently there is indeed a strong trend amongst younger Christians towards traditional Christianity. In her words: "Amid the swirl of spiritual, religious, and moral choices that exist in American culture today, many young adults are opting for the tried-and-true worldview of Christian orthodoxy."[22]

As young adults from "Generation X" and beyond turn to traditional Christianity they choose classical Christian authorities such as the classical Fathers and classical Christian forms of devotion and worship.[23] Throughout her important book Carroll records countless instances of Christians from all denominations (and none) returning to classical Christian figures, theology, morality, and practice. Carroll reports that huge numbers of Christians have been converting from evangelical churches to Roman Catholicism and Eastern Orthodoxy. In fact, Carroll points out that according to a recent Roman Catholic survey, 61% of Roman Catholic coverts (of those surveyed) had converted to Catholicism from other Christian denominations and, on the Eastern Orthodox side, from 1967–1997, the number of American parishes associated with the Antiochene Archdiocese in North America, the Eastern Orthodox church attracting the majority of North American protestant converts to Eastern Orthodoxy, tripled in the number of parishes.[24]

---

21. Regarding the current trend, one newspaper reporter notes: "Now about one-third of all U. S. Orthodox priests are converts — and that number is likely to grow, according to Alexei D. Krindatch, research director at the Patriarch Athenagoras Orthodox Institute in Berkeley, California. A 2006 survey of the four Orthodox seminaries in the country found that about 43% of seminarians are converts, Krindatch said" (Breen, "More Americans").

22. Carroll, *The New Faithful*, 15. As one interviewee puts it: "They're rebelling against the rebellion . . . they want tradition" (36). Carroll notes that the form of this trend is not uniform. Some have become Eastern Orthodox, some Roman Catholic, some have returned to conservative evangelicalism. However, there are shared characteristics, namely, a desire for mystery, guidance from trustworthy sources of authority, and a way to engage culture (15–16).

23. Ibid., 63.

24. Ibid., 64.

A typical North American timeline is that of Peter Gillquist[25] or Thomas Howard,[26] starting out as an evangelical often involved in para-church ministry, a "discovery" of the early church, the subsequent conclusion that "evangelicalism is not enough" (to use Howard's language), and, finally, a conversion to the Roman Catholic (Howard) or Eastern Orthodox (Gillquist) Church.

Carroll puts forward the contention that for contemporary young adult Christians, tradition is "sexy and exotic."[27] These Christians crave classical elements such as mystery, paradox, and Gregorian or Byzantine chant. Indeed, Carroll attributes parts of these desires to "Generation X" Christians' love for the classical Christian counter-cultural attitude. One of Carroll's interviewees noted that more and more young Christians are attracted by classical counter-cultural forms of Christian piety such as monasticism.[28]

Carroll's study has shown that many Christians who have grown up in Protestant evangelicalism are attracted to the liturgical and sacramental life of Eastern Orthodoxy and Roman Catholicism. The rich liturgy and the emphasis on the importance and substance of Communion and Baptism proves attractive to many who have grown up in traditions that view the sacraments as subsidiary to preaching and evangelism due, in part, to a "memorial" sacramental theology which views the sacraments as lacking substance.[29] Regardless of the specific attraction to ancient Christianity, Carroll's study has sociologically documented the movement of *ressource-ment* in which this book is arguing Torrance plays an important role.

There have been, generally, three outcomes to Protestant evangelical retrievals of the Greek Fathers. First, that exemplified by John Henry Newman, Thomas Howard, and Peter Gillquist, namely, the "discovery" of classical Christianity and the conclusion that contemporary Protestantism is not a faithful continuation (or, at least, not the most faithful) of the early church and, accordingly, conversion to either the Roman Catholic Church or the Eastern Orthodox Church. The second type is a more subjective and relative appropriation of the classical Greek Fathers, exemplified by the Emergent/Emerging church, and, though their intentions are good, they lack a consistent objective basis. This group tends to choose their favorite

25. See Gillquist, *Becoming Orthodox*.

26. See Howard, *Evangelical Is Not Enough*; Howard, *Lead, Kindly Light*.

27. Carroll, *The New Faithful*, 83.

28. Ibid., 91.

29. For example, this was one of the reasons Thomas Howard converted. See Howard, *Evangelical Is Not Enough*. Notably, it does not always entail conversion. See, e.g., Kimball's book about incorporating these elements into "Emerging Churches" in Kimball, *The Emerging Church*.

patristic figures and themes based on a (usually subjectively chosen) theme of selection. The third response, which could be broadly labeled "evangelical," is exemplified by Thomas Oden and Robert Webber, who retrieve the classical Church Fathers and appropriate them into their own tradition and context by means of Christological and evangelical appropriation. It will be argued that this third response has the strongest merit out of the three but that Torrance's has much from which they can learn, and therefore Torrance has been and should continue to be used as a legitimate and helpful guide for Protestant, evangelical, and Reformed appropriation of classical Christianity.

CONVERSION: WHEN EVANGELICAL IS NOT ENOUGH

There are numerous figures that have recently converted to Roman Catholicism and Eastern Orthodoxy from Protestant denominations. Indeed, especially in the North American context, it is a growing trend for Protestant evangelicals to "discover" the Greek Fathers and subsequently conclude that the Roman Catholic or Eastern Orthodox communions are the only (or at least more faithful) expression of the church and theology of The Fathers.[30] Numerous books on this topic abound such as those entitled "Evangelical Is Not Enough"[31] and "Coming Home"[32] which describe Protestant evangelical Christians who, having discovered the church of the Greek Fathers, conclude evangelical Christianity, though good as far as it goes, is simply "not enough."

The mindset of Protestants whose return to the Greek Fathers results in conversion to Roman Catholicism or Eastern Orthodoxy is because of their belief that they had found the fruition of the ecclesiastical "golden age" of The Fathers. While their conversion was no doubt owing to pious convictions and they cannot be faulted for this, this section will argue that their conversion was unnecessary and these groups are open to two critiques: (1) buying into the falsehood of the "golden age" conception and (2) an objectivity centered upon external theological systems as opposed to Christ and his Gospel.

---

30. Though it is not exclusive to North America. See e.g., Harper, *The True Light*. Harper was a major evangelical figure in the charismatic movement within the Church of England who converted to Eastern Orthodoxy and became an Orthodox priest. His reasons for conversion were primarily doctrinal and he saw the Church of England as having fallen into theological liberalism.

31. Howard, *Evangelical Is Not Enough*.

32. Gillquist, *Coming Home*.

In order to explore and draw out these arguments this chapter will focus on a selection of case studies: John Henry Newman who converted to Roman Catholicism after life in the Church of England and a selection of North American evangelicals who have converted to Eastern Orthodoxy in recent decades, most notably Peter Gillquist and the Campus Crusade for Christ.

John Henry Newman was the figure who, in many ways, represents the modern return to the Greek Fathers in general and Athanasius of Alexandria in particular. Newman represents those Protestants who, after returning to the Greek Fathers, conclude that their own tradition is not the true and most faithful continuation of the church of The Fathers.[33]

Newman had a certain view, discussed in the previous chapter, which he called "the development of doctrine" and which ultimately led the Oxford theologian to become Roman Catholic.[34] Newman held that one could not understand the early Fathers without the later Fathers and from here began to understand doctrine as having developed throughout the patristic era.[35] After a life of indwelling the life and theology of The Fathers[36] Newman arrived at the conclusion that "modern Catholicism is nothing else but simply the legitimate growth and complement that is the natural and necessary development of the doctrine of the early church."[37] Thus Newman's

33. Bromiley helpfully notes that the Oxford Movement and Anglo-Catholicism appealed to The Fathers for practices that were abandoned with the Reformation. As shall be explored, Newman ultimately concluded that contemporary Protestantism was inconsistent with what he saw in early Christianity. Others, such as Kenneth Kirk adopted such things as Apostolic Succession and Dix developed a view of the liturgy that looked more Roman Catholic than Anglican. Thus, the Anglo-Catholic movement is more in line with the stream of figures who, upon returning to the classical Fathers, convert because their expression of Christianity looks less like evangelicalism and more like Roman Catholicism. Bromiley helpfully elaborates that the Anglo-Catholic method of appropriation tends to read modern views (specifically Catholic) into The Fathers and sees Roman Catholicism as the faithful expression of patristic Christianity thusly either converting or adopting more Roman Catholic practices (e.g., liturgy, Apostolic Succession, etc.). See Bromiley, "Promise of Patristic Studies." See further Webber and Bloesch, *The Orthodox Evangelicals*, 130–31.

34. Newman, *Apologia Pro Vita Sua*, 132–33, 157–58. As Newman worked through writing the text he says his "difficulties so cleared away that [he] ceased to speak of "the Roman Catholics," and boldly called them Catholics" (158). Ultimately Newman concludes: "Modern Rome was in truth ancient Antioch, Alexandria, and Constantinople" (133).

35. King, *Newman and the Alexandrian Fathers*, 51–52.

36. Newman says that he had an early devotion to The Fathers and that from an early age he was convinced that the religion of The Fathers was that of the primitive Christians. See Newman, *Apologia Pro Vita Sua*, 4, 17.

37. Newman, *An Essay on the Development of Christian Doctrine*, 123.

famous phrase: "to be deep in history is to cease to be a Protestant."[38] In fact, Newman resolves: "Were Athanasius to come to life he would undoubtedly recognize the Catholic Church as his own communion."[39] This conclusion caused Newman to convert to Roman Catholicism after a life in the Church of England. In his mind, Roman Catholicism, not Protestantism, is the faithful development of the ancient church.[40]

When he became a Roman Catholic Newman felt as if he was "coming into port after a rough sea."[41] Newman, who had indwelt the life and theology of the Greek Fathers for such a long time desiring to see his own Anglican tradition as faithful to them, ultimately concluded that the Church of England was not the communion of such great heroes of the faith as Athanasius but that in order to join with their tradition he must become Roman Catholic, the development of the church of antiquity.

However, Newman seems to have been committed to a fairly static view of tradition in the form of an ecclesiastical golden age. According to King, Newman held that The Fathers were correct in their interpretation because (a) they were nearer to the apostles in time, (b) they conserved the traditions, and (c) they were pious.[42] Here, Newman was clearly committed to the "golden age" notion embedded within Protestantism, perhaps inheriting it from his own Protestant tradition.

Another excellent example of evangelicalism in the eyes of the evangelical convert to Roman Catholicism or Eastern Orthodoxy can be found in the story of Thomas Howard.[43] Howard, originally a prominent North American evangelical professor at a Christian college journeyed to the Episcopalian and then the Roman Catholic communion. His journey, unique in certain aspects, captures the general mindset of the plethora of evangelicals who continue to follow similar paths to Roman Catholicism and Eastern Orthodoxy.

Howard was convinced that evangelicalism, while generally not wrong on any issues of doctrine, simply "is not enough."[44] Upon discovering more traditional Christianity during time spent in England, Howard confesses,

38. Ibid., 6.

39. Ibid., 71.

40. Newman, *Apologia Pro Vita Sua*, 100: "I could not prove that the Anglican communion was an integral part of the One Church . . . and I could not defend our separation from Rome and her faith."

41. Ibid., 160.

42. King, *Newman and the Alexandrian Fathers*, 45–46.

43. Howard conceptualized evangelicalism as "para-church" and "non-denominational" rather than being any specific ecclesiastical tradition.

44. Howard, *Evangelical Is Not Enough*, 2.

"it opened my imagination backward into history."[45] In addition to being generally a-historical, Howard concluded that evangelicalism had "Manichaean" tendencies[46] liturgically and that evangelicalism in North America was highly individualistic.[47]

Howard represents the greater movement of Protestant evangelicals, mostly in North America, who have discovered that Christianity has a history and was liturgical in her expression in history.[48] In 1985 Howard converted to Roman Catholicism; many evangelical Christians in North America have followed in similar paths since Howard. These Christians' minds are, like Howard's, opened when they discover church history and liturgy. Upon discovering these two aspects they become convinced that evangelicalism, though good enough so far as it goes, is "not enough." They conclude that evangelicalism simply is not a faithful expression of the fullness of the church as seen in history. As Fr. Antony Hughes, former Protestant evangelical turned Eastern Orthodox Priest says of those who convert, "a lot of people discover there is such incredible depth in Christianity. There's two thousand years of this."[49]

The story of the late Peter Gillquist and the North American parachurch organization, Campus Crusade for Christ, is much akin to that of Thomas Howard. Peter Gillquist and the rest of the group documented in Gillquist's ecclesiastical autobiography, *Becoming Orthodox*,[50] were, according to Gillquist, "gung ho" evangelicals.[51] Active in campus outreach and para-church ministry, Gillquist and his group evangelized and ministered on university campuses; however, they decided that their form of ministry was, ultimately, ineffective. Gillquist concluded that the root of the problem lay in the un-ecclesiastical nature of their ministry.[52] For, they were living

45. Ibid., 41. See ibid., 41–61 for a fuller account of Howard's time in England.

46. Ibid., 35.

47. Howard said: "It was as though the Bible had been written yesterday and I were the first man to open it" (*Evangelical Is Not Enough*, 67). Though, he admitted, evangelicalism never actually said this as such but somehow he left evangelicalism with this "feeling."

48. In Howard's estimate: "Enough people are following a similar route to call it a 'movement in the Church'" (*Evangelical Is Not Enough*, 149).

49. Quoted in Carroll, *The New Faithful*, 60.

50. Gillquist, *Becoming Orthodox*.

51. Ibid., 4–5.

52. Ibid., 9–14. Gillquist states: "We get decisions, we get the commitments to Christ, we are building the organization and recruiting the staff, but we are not affecting a change. We are a failure in the midst of our own success" (9).

out a Christianity of "Christ without church."[53] Indeed it seemed to Gillquist that they were evangelizing but sending out countless Christians without any type of discipleship.

Owing to Gillquist and his fellow Campus Crusaders' dissatisfaction with their ministry they decided to explore what the early church really looked like. They soon discovered that the early Christian church was indeed not parachurch but rather more organized; and thus they wished to turn the Campus Crusade organization into a church; a desire quickly squelched by the leaders in the organization.[54] Therefore, they left the Campus Crusade and began a grand attempt at forming an ecclesiastical body on the basis of what they read in the New Testament and classical Christian texts.

After leaving Campus Crusade, Gillquist and his fellows split up and formed a number of house and small congregations throughout the United States. Soon, however, they concluded that they needed to work together and formed a conglomerate of parishes.[55] The group decided to figure out what the early church really was all about and accordingly they each took a different element to study about classical Christianity, church history, classic doctrine, worship, and the person of Christ ultimately gathering for a retreat in 1975 and comparing notes.[56] Their conclusion was that the classical church was liturgical, episcopal, and defined in doctrine by the ecumenical councils.[57] They decided to form an ecclesiastical community based on their findings. Initially they called themselves the "New Covenant Apostolic Order" but eventually became the "Evangelical Orthodox Church."[58]

Thus far Gillquist and his fellows were committed evangelicals who were intentionally returning to classical Christian figures and practice. They were appropriating these themes and figures into their own tradition, albeit rather statically akin to the Anglo-Catholics. However, they had no objective guiding principle other than discovery of the early church for the purpose of contemporary imitation and application. During this process, one or two of their leaders had converted to the Eastern Orthodox Church; one who still received their literature noticed they were sounding more and more Eastern Orthodox and accordingly put them in touch with Russian Orthodox Church leader and professor at St. Vladimir's Orthodox Theological Seminary in New York, Alexander Schmemann. Upon meeting the Evangelical

53. Ibid., 13–14.

54. Ibid., 18–21.

55. Ibid., 22–26. Leaders over the age of 40 became elders.

56. Ibid., 29–33.

57. Ibid., 34–48.

58. Ibid., 49–50.

Orthodox, Schmemann apparently commented, "they're Orthodox, but they don't know it yet."[59] Eventually the Evangelical Orthodox stepped inside an Eastern Orthodox Church and, to their surprise; everything they had read about in the classical Christian church had materialized.[60]

The Evangelical Orthodox Church ultimately decided they wanted to formally enter into communion with the Eastern Orthodox Church. So, they headed for Istanbul to see the Ecumenical Patriarchate of Constantinople.[61] To their dismay they were turned back and told to work towards communion with the Orthodox in America.[62] The Evangelical Orthodox Church then met with the Patriarchate of the Antiochene Orthodox Church and the Antiochene Metropolitan of North America, who was significantly more open to their desires.[63] Soon after (in 1987) the majority of the parishes of the Evangelical Orthodox Church were incorporated into the Antiochene Orthodox Church.[64] The conclusion of Gillquist and their community was that Orthodoxy was simply a fuller and truer evangelicalism.

The desire to appropriate classical Christianity into the contemporary church is commendable; however, to feel the need to convert to another denomination because "evangelical is not enough" is, at best, unnecessary and, at worst, conforming to an external notion of ecclesiology and commitment to external definitions of Christianity.[65] The evangelicals who convert often conclude that appropriation of classical Christianity necessarily entails conforming to the practice of the early church, much of which may have had

59. Ibid., 139.

60. Ibid., 137.

61. Ibid., 143–44.

62. Ibid., 149–52.

63. Ibid., 154–56.

64. Ibid., 161–72; Metropolitan Philip, "Metropolitan Philip's Address," 4–10. A number of parishes, mostly in the Midwest, remained as the Evangelical Orthodox. They exist to this day committed to evangelicalism. According to one former member in personal interaction, their worship is the Liturgy of St. John Chrysostom chanted in a monotone and, according to Peter Gillquist in personal interaction, "half Liturgy of St. John Chrysostom and half 'make-it-up.'" See the Evangelical Orthodox Church website for further information: http://www.evangelicalorthodox.org/.

65. Sauve's critique of George's Florovsky's retrieval of the Greek Fathers is applicable here as well. Though Sauve generally approves of Florovsky's appropriation of The Fathers he says of the Russian theologian's "neopatristic synthesis" that "if one holds to the neopatristic synthesis as an absolute methodology for doing theology . . . one treats The Fathers in the same way that Protestants treat the Scriptures; *sola scriptura* is replaced with *sola patristica*. The Fathers are used as proof-texts . . . " The figures and groups discussed in this section who feel the need to convert once "discovering" church history also, quite legalistically, use The Fathers in a manner similar to proof-texting. See Sauve, "Georges V. Florovsky," 83.

more to do with culture than solely theological commitment. Thus, they consider it impossible to retrieve the life and work of The Fathers within their own Protestant traditions. This is ultimately a convoluting of the distinction between faith and order and it contains elements of legalism.[66] These figures felt the need to conform to the external aspects of patristic theology and life far too literally.[67] Their static approach is similar to what, as shall be more fully examined in chapter 5 of this book, Torrance sees in the Western church, namely, the "Tertullian type of approach" towards both Scripture and confession[68] where, as he sees it, they reduce "the church's Confession of the Faith to systems of doctrinal presuppositions which are invested with prescriptive authority."[69] Ultimately, Torrance views this as dualist and argues for a separation of the substance of the faith from its formulation.[70] Torrance's helpful separation of faith and order as well as the object of faith from its formulation will be discussed later in this book. As the subsequent chapters on Torrance shall explore, Torrance saw a distinction between the substance of the faith (which he saw as core) and forms of piety (which he saw as peripheral).

THE EMERGENT/EMERGING CHURCH

Whereas some evangelicals, upon returning to The Fathers, saw the need to convert, others appropriate classical Christianity in, at best, a more subjective manner and, at worst, perhaps even tendentiously. One example of this approach is the Emergent/Emerging church.[71] These figures are, in many

66. This is not to say that converting to another denomination such as Roman Catholicism or Eastern Orthodoxy is inherently wrong; it can indeed be done rightly.

67. As Sauve helpfully puts it about Georges Florovsky: "Florovsky's admonition to 'follow The Fathers' does not mean just to quote their words (especially out of context) but to 'acquire their mind' . . . This recovery of the 'mind' of The Fathers—a recovery not only of their theology but of their existential attitude, their spiritual orientation, their piety and holiness—is behind his concept of *neopatristic synthesis*" (Sauve, "Georges V. Florovsky," 69). The group discussed above often tended towards the view that adopting the "mind" of The Fathers entailed literal imitation of their way of life. As will be argued, the "evangelicals" below, especially Torrance, were most in line with Florovsky's conception of adoption of the "mind of The Fathers."

68. See Torrance, *Theological Dialogue*, 1:107.

69. Ibid.

70. Ibid.

71. This is a largely North American Christian movement which, strongly dissatisfied with their usually seeker-sensitive and conservative evangelical Protestantism, is embracing a broader Christianity; a door opened by postmodernism. One could distinguish between "emerging" and "emergent," the former being the generic, umbrella term

ways, at the forefront of the contemporary "return to" the classical Greek
Fathers and, along with Torrance and the evangelical movement which will
be discussed below, very commendably set the stage for others to return to
the classical Fathers. However, they lack any objective guiding principle.[72]
Accordingly, their appropriation of The Fathers often tends towards subjec-
tivity and tendentiousness.

The first aspect to Emerging Christianity's appropriation of classical
Christianity entails their overall approach to theology. As many theologians from both within and without the movement point out, Emerging
Christianity adheres to a "post" theology, meaning, they define themselves
in relation to being after ("post") a number of elements. Herein, Emerging
Christianity is "post" a plethora of rudiments of traditional Christianity and
traditional Christian theology. For example, as Scot McKnight points out,
they are "post systematic theology." In his words:

> The emerging movement tends to be suspicious of systematic
> theology. Why? Not because we don't read systematics, but be-
> cause the diversity of theologies alarms us, no genuine consensus
> has been achieved, God didn't reveal a systematic theology but
> a storied narrative, and no language is capable of capturing the
> Absolute Truth who alone is God. Frankly, the emerging move-
> ment loves ideas and theology. It just doesn't have an airtight
> system or statement of faith. We believe the Great Tradition of-
> fers various ways for telling the truth about God's redemption in
> Christ, but we don't believe any one theology gets it absolutely
> right. Hence, a trademark feature of the emerging movement
> is that we believe all theology will remain a conversation about
> the Truth who is God in Christ through the Spirit, and about
> God's story of redemption at work in the church. No systematic
> theology can be final. In this sense, the emerging movement is
> radically Reformed.[73]

---

and the latter a specific group of the former. See Tickle, *The Great Emergence,* 163; See
also McKnight, "Five Streams," 1. The terms "Emerging Christianity," "Emergent," and
"Emerging" will be used synonymously in this book.

72. It should be noted that it is difficult to identify specifically emerging beliefs because their identity is defined more in terms of a generous approach and mindset than
actual set beliefs or ecclesiastical structures. Scot McKnight helpfully articulates that
their approach to theology is: "This is what I believe, but I could be wrong. What do you
think? Let's talk" (McKnight, "Five Streams," 5). Indeed, it is "a conversation" more than
anything. Byassee notes this also. See Byassee, "Emerging From What?" 251.

73. McKnight, "Five Streams," 5.

Additionally, Emergents are "post" modern.[74] Different members are more "postmodern" than others; they all, however, see themselves as responsive to and following from the Christianity of the modern age.[75]

Along similar lines, Emerging Christianity is, in many regards, a protest movement. So, along with being "post" systematic theology and "post" modern (and, indeed, sometimes "postmodern"), the movement is a response to the Christianity within which the leaders of the movement were reared. Indeed, as D. A. Carson in his critique of Emerging Christianity puts it, "the reforms that the movement encourages mirror the protests of the lives of many of its leaders."[76] Owing to Emerging Christianity's "post" mindset, they are, as a whole, suspicious of tradition, especially modernism, and especially the last twenty or so years.[77] Accordingly, they are often strongly allergic of anything hinting of "imperial Christianity" and often attempt a process akin to "de-Hellenization" in places they see necessary.[78]

Notably (perhaps even ironically), Emerging Christianity's suspicious attitude towards the past in general and modernism in particular has opened a door into the world of the classical Christianity of pre-modernity. The founders of Emerging Christianity arose out of the same seeker-sensitive mega-church evangelicalism that figures discussed above such as Peter Gillquist and Thomas Howard converted from; and, for both groups, this opened the door to the classical Christianity of the Eastern, Greek Fathers. However, Emerging Christianity's appropriation led not to conversion to a more historically rooted Christian denomination, as it did for Howard and Gillquist, but something rather different.

Overall, leading figures in Emerging Christianity are interested, at least in theory, in anything Christian before the modern era. However, other than this there is no other guiding principle for reading or appropriation.

---

74. Carson, *Becoming Conversant with the Emerging Church,* 29.

75. Dan Kimball is illustrative. He considers Emerging Christianity to be "post" seeker sensitive and mega-church. See Kimball, *The Emerging Church,* 27; See also Carson, *Becoming Conversant with the Emerging Church,* 38.

76. Carson, *Becoming Conversant with the Emerging Church,* 14.

77. As one Emerging author puts it: "In Emergent circles I sometimes find a nagging suspicion about the past—specifically, the near past—born of our heightened sensitivity to the compromises of the church within modernity. We're working to be something new—new theology and new ecclesial forms that are free or at least loosened from uncritical compromises with the modern ideologies make us anxious. Sometimes the past is problematic (at least the past that's closest to us, where we see such troubling compromises); other times, the past is our companion (many of us find great encouragement from the ancient, premodern church)" (Eerdman, "Digging Up the Past," 236–37).

78. See the account of Phyllis Tickle: Tickle, *The Great Emergence,* 161–62; McLaren, *Why Did Jesus?,* 81–86.

Indeed, their approach is, at best, highly eclectic. One recent Emerging author contends that Emergents follow a use of tradition which is "extemporaneous, free, meandering, playful."[79] Freedom as a general guiding principle shows up regularly in many Emerging authors both implicitly and explicitly. For example, one of the better-known Emerging authors, Tony Jones, wrote a book on the spiritual disciplines[80] following in the vein of authors such as Richard Foster.[81] Here, Jones' guiding principle for the appropriation of classical Christianity was simply spiritual disciplines and exercises and his discussion ranges from the Byzantine "Jesus Prayer" to contemporary Roman Catholic spirituality. Jones, in an attempt to stray from modern and seeker-sensitive forms of spirituality, wants to go deeper. Though a very helpful book on the spiritual disciplines across all the traditions and covering a great span of history, Jones' appropriation seems to be based on nothing more than his own selective reading of classical Christianity.

Another notable figure from Emergent Christianity, Shane Claiborne who lives as a "neo-monastic" in Philadelphia, Pennsylvania,[82] returns to The Fathers idiosyncratically. These "neo-monastics" of Emerging Christianity are communities of married and single Christians living intentionally in a community devoted to charity. They have chosen this one, arguably very important, element of classical Christianity and appropriated it for themselves. However, in practice, their way of life resembles very little of the ancient monastic tradition other than a shared name.[83] This, once again, portrays the highly eclectic method of appropriation.[84]

The selectivity and eclecticism of Emerging Christianity's appropriation of classical Christianity is perhaps clearest in the writings of Brian McLaren, particularly in his book "Generous Orthodoxy."[85] Here, McLaren identifies orthodoxy with humility, charity, courage, and diligence.[86] In

79. Eerdman, "Digging Up the Past," 242.

80. Jones, *The Sacred Way.*

81. Foster, *Celebration of Discipline.*

82. See Claiborne, *Irresistible Revolution.*

83. Upon hearing about the "neo-monastics," a Greek Orthodox monk once said in personal conversation, with a cheeky grin on his face, "tell him to come see us 'old monastics'" (the contextual implication being that the "neo-monastics" have nothing to do with—and want nothing to do with—the "old monastics."

84. Byasee is less critical. He believes that the neo-monastic movement is bringing a much-needed element back into evangelicalism. See Byasee, "Emerging From What?" 258. While it could be argued that monasticism is indeed a much-needed element, neo-monasticism is nothing like monasticism.

85. McLaren, *A Generous Orthodoxy.*

86. Ibid., 30.

short, for McLaren orthodoxy and orthopraxy cannot be separated and, indeed, mutually inform one another.[87] McLaren's generous orthodoxy looks to all traditions and historical time periods (other than the most recent) and even "seeks to see members of other religions and non-religions . . . as dialogue partners and even collaborators."[88]

When McLaren identifies precise elements of his generous orthodoxy he lists the "seven Jesus' whom he has known," the conservative protestant Jesus, the Pentecostal-charismatic Jesus, the Roman Catholic Jesus, the Eastern Orthodox Jesus, the liberal protestant Jesus, the Anabaptist Jesus, and the Jesus of the oppressed.[89] He explains that, therefore, he is missional, evangelical, post-protestant, liberal/conservative, mystic/poetic, biblical, charismatic/contemplative, fundamental/Calvinist, (ana)Baptist/Anglican, Methodist, catholic, Green, incarnational, Depressed-yet-hopeful, emergent, and unfinished.[90] On a practical level, typical of the Emergent movement in this regard is St Gregory of Nyssa church in California and their combination of Eastern Orthodox, Coptic, and Anglican practices and theology.[91]

Ultimately, McLaren concludes that orthodoxy must be viewed as an ongoing process.[92] Throughout his book McLaren refers to elements and figures from classical Christianity,[93] advocating a return to any and all aspects of pre-modern and contemporary church tradition. McLaren proposes, finally, that Emergents, rather than working within their own tradition, ought to embrace the whole, "capital T" Tradition. In the words of one commentator on the movement, their view is: "Don't fret so much about denominational distinctives. Embrace the entire Christian tradition as your own."[94]

---

87. Ibid., 30ff. At first glance this close connection of orthodoxy and orthodopraxy looks akin to Torrance's appropriation of the patristic notion of εὐσέβια (piety) and θεοσεβία (godliness) which will be discussed in chapters 3 and 4 of this book. However, the identification between the two is much closer in McLaren than it is in Torrance and Athanasius for whom piety/godliness flow from true theology. See the following chapter of this book for elaboration upon Torrance's view. For McLaren, the two are essentially amalgamated; orthopraxy is orthodoxy.

88. Ibid., 35.

89. Ibid., 43–67.

90. Ibid., 105–297.

91. Phyllis Tickle labels them "Angli-emergent'" (Tickle, *Emergence Christianity*, 86). Hyphenations of this sort are common for Emergents.

92. McLaren, *A Generous Orthodoxy*, 293ff.

93. E.g., Athanasius. See McLaren, *A Generous Orthodoxy*, 57–58.

94. Carson, *Becoming Conversant with the Emerging Church*, 128.

As discussed earlier, Emerging Christians are self-admittedly having more of a "conversation" than doing scientific theology as such. Accordingly, their appropriation of classical Christianity is, even at the "formal" (if Emergent theologians would ever even call it that) theological level, extremely unorganized and eclectic. At the "grassroots" level of orthopraxy, their appropriation is no less eclectic. Overall, Emerging Christians want to move far away from seeker-sensitive and mega-church models towards, seemingly, any other model. Thus, for them classical pre-modern Christianity holds certain attraction.

Dan Kimball, further illustrating the eclectic appeal to the ancient Christian tradition, advocates bringing candles and darkness into worship services.[95] Additionally, Kimball urges for Christ-centered and simple worship, referring to Justin Martyr's account on early Christian worship in his First Apology.[96] Notably, for Kimball, this means a return to the centrality of communion[97] and theocentric preaching.[98] Thus, Kimball, while foregoing more recent Christian practices of his own broadly evangelical tradition from whence he came, is returning to practices of other traditions and pre-modern Christian traditions.[99]

The Emerging movement's return to and appropriation of classical Christianity is commendable and they are in many ways at the forefront of a *ressourcement* movement in evangelical circles. Whereas their intentions are indeed commendable, their lack of any objective guiding principle for appropriation of classical Christianity causes their reading to be highly subjective, eclectic, and often tendentious. As Carson helpfully notes, Emergent theology tries to work somewhere on the spectrum between the polarized extremes of absolutism and relativism.[100] In regards to a return and appropriation of classical Christianity this has become a basically eclectic appeal to tradition.[101] This Emergent return to Tradition and classical Christianity,

95. Kimball, *The Emerging Church*, 35.

96. Ibid., 113.

97. Ibid., 162.

98. Ibid., 251–54.

99. D. A. Carson notes this trend towards such classic practices as candles, crosses, and retreats. Emergents want to be linked to historic Christianity and not only modern evangelicalism/fundamentalism. See Carson, *Becoming Conversant with the Emerging Church*, 55.

100. Ibid., 31.

101. Carson argues that the Emergent "appeal to tradition" tends to work itself out in one of three ways: (1) picking and choosing elements from classical Christianity, (2) because every Christian is a part of some tradition related to other traditions, Christians must learn to see the "bigger picture," or, at the most defined and rigorous level, (3) following Jonathan Wilson's interpretation of Alasdair MacIntyre's view of tradition,

as opposed to allowing the Emergent church to be informed and reformed by classical Christianity, causes them to simply be unfaithful to and misunderstand classical Christianity.[102]

Ultimately, then, the Emergent church, while valiantly and commendably leading the way to a return to the classical Fathers, often misunderstands them completely.[103] This is perhaps owing to the fact that, rather than allowing the ideas of the classical Fathers to guide them, the Emergent church is basically guided by their own eclecticism and idiosyncrasy, indeed; they have become absolute in their "emergentedness[104] and they have an overly strong confidence in modern progress.[105]

Unfortunately, the Emergent return to Tradition often amounts to an unfair treatment of specific traditions.[106] Typical is Phyllis Tickle's statement: "Christianity, in its early days, had no theory of the atonement or of its mechanics; or, if it did, there is no written record left to bear witness to that fact."[107] Also typical is Brian McLaren's statement:

> Constantine gave Roman-Imperial Christians a compelling reason to reject Mohammed (since Mohammed didn't submit

Christians should embrace one overarching tradition in order to combat fragmented individualism of traditions which modernism taught. See ibid., 139–140. See also MacIntyre, *After Virtue* and Wilson, *Living Faithfully*.

102. Carson provides two further helpful critiques: (1) the irony of the Emergent appeal to Tradition but dissimilarity to any tradition in their own practice. He states: "As long as you can pick and choose from something as vast as the great Tradition, you are really not bound by the discipline of any tradition. While thinking yourself most virtuous, your choices become most idiosyncratic." Secondly, (2) there were and continue to be core contradictions between the different traditions (Carson, *Becoming Conversant with the Emerging Church*, 140–42).

103. Carson states: "[McLaren] has constructed his own Jesus from disembodied slips of presentation he happens to have stumbled across within these various traditions" (ibid., 162).

104. Alan Torrance's helpful account and study of the collapse of the threefold typology (exclusivism, inclusivism, and pluralism) of Alan Race and Gavin D'Costa perhaps sheds light on the Emergent approach to tradition. According to Torrance, "the logical impossibility of a pluralist view of religions means that the typology of exclusivism, inclusivism and pluralism is untenable" because logically "pluralism must always logically be a form of exclusivism and nothing called pluralism really exists" collapsing the threefold typology at the base on the basis of the fact that "all pluralists are committed to holding some form of truth criteria . . . " (Torrance, "Towards Inclusive Ministry," 257–58). See also D'Costa, "The Impossibility of a Pluralist View of Religions," 223–32. The "truth criteria" of the Emergent church seems to be "being Emergent."

105. See further Byasee, "Emerging From What?" 255.

106. Jason Byasee gave an example of Doug Pagitt's complete misreading of the debate between Augustine and Pelagius. See Byasee, "Emerging From What?" 254.

107. Tickle, *Emergence Christianity*, 197.

to the theopolitical entity Constantine had created) and Constantine also gave Mohammed a compelling reason to reject so-called orthodox Roman Christianity (since Christianity required submission to the Roman theopolitical system).[108]

Thus, according to McLaren, Mohammad could not possibly have identified as a Christian and was forced to form his own religion.[109] The Emergent reading in both these illustrative instances portrays their turn to classical Christian history but a reading through the lens of their own critiques of more organized and imperial Christianity.[110] However, Athanasius, for example, had a very robust view of the atonement[111] and one could point to John of Damascus' discussion of Islam to see the important theological differences between to two religions in the mind of one of The Fathers.[112]

While Emergents often misread the classical Christian tradition owing to their eclecticism and subjectivism, their genius is in the application of The Fathers.[113] Emergents want to retrieve helpful elements (albeit as they see it) and directly apply them to church life today. Herein, they are at the forefront of a return to The Fathers and their example will, no doubt, continue to lead many towards further retrieval of classical Christianity. Ultimately, however, they are unfair to The Fathers themselves on account of their tendentiousness.

ANCIENT-FUTURE CHRISTIANITY AND PALEO-ORTHODOXY

The third approach to The Fathers among evangelicals is more objective than the previous group, however, they tend to approach them through Western, Protestant, and Augustinian lenses. Some have provided very practical

---

108. McLaren, *Why Did Jesus?*, 91.

109. Ibid., 90.

110. McLaren's reading in this particularly instance is guided by his agenda for a more generous and charitable approach to other religions. In his chapter on the doctrine of the Trinity he refers to Gregory Nazianzen, the other Cappadocian Fathers, and John of Damascus, in his proposal for social Trinitarianism as a way to view God and social interactions in order for better Christian interactions with others. See ibid., 125–32.

111. E.g., *De Incarnatione*, 7–9.

112. E.g., *De Haeresibus*, 101.

113. See Byasee, "Emerging From What?" 257–63.

guidelines for appropriation. Their chroniclers have called them by many different titles including "young fogeys"[114] and "younger evangelicals."[115]

Robert Webber's influence on evangelical appropriations of classical Christianity was significant during his time and continues to this day.[116] In many ways, Webber is looked to as the father of this movement. Webber's appropriation of classical theology is perhaps best elaborated upon in his book *Ancient-Future Faith*. Here he attempts to return to classical Christianity while also applying it to contemporary Christianity. The "Webberian" retrieval of classical Christianity began in May 1997 with the "Chicago Call," a call for evangelicals to return to historic Christianity.[117] The *Chicago Call* urged evangelicals to return to historic roots and creedal identity.

The core of Webber's appropriation of classical Christianity is a Christocentrism of his reading and appropriation. Webber proposes a "Christocentric method" of appropriation.[118] Webber urges Christians to interpret the Bible, appropriate The Fathers, and do theology with a focus upon the *regula fidei* (Rule of Faith) and also the *kerygma*.[119] Indeed, he states that the "tapestry of faith begins with the person and work of Christ."[120] Webber applies this approach directly to Christology, as well as ecclesiology,[121] worship,[122] spirituality,[123] and mission, typically Western and Protestant themes.[124] The outcome of his project is a more holistic conception of the atonement than typically found in Protestantism, a more mystic spirituality focused upon union with Christ, and emulation of early Christian mission practice. Thus, his evangelical tradition is somewhat reformed on the basis of what he finds. Webber's notion of the *regula fidei* is somewhat rigid,

114. Oden, *Requiem*, 137–39; Oden, *The Rebirth of Orthodoxy*, 10–11.

115. Webber, *Younger Evangelicals*.

116. For example, Joel Scandrett was recently appointed as the director for the recently formed Robert E. Webber Center at Trinity School for Ministry, an evangelical seminary in the U.S. See Scandrett, "The Robert E. Webber Center," 6–8 for a projection of his hopes.

117. See Webber and Bloesch, *The Orthodox Evangelicals*, 11–18 for the text of the *Chicago Call* and subsequent pages for comments on the *Call*.

118. Webber, *Ancient-Future Faith*, 31.

119. Ibid., 185. Webber proposed a theological reading of Scripture (190). Cf. Torrance, *Reality and Evangelical Theology*.

120. Webber, *Ancient-Future Faith*, 189.

121. Ibid., 73–91.

122. Ibid., 97–115; Webber, *Planning Blended Worship*, 17; Webber, *Ancient-Future Worship*. See e.g., ibid., 89–117, 167–78.

123. Webber, *Ancient-Future Faith*, 121–38.

124. Ibid., 141–73.

however, akin to the static approach of those who convert after discovering The Fathers. Webber's project is, however, on the whole highly practical in orientation. Throughout his many publications he sought to explore *how* the theology and faith of classical Christianity might be applied in contemporary settings; indeed very precisely in most cases.

This is an element taken up more fully by Thomas Oden. Whereas Webber's work was more epistemological and methodological in nature Oden's work is perhaps the most comprehensive appropriation of The Fathers and his reading is more extremely holistic and synthetic. Most importantly, Oden offers a very helpful and practical guide for appropriation. Oden labels the movement in which he stands "paleo-orthodoxy," a term which he uses to set this movement apart from other movements with the term "orthodox" embedded in them such as "neo-orthodoxy."[125] For Oden, what sets the paleo-orthodox apart is their return to ancient Christian orthodoxy, which he views as the "vital center" and the "central thread" running throughout Christianity.[126]

In an attempt to return to the "vital center" Oden proposes a return to the "Vincentian Canon" and, like Webber, the Rule of Faith. Oden calls for a return to "orthodoxy" by which he means "integrated biblical teaching as interpreted in its most consensual period . . . classic Christian teaching."[127] This is, for Oden, a return to the "fountain" as he calls it.[128] Oden proposes that in order to focus upon orthodoxy, Christians return to a focus upon the Rule of Faith by means of the "Vincentian canon."[129] Herein Oden contends that paleo-orthodox theologians should return to that truly consensual period of Christian orthodoxy and "guard the Deposit of Faith."[130] For Oden, Vincent of Lérins' method of "consensual recollection" should be applied very literally.[131] For Oden, following Vincent, then the best attempt (guided by the Holy Spirit), is to believe only that which has been believed "everywhere, always, and by all."[132] Thus, for Oden, the key is to always

---

125. See e.g., Oden, *Requiem*, 130–31; Oden, *The Rebirth of Orthodoxy*, 33–34. Oden lists a number of Protestant, Catholic, and Orthodox writers he saw as part of the movement (*Requiem*, 165–66). He says: "This list is much healthier than the few souls I could name in Agenda for Theology in 1979 . . . then it was a cloud the size of a man's hand; now it is misting; in a decade it will shower; someday there may be a hurricane."

126. Oden, *Agenda for Theology*, 115–16.

127. Oden, *The Rebirth of Orthodoxy*, 29.

128. Ibid., 33.

129. Ibid., 37.

130. Ibid., 122–23.

131. Ibid., 157.

132. Ibid., 159–86.

seek universality, antiquity, and conciliar consent.[133] Herein, there are "key ecumenical teachers" which are to be followed.[134] Oden applies his method very widely in the fields of dogmatic theology[135] and pastoral theology[136] as well as in very extensive and ecumenical compendiums of patristic writings in the *Ancient Christian Commentaries on Scripture* and *Ancient Christian Doctrine* series.

D. H. Williams, following in the vein of Oden, proposes a retrieval of classical Christianity and application of it into "current theological reflections of evangelicalism."[137] Calling the evangelical mindset towards tradition "amnesia" he calls, in response, for a remembering of tradition.[138] Accordingly, much of Williams' work has been a re-presentation of the tradition for Protestants, which he calls "the foundational legacy of apostolic and patristic faith, most accurately enshrined in Scripture and secondarily in the great confessions and creeds of the early church."[139] Ultimately, Williams believes that the patristic tradition was "canonical" and should be normative; the core to which was God's self-revelation in Jesus Christ, indeed, the Rule of Faith.[140] Again, his notion of the Rule of Faith is fairly general and he looks to the whole of tradition.

Other figures have followed in this same stream of a more holistic approach to The Fathers. For example, James Cutsinger in his book *Reclaiming the Great Tradition*,[141] Rodney Clapp in his book *Border Crossings*,[142] Christopher Hall's work with Thomas Oden in the *Ancient Christian Commentary* series already discussed above as well as his theological reworking of The

---

133. Ibid., 162–70.

134. Ibid., 171. Oden, following the early councils, lists Cyprian, the Cappadocians, Athanasius and Cyril, Ambrose, Augustine, John Chrysostom, Theophilus, Hilary, Jerome, Prosper, and Leo. Very helpfully Oden notes that The Fathers could be quoted as holding wild views but that they should be viewed, according to Vincent, sympathetically and in light of one another; just like reading the Bible (ibid., 172–73). Holmes argues that this was the Reformation method and that Calvin, when disagreeing with, for example, Augustine, would simply say "someone has said," not because he did not know who it was but because he was disagreeing with him charitably. See Holmes, *Listening to the Past*, 16.

135. Oden, *Classic Christianity*.

136. Oden, *Pastoral Theology*.

137. Williams, *Retrieving the Tradition*, 4–5.

138. Ibid., 9, 16.

139. Williams, *Evangelicals and Tradition*, 24, 47–84.

140. See further ibid., 47–84.

141. Cutsinger, *Reclaiming the Great Tradition*.

142. Clapp, *Border Crossings*.

Fathers in his other more distinctively theological texts,[143] and also William J. Abraham's *Logic of Renewal.*[144]

These groups, while calling for a return to the East, typically remain fairly Augustinian and Protestant in their emphases. Throughout Webber's book he attempts to allow the Great Tradition to inform basically Protestant themes such as justification, church, mission, worship. Williams attempts to prove that the early Greek Fathers asserted a basically Protestant version of justification by faith.[145] These theologians' intentions are good, namely, freeing The Fathers from accusations of doing theology through the spectacles of Greek philosophy and seeing Protestantism as in line with patristic Christianity. However, they tend towards reading Western, Protestant, Augustinian theology back into Fathers who were not always Western, Protestant, or Augustinian. As this this book shall explore in subsequent chapters, Torrance, while remaining faithfully Reformed and evangelical returned to The Fathers on their own terms, and thus offers a helpful corrective to the Augustinian-leaning approach of paleo-orthodoxy.

CONCLUSION

This chapter has argued that by the mid-twentieth-century Protestant evangelicalism founds itself in the midst of widespread "discovery" of the patristic tradition. Torrance stands within and, in many ways at the cutting edge of, these evangelical theologies of retrieval. These evangelical movements of retrieval tended to have one of three outcomes: conversion to Roman Catholicism or Eastern Orthodoxy, subjective appropriation, or synthetic and holistic appropriation, often via an unspoken (or, sometimes not so unspoken) Western and Augustinian lens.

Torrance, a theologian who saw himself squarely in the Scottish Reformed and evangelical tradition of indebtedness to the Greek Fathers[146] in addition to, more generally, the Reformed and Calvinist tradition of faithfulness to the *Consensus Patrum*,[147] is a unique figure during his own immediate setting owing to, on the one hand, the widespread ignorance of The

---

143. Hall, *Learning Theology*; Hall, *Reading Scripture*; Olson and Hall, *The Trinity*.

144. Abraham, *The Logic of Renewal*.

145. Williams, *Evangelicals and Tradition*, 130–39. Though Oden's is the most blatant attempt. See Oden, *Justification Reader*.

146. See Torrance, *Scottish Theology*, 66–74, 79–90 for a discussion of Robert Boyd and John Forbes of Corse.

147. See Torrance, *Trinitarian Perspectives*, 21–76 for a discussion of the connections Torrance saw between Calvin and the Greek Fathers.

Fathers and, on the other hand approaches of varying levels of tendentiousness or conversion. Torrance remembers himself always being informed
to a certain extent by The Fathers, even before he entered his studies in
divinity.[148] Patristic themes and figures are indeed present in many of Torrance's early works.[149] However, the *Consensus Patrum* as an explicit entity
only begins to emerge as a central theme in Torrance's later texts. Notably,
it flowers during the Reformed-Orthodox Dialogue in the late 1980s[150] and
was likely influenced by Torrance's interaction with the Eastern Orthodox
for whom the notion of a *Consensus Patrum* is absolutely central, as the
previous chapter explored. Torrance's *Trinitarian Faith*, published in 1988,
is the clearest statement of Torrance's version of the consensual patristic
tradition out of all of Torrance's many published and unpublished writings.

Torrance is of great relevance as an example of a Reformed evangelical
retrieval of the Greek Fathers. Furthermore, Torrance saw his role as necessarily involving criticism of the Western, Augustinian tradition (particularly
the epistemological, cosmological, and theological dualism embedded in it)
by means of the Greek Fathers. Thus, as this book will argue in the following
chapters, Torrance's approach is unique amongst other Protestants who traditionally emphasized Augustine (either explicitly or implicitly) by reading
the Greek Fathers through Augustinian and Western theological themes.
Torrance returns to and adopts Greek patristic themes such as *theosis* and
the vicarious humanity of Christ while remaining faithfully Reformed and
evangelical.

The subsequent chapters of this book will explore the way in which
Torrance allows his own tradition to be reconstructed on the basis of what
he discovers in The Fathers and also reconstructs The Fathers in light of
his own Reformed evangelical tradition, allowing the two sides to mutually
inform one another in a very dynamic way. While truly returning to the
Greek Fathers on their own terms Torrance was, at his core, an evangelical
and Reformed theologian and churchman, and he approached The Fathers
from this perspective.

Torrance was an evangelical. He was born into a missionary family
in China, sent to China by the China Inland Mission.[151] Throughout his

---

148. *Itinerarium Mentis In Deum: T. F. Torrance—My Theological Development.* The
Thomas F. Torrance Manuscript Collection. Special Collections, Princeton Theological
Seminary Library, Series II, Box 10.

149. E.g., Torrance, *Space, Time and Incarnation* where he argues for the importance of the Nicene conception of space and time over and against various forms of
epistemological and cosmological dualism.

150. See Torrance, *Theological Dialogue*, volumes 1 and 2.

151. *Itinerarium Mentis In Deum: T. F. Torrance—My Theological Development.* The

life Torrance viewed himself more as a missionary and evangelist than an academic. Though he entered an academic vocation, he considered himself an evangelist throughout his entire life, an evangelist to the Western worldview and culture.[152] Prior to the flowering of his academic career, Torrance was ordained as a Minister in the Church of Scotland and has approached theology not as a purely academic discipline but as something that requires a pious and repentant approach.[153] Theologically, as shall be seen in the following chapters, Torrance considered the historical Jesus Christ to be absolutely central. Though he strayed away from typical evangelical emphases such as the atonement and emphasized rather the incarnation he clearly remained committed to these central doctrines; he simply emphasized others (and viewed the traditional evangelical themes in light of other, more ecumenical, themes).

Torrance was a Reformed theologian. His early studies in theology were under the Reformed theologian H. R. Mackintosh, a major conduit of Barthian theology into Scotland and the English-speaking world. Torrance considers Mackintosh to have had no small influence upon his own theological development and remembers his time with him at New College fondly.[154] Torrance's earliest published works are on Reformed theology. His *School of Faith*,[155] originally published in 1959 is a collection of Reformed catechisms and contains a lengthy introduction to Reformed theology by Torrance. In addition to this Torrance wrote *Calvin's Doctrine of Man*[156] early in his academic career (1957) and co-edited John Calvin's commentaries (with his brother D. W. Torrance). Torrance was also an early commentator

---

Thomas F. Torrance Manuscript Collection. Special Collections, Princeton Theological Seminary Library, Series II, Box 10.

152. Jock Stein notes, referencing Robert T. Walker's recent PhD thesis, that Torrance never saw himself as an academic. Rather, he primarily saw himself as a missionary evangelizing the foundations of modern scientific culture, which involved four aspects: (1) Fashioning a modern Christian dogmatics, (2) reconstructing the concept of reason as controlled by its object, (3) overcoming dualism, and (4) reshaping fundamental presuppositions. See Jock Stein, "Introduction" in Torrance, *Gospel, Church, and Ministry*, 2. These elements of Torrance's "mission statement" surely drove his work in constructing the Torrancian *Consensus Patrum*.

153. See Torrance, *Atonement*, 437–47. At the bi-annual T. F. Torrance Conference in Scotland run by Torrance's former student and nephew Robert T. Walker, those present who studied theology under Torrance continually bring up the fact that Torrance emphasized this element very strongly in his dogmatics lectures at New College.

154. *Itinerarium Mentis In Deum: T. F. Torrance—My Theological Development*. The Thomas F. Torrance Manuscript Collection. Special Collections, Princeton Theological Seminary Library, Series II, Box 10.

155. Torrance, *The School of Faith*.

156. Torrance, *Calvin's Doctrine of Man*.

on Barth[157] and he spearheaded the translation of the *Church Dogmatics* into English. Finally, Torrance spent his early years in the academy at Auburn Seminary in New York and he was a long-time friend of Princeton Theological Seminary.[158] Throughout his years Torrance was no stranger to Princeton and spent much time there. Theologically, Torrance emphasized typically Reformed theological themes such as election, *solus Christus* (Christ alone), *sola fide* (faith alone), and *sola gratia* (grace alone). Though, there were limits to Torrance's engagement with Reformed theology[159] and the subsequent chapters of this book will show that Torrance's appropriation of Reformed theology influenced him to offer major reformulation of some of these classical Reformed tenets.[160]

This evangelical and Reformed perspective informed Torrance's approach to the church fathers. However, as this book shall argue, Torrance was not rigidly Reformed in that anything which did not fit into Reformed theology was removed from The Fathers. Rather, Torrance allowed The Fathers and his own Reformed evangelical tradition to dynamically inform and reform one another. Indeed, the Torrancian *Consensus Patrum* is a reformulation of both Greek patristic theology and Reformed evangelical theology on the basis of one another. This was due, in part, to Torrance's conception of the Reformed tradition. Torrance states, "The Reformation was not a movement to refound the Church, or to found a new Church . . . "[161] Accordingly, Torrance, as a member of the Reformed tradition, saw

157. Torrance, *Karl Barth: An Introduction to His Early Theology.*

158. See McGrath, *T. F. Torrance*, 47–58 for an account of Torrance's work in Auburn and early years in Princeton and 59–85 for an account of Torrance's time as a chaplain. Torrance returned to Europe when World War Two broke out. However he came back to Princeton often and his intellectual legacy (in the form of his manuscript collection) is stored in the archives at the seminary.

159. For example, he did not really engage Dutch Reformed theology.

160. For example, Torrance is critical of the hyper-Calvinism of Westminster Standards, preferring the more biblical approach of the earlier Reformed catechisms (as opposed to the idiosyncratic approach of Westminster), the more Christological and evangelical approach of the early Reformed catechisms (as opposed to the more abstract approach of Westminster), the more scientific approach of the earlier Reformed catechisms expounding doctrine in light of "its own inherent patterns" (as opposed to the more rationalistic approach of Westminster), and the emphasis on the incarnation of the earlier catechisms (as opposed to the emphasis on human appropriation of salvation in Westminster). See Torrance, "Introduction" in *School of Faith*, xvii–xvii. Torrance prefers, more broadly, an approach of "Christological criticism" whereby the Person and Work of Christ act as a corrective to various forms of doctrinal and pietistic perversions. He sees this is in line with Calvin and the classical Reformed theologians. See Torrance, *Conflict and Agreement*, 89–103.

161. Torrance, *Conflict and Agreement*, 1:77. This chapter in *Conflict and Agreement* outlines Torrance's conception of the Reformed tradition (1:76–89).

himself standing within an ongoing movement of reform with the catholic church.[162] Furthermore, conceiving of himself as standing with the Reformers, Torrance understood a recovery of the patristic tradition as the means of reform and he tries to combat perversions of the Gospel in the modern church in the same manner as the Reformers where " . . . the teaching of The Fathers was resurrected against the schoolmen."[163] Accordingly, Torrance did not consider the recovery of the *Consensus Patrum* to be something novel; rather, he considered it to be the traditional means of reformation of corruption in the church.

Torrance provides a helpful example for others within the evangelical tradition who are currently returning to The Fathers inasmuch as these theologians often lack both an objective guide for appropriation and tend towards a numerical *consensus,* a magnified "golden-age" view of the early church, an emphasis on Augustine, an overly synthetic, or an overly eclectic view of The Fathers. Indeed, Torrance stands unique as objectively Christocentric, faithful to his own tradition, and seeing both the interrelation between The Fathers and his tradition as dynamic enough to allow them to be mutually informative. It is therefore to an exploration of the Torrancian *Consensus Patrum,* consisting of truly catholic (ecumenical) themes and figures, to which this book shall now turn. Chapter 3 will explore the catholic themes and chapter 4 will explore the catholic figures.

162. Torrance's conception of his own Reformed and evangelical tradition as part of the wider catholic tradition goes deeper than these theological assertions. He sees a version of Presbyterianism (really, a Presbyterian-Episcopal hybrid) to have been the preferred ecclesiastical order of the ancient church, the Reformers, and large parts of the Scottish Reformed tradition. See *Conflict and Agreement,* 1:85–89. See also Torrance, *Royal Priesthood* for a much fuller elaboration upon this point. See chapter 5 of this book for further expansion of this topic.

163. Torrance, *Conflict and Agreement,* 1:79.

CHAPTER 3

T. F. Torrance's *Consensus Patrum*

CATHOLIC THEMES

*The ὁμοούσιος τῷ Πατρί was revolutionary and decisive: it expressed the fact that what God is 'toward us' and 'in the midst of us' in and through the Word made flesh, he really is **in himself**; that he is in the **internal relations** of his transcendent being the very same Father, Son and Holy Spirit that he is in his revealing and saving activity in time and space toward mankind.*

Thomas F. Torrance, *The Trinitarian Faith*, 130.

INTRODUCTION

Chapter 1 of this book explored the different approaches to the *Consensus Patrum* in Roman Catholicism, Eastern Orthodoxy, and Protestantism. Chapter 2 argued that by Torrance's time The Fathers were basically viewed as the inheritance of Catholics, Orthodox, and, perhaps, liberal Protestants and that, because of this, many evangelicals have, relatively recently, begun to "discover" the Greek Fathers but continue to approach them with, at best, a somewhat Western lens. However many of the evangelicals explored approach The Fathers with a subjective lens or, conversely, conclude there is a need to convert to Orthodoxy or Catholicism. Therefore, Torrance's approach to the Greek Fathers on their own terms as a Reformed evangelical is unique.

In a letter to Torrance from 1988, Torrance's friend and ecumenical dialogue partner and the then Eastern Orthodox Archbishop Methodios of Aksum, writes "I admire your patristic expressions and your use of catholic terms . . ."[1] The central claim of this book is that Torrance's use of The Fathers is an imaginative and creative reconstruction[2] of The Fathers into a Reformed and evangelical version of the *Consensus Patrum*, centered on Christology and involving substantial changes to his own tradition and fresh insight into and sometimes even reformulation of traditional readings of the patristic tradition, portraying The Fathers as the inheritance of the Reformed evangelical tradition. This chapter shall examine how this involves (from the Reformed evangelical side) a focus upon the Word of God and a centeredness on the fulcrum of the Nicene ὁμοούσιον (and therein Trinity and Christology) and an evangelical commitment to salvation by grace and the divine initiative[3] in salvation and revelation and (from the patristic side) a commitment to truly Greek patristic themes. Torrance departs from emphasizing traditional Reformed creeds and confessions (though he considers many of them to have merit) and returns to classical and ecumenical theological themes. However, his return to The Fathers is not simply a reading of them; to take the language of Archbishop Methodios a step further, Torrance not only imaginatively uses "patristic expressions" and "catholic terms" but his reading and appropriation of the classical Church Fathers consists of an imaginative reconstruction of "catholic themes and catholic figures" into the Torrancian Reformed evangelical version of the *Consensus Patrum*.

Torrance's imaginative reconstruction allows Torrance to draw out elements and nuances not previously seen in patristic theology. Torrance is a *western* theologian approaching the *Greek* Fathers, a unique endeavor in itself. As chapter 1 of this book showed, the Western tradition (both Protestant and Roman Catholic) has generally seen itself in line with the ancient church but their emphasis has tended to be upon Augustine and the Augustinian tradition. Furthermore, Torrance does more than simply

---

1. The Thomas F. Torrance Manuscript Collection. Special Collections, Princeton Theological Seminary Library. Box 172.

2. Torrance uses the language of "reconstruction" throughout his many texts. In this instance, the term is being used akin to Torrance in his dogmatics lectures where he reconstructs "classic doctrines" by combining patristic and Reformed theology. See e.g., Torrance, *Incarnation*, 85–86.

3. The term is H. R. Mackintosh's and this commitment drives much of Torrance's theology. See Mackintosh, *The Divine Initiative*.

interpret The Fathers; rather, he uses them as theological conversation partners at the great ecumenical and historical table of Christianity. Whilst using The Fathers as theological dialogue partners, Torrance employs The Fathers imaginatively in two primary ways, first by having a ὁμοούσιον and Athanasian centered reading of The Fathers and second, by reading and appropriating The Fathers theologically as opposed to patrologically.

It is important to note that Torrance interprets The Fathers as a theologian and a dogmatician rather than as a patrologist.[4] As such, rather than historically, Torrance reads The Fathers theologically and, more specifically, Christologically. Thus, Torrance's reading and use of The Fathers neither simply resembles traditional patrology nor indeed Reformed dogmatic theology; it is rather a uniquely construed Reformed evangelical reconstruction of The Fathers and their theology. Herein, Torrance's project has much to offer contemporary systematic and evangelical theology, and, indeed, patrology as a unique "evangelical patristic dogmatics." In his reading of The Fathers Torrance remains centered upon this reconstructive approach. This allows him fresh insight into The Fathers by means of his imaginative connections, re-reading, and re-situating of The Fathers by bringing fresh questions to The Fathers and attempting to imaginatively reconstruct their answers in order to explore their relevance in his own theological context.

Torrance's book *The Trinitarian Faith: The Evangelical Faith of the Ancient Catholic Church* was originally delivered as the Warfield Lectures at Princeton Theological Seminary in 1981 and later published in 1987.[5] The book is, in many regards, his *magnum opus*, indeed the flowering of both his dogmatic and scientific theology not to mention his interpretation and appropriation of the patristic tradition and construction of the Torrancian *Consensus Patrum*. Owing to the Reformed-dogmatic centeredness of the book, the historical and ecumenical scope, and the evangelical commitments, the book is a truly unique work.[6] The book is not simply a work of patrology nor is it purely a systematic theology. It stands rather as an example of Torrance's reading of the *Consensus Patrum* and as such provides a

---

4. John Behr contends that there are many problems with modern studies of The Fathers, primarily because it has become mainly a study of Late Antiquity rather than theology. See Behr, *The Mystery of Christ*, 18. *Trinitarian Faith* is not a study of Late Antiquity. In fact, there is hardly any pure historical discussion; rather, it is an entirely theological reading of early Christian history (i.e., reconstructed in light of God's self-revelation).

5. Torrance, *Trinitarian Faith*, 1–10.

6. George Hunsinger states: "If I could recommend only one book that explains the faith that unites the world's more than 2 billion Christians—Protestant, Catholic and Orthodox—this would be it. Learned and profound, it is perhaps Torrance's most readable work" (Hunsinger, "5 Picks," 38).

helpful starting point for a case study in this book. Torrance is generally an extremely consistent theologian and thus his multitude of other texts dealing with The Fathers will be used to supplement the material in *Trinitarian Faith* and any divergence or development will be examined.

Throughout *Trinitarian Faith* (and also elsewhere) Torrance orchestrates his patristic dogmatics by means of various themes and figures. Many of the themes are traditional Torrancian themes, albeit with patristic nuances, whereas he extrapolates others directly from The Fathers and are accordingly more explicitly patristic in nature. For Torrance, reading and appropriating The Fathers in this way is an essential part of his much greater theological methodology of evangelizing the foundations of Western thought discussed in the previous chapter.

This chapter will first explore Torrance's methodology as it pertains to his reading of the *Consensus Patrum*. Herein, the Torrancian *Consensus Patrum* will be introduced and Torrance's conception of theology as dogmatic, scientific, and ecumenical/historical will be discussed. Secondly, Torrance's use of The Fathers in *Trinitarian Faith* will be explored in detail. In this section, the editions, figures, and texts in use on Torrance's *Consensus Patrum* palate will be unpacked, Torrance's possible filters for reading The Fathers will be unpacked, and his indwelling of the patristic mind will be explored. Following this, the major themes in the Torrancian *Consensus Patrum* as found most clearly in his magisterial text *The Trinitarian Faith* will be discussed: Christology and the ὁμοούσιον, Trinity and Pneumatology, epistemological objectivity, creation, ecclesiology and the sacraments, asceticism, the vicarious humanity, and the Latin and Greek views of the atonement. This chapter shall explore how Torrance returns to these explicitly Greek patristic themes on their own terms. However, Torrance does not return to them in a narrowly patristic way becoming a patristic fundamentalist; rather, Torrance retrieves these Greek patristic themes in a Reformed and evangelical way. However, Torrance is also not narrowly Reformed. Rather, Torrance creatively constructs the Torrancian *Consensus Patrum* by allowing the Greek patristic tradition and his own Reformed evangelical tradition to mutually inform and, indeed, reform one another in a very dynamic way. Thus, this chapter shall explore how Torrance's approach to these themes is through a Reformed evangelical lens; however, his own Reformed evangelical lens is, in turn, reformed by means of what Torrance finds in the Greek Fathers.

TORRANCE'S PATRISTIC DOGMATICS

Though The Fathers undergird Torrance's entire theology, lying behind all of his dogmatic thought,[7] *Trinitarian Faith* is absolutely distinctive among his works inasmuch as in it Torrance explores the patristic theological tradition as it was put forward in the Nicene-Constantinopolitan Creed. Furthermore, it is essential to keep in mind what Torrance is trying to do and not trying to do in *Trinitarian Faith*.[8] First, there are two things that Torrance is not trying to do. On the one hand, Torrance is not attempting to offer a systematic theology text. He had hopes of doing this at some point in his life and his recently published dogmatics lectures from New College are, in many ways, a posthumous actualization of this vision.[9] By any account, *Trinitarian Faith* is dogmatic and systematic but it is not a systematic theology text. Secondly, *Trinitarian Faith* is not a work of patrology.[10] In *Trinitarian Faith* Torrance is not attempting to offer a study of the fourth century in particular or late antiquity in general. Rather, *Trinitarian Faith* is a study of the classical theology of the church fathers. The book is a discussion of the "evangelical and apostolic faith"[11] of the fourth century and Torrance means it as an introduction and handbook for students.[12] Within the text Torrance traces the "inner theological connections that gave coherent structure to the classical theology of the ancient Catholic Church."[13] The organization of

7. Torrance says that the Greek fathers shaped his work from the beginning of his theological development. See *Itinerarium Mentis In Deum: T. F. Torrance—My Theological Development*. The Thomas F. Torrance Manuscript Collection, Series II, Box 10: Autobiographical Writings of Thomas F. Torrance, Princeton Seminary.

8. It is notable that even the title of the book discloses Torrance's approach: The *Trinitarian* Faith: The *Evangelical* Theology of the Ancient *Catholic* Church. In other words, *The Trinitarian Faith* is Torrance's exposition of a truly ecumenical faith which he sees as both Trinitarian and evangelical.

9. Compiled and published by his nephew and former student Robert Walker. See Torrance, *Incarnation*; Torrance, *Atonement*.

10. "The scientific study of the church fathers." Quasten's is the classic work, however there are a plethora of them. See Quasten, *Patrology: V. 1–5*. The text was first published in English in 1950.

11. Torrance, *Trinitarian Faith*, 1.

12. Ibid. Perhaps taking for his inspiration the magisterial text of his beloved teacher on Christology. See Mackintosh, *The Person of Jesus Christ*, vii.

13. Torrance, *Trinitarian Faith*, 2. Robert Walker helpfully clarifies that in Torrance's theological jargon "the phrase 'inner logic' represents a concept which is central to Torrance's theology and which he uses at key points to denote the essential structure and inherent significance of something. The word 'inner' refers to its intrinsic nature, underlying fundamental pattern, and the precise relations embedded within and constitutive of it, while 'logic' refers to its meaning and significance, the rationale and intelligibility inherent in it and its internal structural relations. Torrance uses 'inner logic'

Trinitarian Faith follows the Nicene-Constantinopolitan Creed (especially its lynchpin according to Torrance, the ὁμοούσιον) and each chapter consists of an explication of the main elements of the Creed on the basis of what Torrance considers to be "classical theology."

Torrance garners a number of elements from The Fathers which, in turn, guide his reading of the "inner connections" of classical theology, namely, that theology is inherently dogmatic, scientific, ecumenical, and historical. Thus the Torrancian *consensus* is a very dynamic entity. Torrance sees the classical Fathers following these same commitments and thus extracts them from The Fathers; he also applies these commitments to his reading of The Fathers. It is essential to briefly unpack these core elements of Torrance in order to understand how he does theology and how he appropriates The Fathers and constructs them into a truly Torrancian *Consensus Patrum*. These themes are absolutely foundational for Torrance and drive his reconstruction of The Fathers. They will arise more concretely in the patristic themes that Torrance sees as core to the *consensus* as put forward in *Trinitarian Faith* and even more concretely in the specific themes Torrance sees in the major Fathers of the *consensus*.

First, theology is inherently dogmatic. By dogmatic, Torrance means a binding centeredness on the Word. As Torrance puts it:

> In the set of theological disciplines, dogmatics is the 'pure science' in which we are concerned to penetrate down to the basic realities about which we must view an account, and which we are compelled to think out in accordance with their own nature and the basic principles we derive from them. In dogmatics, then, theology is bound to its given object, God's Word addressed to us in Jesus Christ, and develops its understanding of it in accordance with its nature and with the way in which it is actually disclosed to us in history.[14]

This means that theology and theological exercises must necessarily always be focused on the Word of God, that is, Jesus Christ. This is, in many regards, a commitment to doing theology in the Reformed fashion and thus "dogmatic" could very well be considered synonymous with "Reformed" for

---

or 'interior logic' with reference to the bible, Christology and theological knowledge and sometimes simply 'logic' to speak of 'the logic of grace' and 'the logic of Christ." (Walker, "Incarnation and Atonement," 5). Thus, for Torrance, to study the "inner logic" of something meant to look at the meaning behind it, which necessarily entails going beyond its surface meaning.

14. Torrance, *Incarnation*, 6. According to Torrance, Reformed theology positively developed dogmatics in a significant way.

Torrance.[15] Therefore, whether one does theology on the basis of the Scriptures, the classical theology of a figure such as Athanasius, or simply reflects theologically, the activity must always remain dogmatic. To be otherwise focused ultimately causes the activity to no longer be theology but mythology, a distinction Torrance sees in Athanasius, as shall be seen later in this chapter. Equally important for Torrance in this regard is the "evangelical" nature of theology, particularly his study of The Fathers. Torrance believes that the Greek Fathers can be best understood in light of the evangelical, grace-based perspective of the Reformation.[16]

Secondly, theology is inherently scientific. This means that theology has to do with study of an object as it is in itself and therefore must be defined by terms in accordance with that object in itself.[17] Thus, in truly scientific theological study, the focus must be on God and the object (God) must define the way in which theologians speak about God. In the case of theology, because of the Creator/creature divide, talk about God can only be done on the basis of what God says about himself; that is, in his Word by his Holy Spirit.

Thirdly, theology is inherently ecumenical and historical. The ecumenical and historical character of theology has to with its dogmatic and scientific nature. Since theology is rooted in the Word and is conversation about and dialogue with God, it must necessarily engage with what others have said in their own dialogue with God, both ecumenically and historically.[18] Therefore, when doing theology dogmatically and scientifically, theology must also engage with those who did theology in the past and who do theology in the present. As will be seen in this and the following chapter, this is not a simple interpretation of The Fathers, however. Rather, it means bringing contemporary theological questions and issues to The Fathers and

15. See Torrance's discussion of Reformed theology's championing of "dogmatic science" in endnote 1 to *Incarnation*, 257–60.

16. Torrance, *Trinitarian Perspectives*, 21–22.

17. Torrance, *Trinitarian Faith*, 51: "Scientific knowledge was held [by The Fathers, specifically the Alexandrian Fathers,] to result from inquiry strictly in accordance with the nature of the reality being investigated, that is, knowledge of it reached under the constraint of what it actually and essentially is in itself, and not according to arbitrary convention."

18. Torrance, "Introduction" in *The School of Faith*, lxvii–lxviii: "Theology must engage in historical studies just because it is historical dialogue with God. It must seek to understand the mind of all the previous generations in the Church, and in the light of their hearing of the Word and understanding of the Truth hear the Word and seek to understand the Truth anew for itself . . . Theology must engage in ecumenical studies just because it is the dialogue of the one Covenant people with God, and therefore the exposition of theology as hearing of the Word and understanding of the Truth cannot be private to one particular Church any more than it can be private to one generation."

constructing answers by means of dogmatic and scientific theology. Thus, by historical Torrance really means "historically informed."

TORRANCE'S USE OF THE FATHERS IN TRINITARIAN FAITH

The most notable aspect to Torrance's *Trinitarian Faith* from a constructive-theological perspective is the way in which he positively and imaginatively reconstructs and appropriates the theology of The Fathers. However, before exploring this "meat" it is essential to first look at the "bones" of the text, namely, the major texts, editions, and figures that are in use in *Trinitarian Faith* and drive Torrance's reconstruction of the *Consensus Patrum*.[19] Following this it will then be possible to look at the themes that Torrance extrapolates from The Fathers and constructs into the Torrancian *Consensus Patrum*.

Though there are notable exceptions,[20] Torrance rarely cites a particular edition of a text. Rather, he simply cites the patristic figure and text (e.g., "Athanasius, *Con. Ar.*, 3.4"); but he does provide his readers with clues as to what the particular edition might be. In the *Foreword* to *Trinitarian Faith*, he says:

> I am very conscious of the great tradition in Patristic scholarship which I have enjoyed for many years, and of my indebtedness to those who have made the original texts so readily available. I have in mind the immense work of J. P. Migne, *Patrologia, Series Graeca et Series Latina*;[21] *Die grieschichen christlichen Schrift-steller der ersten drei Jahrhunderte*[22] of the Berlin Academy; and not least the new *Library of Greek Fathers and Ecclesastical*

---

19. See the appendix of this book for a full chart of all the patristic sources Torrance cites in *The Trinitarian Faith*.

20. For example, Gregory of Nyssa, for whom he often notes that he used one of Werner Jaeger's editions and Basil the Great, for whom he often notes that he used the *Library of Greek Fathers and Ecclesiastical Writers*. See below.

21. Migne, *Patrologiae Cursus Completus. Series Latina* and *Patrologia Cursus Completus Series Graeca*, 165 vols. J. P. Migne (d. 1875) was a French priest who opened a publishing house and published the Greek Fathers in Greek along with a Latin translation and the Latin Fathers cheaply in order to make them more readily available for wide consumption

22. Harnack and Mommsen, *Die Grieschichen Christlichen Schriftsteller Der Ersten Drei Jahrhunderte*. This is a text critical collection of Greek patristic writings compiled by Adolf von Harnack and Theodor Mommsen.

Writers[23]still in process of being published in Athens which is very helpful. I have gratefully availed myself of translations in the *Ante-Nicene and Post-Nicene Fathers*,[24] and C. R. B. Shapland *The Letters of St Athanasius Concerning the Holy Spirit*,[25] but have often revised or given a new rendering of passages cited.[26]

Torrance's shorthand labeling of these texts is not always traditional; but it is generally intuitive; though occasionally there are some ambiguously abbreviated titles.[27] He often cites an abundance of patristic texts in one footnote separated by either a comma or a semi-colon. In such situations, it is usually clear that Torrance intends the semi-colon to denote a separate reference,[28] however, occasionally, he seems to separate references by means of a comma.[29]

---

23. ΑΠΟΣΤΟΛΙΚΗΣ ΔΙΑΚΟΝΙΑΣ ΤΗΣ ΕΚΚΛΗΣΙΑΣ ΤΗΣ ΕΛΛΑΔΟΣ. *ΒΙΒΛΙΟΘΗΚΗ ΕΛΛΗΩΝ ΠΑΤΕΡΩΝ ΚΑΙ ΕΚΚΛΗΣΙΚΩΝ ΕΥΓΓΡΑΦΕΩΝ (Library of Greek Fathers and Ecclesiastical Writers)*. This is a series published by the Greek Orthodox Church's official publishing house which was being published in Greece during Torrance's time. It was a mass production in Greek of the critical editions of the Greek Fathers without the textual apparatus. It was made readily available because of less stringent copyright laws in Greece in comparison with, for example, Western Europe and North America. During Torrance's time they were widely available in theological bookstores in Britain. Today, the editions are still readily available in Greece but less so elsewhere.

24. Roberts, Schaff, and Donaldson, *The Ante-Nicene Fathers*; Roberts, Schaff, and Donaldson, *Nicene and Post-Nicene Fathers: First Series, 14 Volumes*; Roberts et al.,*Nicene and Post-Nicene Fathers: Second Series, 14 Volumes*. This is the collection of texts originally translated by Newman, Pusey, and other figures from the Anglican tractarian movement.

25. Shapland, *The Letters of Saint Athanasius Concerning the Holy Spirit*. Until recently this was the only available English translation of this collection of these letters by Athanasius. See St. Athanasius the Great and Didymus the Blind: Athanasius, *Works on the Spirit PPS43* for the most recent translation into English published by St. Vladimir's Orthodox Seminary.

26. Torrance, *Trinitarian Faith*, 11.

27. To illustrate: Epiphanius, *Ref. Aet.* is *Refutation of the Aetians*, a text which is part of *Haereses* and *De Fide* is a work titled *Expositio Fide*, which is at the end of *Haereses*. See *Trinitarian Faith*, 223 and 244, respectively, for example. It is clear that Torrance is consistent with his own abbreviations and he often uses the accepted patristic abbreviation or, if not, an abbreviation that is fairly obvious. Only occasionally does he use an unclear abbreviation. However, once the text is discovered, it becomes clear why Torrance uses the abbreviation he does.

28. For example, *Trinitarian Faith*, 221.

29. For example, ibid., 292.

Historically, Torrance is informed primarily by the *Ecclesiastical Histories* of Socrates, Sozomen, Eusebius, and Theodoret.[30] Largely absent from Torrance's texts and their footnotes are secondary texts on patrology, however. Torrance is not concerned with historical studies.[31] His approach to the Greek Fathers is as a Reformed and evangelical theologian. Nevertheless, there are clearly both very explicitly acknowledged (such as Karl Barth and H. R. Mackintosh) and less explicitly acknowledged influences (such as John McLeod Campbell, James Orr, and Adolf von Harnack) upon Torrance's reading of The Fathers.[32] Furthermore, there are a few "guides" whom Torrance acknowledges to follow in his reading of The Fathers and the patristic era which seem to have influenced his work in *Trinitarian Faith*. Occasionally Torrance hints at figures who influenced his reading of The Fathers directly such as G. L. Prestige,[33] Georges Florovsky,[34] Methodios

30. He cites Socrates' *Historica* a total of six times, Sozomen's once, Theodoret's twenty-seven times, and Eusebius of Caesarea's once. He also cites Athanasius' *Historia Arianorum ad Monachos* once. Many scholars accuse Torrance of a one-sided reading of history. See, for example, Behr, Review of *Divine Meaning*, 107. He accuses Torrance of painting a one-sided picture of Athanasius that makes it seem as if there is no disagreement amongst patristic scholars about Athanasius.

31. John Behr speaks somewhat approvingly of Torrance in this regard. Behr, Review of *Divine Meaning*, 104–5. But, as noted above, Behr wants Torrance to be fairer in his depiction of the fourth century.

32. Duncan Rankin argues that Torrance's view of Athanasius on the atonement was directly from Melville Scott. See Rankin, "Carnal Union with Christ" 268; 209; A 83–A 115 referring to Scott, *Athanasius on the Atonement*. Rankin's critique seems to be somewhat of an afterthought (it was only in an appendix to his thesis) and his evidence is somewhat weak. He bases his conclusions on the fact that he discovered evidence of Torrance checking Scott's text out of the New College library while a student. See the appendix to Rankin, "Carnal Union with Christ."

33. Torrance, *The Christian Doctrine of God*, 130. The primary way in which Torrance uses Prestige was in regards to specific definitions of theological terms in The Fathers. For example, Torrance adheres to Prestige's definitions of ὁμοούσιον (see *The Christian Doctrine of God*, 80, especially footnote 38) and ὑπόστασις (*The Christian Doctrine of God*, 130). Specifically, Torrance, with Prestige, holds that οὐσια refers to the "intrinsic constitution" in the Godhead, and ὑπόστασις refers to "concrete independence" in the Godhead (see Torrance, *Theological Dialogue*, 2:10). As shall be seen later in this chapter and in the following chapter, this definition of οὐσια and ὑπόστασις undergirds much of Torrance's reading of The Fathers on the doctrine of the Trinity.

34. In one of Torrance's early works he ruminates upon the ecumenical relevance of the fact that at a recent dialogue he found "Calvin's language on the lips of Professor Florovsky . . . " See *Conflict and Agreement*, 1:227. The most significant references have to do with reading Athanasius over and against the traditional Alexandrian view of Origen and Clement. For example, Torrance argues, citing Florovsky, that Athanasius destroyed the Origenist position that the created universe is necessary to God's own being (Torrance, *The Christian Doctrine of God*, 4).

Fouyas,[35] and George Dragas.[36] These figures occasionally appear in Torrance's footnotes but it is clear that their approach influenced him more significantly than would seem at first glance. Torrance relies upon each of these theologians in different ways and in different aspects of his theology.

Theologically, Torrance is informed by a large corpus of patristic figures. Throughout *Trinitarian Faith* Torrance cites Epiphanius of Salamis a total of 382 times, the majority of which are in *chapter 6: The Eternal Spirit*; he cites Irenaeus of Lyons a total of 293 times; he cites Gregory Nazianzen a total of 284 times, throughout *Trinitarian Faith*; he cites Basil the Great a total of 276 times, throughout the book, but notably in *chapter 6*; he cites Origen a total of 192 times, mostly in the first chapter, *Faith and Godliness*; he cites Didymus the Blind a total of 185 times, most often in *chapter 6*; he cites Hilary of Poitiers a total of one 180; and he cites Cyril of Jerusalem a total of ninety-five times.

By far, the figure Torrance cites and references the most in *Trinitarian Faith* is Athanasius of Alexandria. Torrance cites Athanasius a total of 1,197 times throughout the book. Torrance cites him consistently throughout the text and Torrance's reading of Athanasius' theology clearly informs Torrance's conception of the *Consensus Patrum* in a major way. However, there are certain Fathers that do show up more than Athanasius in specific chapters, such as Origen in chapter 1 (on faith and godliness), who, in this chapter, shows up nearly twice as many times as Athanasius.

By far the text Torrance cites the most overall is Athanasius' *Contra Arianos* which he cites over 450 times.[37] Torrance also cites Irenaeus' *Ad-*

---

35. Methodios Fouyas was a Greek Orthodox bishop and patristics scholar with whom Torrance had a close friendship. Fouyas was also the bishop who gave Torrance the honorary office of proto-presbyter in the Greek Orthodox Patriarchate of Alexandria. *The Thomas F. Torrance Manuscript Collection* in the Princeton Theological Seminary archives contain some interesting photographs of Torrance post-ordination and the pectoral crosses he was given upon ordination. See Box 214 which contains a slew of pectoral crosses, some of which are only given to ordained Orthodox priests. There is also a picture of Torrance wearing the cross, surrounded by a number of Orthodox bishops in Box 202. Along with Prestige, Torrance often cites Methodios Fouyas as support for his understanding of theological terms, such as οὐσία (Torrance, *The Christian Doctrine of God*, 80).

36. Torrance, *The Christian Doctrine of God*, 96. George Dragas, a former student of Torrance's and patristics scholar, is often referred to in Torrance's later writings. A significant citation occurs when Torrance refers to Dragas, a scholar of Athanasius and Cyril, to support his view that both Athanasius and Cyril held that the Spirit proceeds from the οὐσια and not ὑπόστασίς of the Father (Torrance, *The Christian Doctrine of God*, 192). Torrance agrees with Dragas on a number of issues and includes him in his text *The Incarnation: Ecumenical Studies in the Nicene-Constantinopolitan Creed* (Dragas, "The Eternal Son," 16–57).

37. Whilst the current scholarly consensus tends to view *Contra Arianos IV* as

versus Haereses frequently, which Torrance references 269 times. He also cites Gregory Nazianzen's orations and Basil the Great's epistles in large quantity. Torrance cites Basil's 110 times. He refers to Gregory's orations 291 times, most notably, Oration 31 (the *Fifth Theological Oration, On the Holy Spirit*) which he cites forty-eight of those times. He cites Epiphanius' *Haereses* 267 times and his *Ancaoratus* ninety-five times. He cites Cyril of Jerusalem's *Catecheses* ninety-four times and Hilary's *De Trinitate* 176 times. He cites Basil's *On the Holy Spirit* sixty-one times. As with the other authors, while this represents the overall citations and references, in each individual chapter certain figures sometimes dominate the scene.[38]

An examination of *Trinitarian Faith* portrays Torrance as a theologian who was intimately acquainted with The Fathers' writings and mindset.[39] He knew their works intimately and truly indwelt their life and thought.[40] Indeed, on each page there is likely to be five or so footnotes, each footnote containing anywhere from ten to fifty patristic citations and references.[41] Scholars commenting on Torrance's many works in patristic theology have been impressed with his indwelling of primary sources.[42]

Furthermore, Torrance not only reads The Fathers analytically but according to Fr. George Dion. Dragas, "synthetically" and thereby "appropriates the principles of Patristic Theology."[43] Torrance indwells the life and thought of The Fathers. According to Dragas, "few contemporary theologians in his tradition have so thoroughly and consistently appropriated the spiritual wealth of Greek Patristic Theology."[44] In many ways, this is because of Torrance's indwelling The Fathers' mindset and imitating their life of piety as well as appropriating their theology into his own context; and, *Trinitarian Faith* is the outcome of this in its purest form. Torrance

---

Pseudo-Athanasian in authorship, Torrance considers it Athanasian.

38. See appendix.

39. See the appendix for the full listing of patristic figures, sources, and numbers of times cited in *Trinitarian Faith*. While Athanasius, Hilary, Gregory Nazianzen, Irenaeus, and the other "usual suspects" are present as one might expect there are a few surprises which shows that Torrance had read widely and deeply in patristic literature; a suspicion a reader would have upon a study of nearly any of Torrance's texts on The Fathers.

40. Torrance says: "In the course of preparing [*Trinitarian Faith*] for publication I re-read the works of the great fathers for each chapter" (*Trinitarian Faith*, 1).

41. For this and all further references to number of times Torrance referred to an author or texts see the appendix.

42. Behr, Review of *Divine Meaning*; Wilken, Review of *Divine Meaning*, 743–44; Morrison, Review of *The Trinitarian Faith*, 117–19.

43. Dragas, "The Significance for the Church" 216.

44. Ibid., 216.

applies this vision and methodology to all areas of his theology, not least his reading of the *consensus*. As perhaps an outcome of Torrance's indwelling of The Fathers, scholars have furthermore noted that Torrance's enterprise was done "with the spiritual warmth of a praying theologian."[45]

CATHOLIC THEMES

In *Trinitarian Faith* Torrance discusses a plethora of catholic themes that he sees contained within The Fathers and their inner connections.[46] These themes, like the catholic figures and streams, which will be explored in the following chapter of this book, are a part of Torrance's creative Reformed evangelical reconstruction of The Fathers. In the themes Torrance's imaginative Christ-centered *Consensus Patrum* shines clear. The rest of this chapter shall explore the way in which Torrance approaches these Greek patristic themes on their own terms but reformulates them in a Reformed and evangelical fashion, allowing the Greek Fathers and his Reformed tradition to dynamically inform one another. This chapter will explore how a number of these themes comprise great contributions to contemporary understanding of theology and The Fathers and have much to offer modern systematic theology and patrology. The rest of this chapter will explore the themes in order to see precisely what Torrance is up to in his imaginative reconstruction of The Fathers into his Torrancian Reformed evangelical *Consensus Patrum* and point out Torrance's unique insight and contribution as well as where the possibility of critique exists. The following chapter shall explore the streams which Torrance constructs around the themes and offer comment on the gains of Torrance's *consensus*.

The Centrality of Christology: The ὁμοούσιον

The Nicene doctrine of ὁμοούσιον τῷ Πατρί[47] serves as the cornerstone of Torrance's creative Reformed evangelical reconstruction of the church

---

45. Copan, Review of *The Christian Doctrine of God*, 246.

46. The catholic themes and catholic figures/streams which comprise the Torrancian *Consensus Patrum* are intricately connected to one another and, thus, either could probably be discussed first. However, if one had to point to one undergirding the other, it must be said that the catholic themes drove the catholic figures. For, Torrance constructs his streams and made his imaginative connections by means of the underlying themes to which the figures were committed. Therefore, this chapter will discuss the themes and the following chapter will discuss the figures/streams.

47. The word ὁμοούσιον comes from the combination of the Greek words ὁμο (same) and οὐσια (stuff/essence) and means "of the same substance or stuff." See Lampe, ed.,

fathers into the Torrancian *Consensus Patrum*.[48] Torrance's ὁμοούσιον is re-trieved from Nicene theology and it is, in many ways, a reconstruction of the Reformation principle of *Solus Christus* (Christ alone) in light of the theology of The Fathers and it exemplifies Torrance's approach to doctrine of the Greek Fathers (the ὁμοούσιον) from his own Reformed and evangelical perspective (Word-centeredness). Torrance sees the flowering of the evan-gelical theology of the *consensus* in the Nicene doctrine of ὁμοούσιον, which, according to Torrance, implies that "God Himself is the actual content of his revelation and God Himself is really in Jesus Christ reconciling the world to Himself."[49] The core of Torrance's *consensus* is the ὁμοούσιον and, as such, theology must be centered upon it in an objective and realist manner. In this way it affects all doctrine and serves as a lynchpin for theology.[50] As such the ὁμοούσιον is the center of the Torrancian *Consensus Patrum* and Torrance's entire imaginative reconstruction of The Fathers is done on the basis of it and through it and he reconstructs everything around it. So, Torrance's re-construction of the patristic dogmatic tradition begins with Christology, for which the ὁμοούσιον is central, and is always tethered to this fulcrum.[51] For him, everything in theology rests upon this Father-Son relationship and,

---

A Patristic Greek Lexicon, 958–60 for lexical information. It comes from the Nicene-Constantinopolitan Creed: "We believe . . . in the Son . . . who is light of light, very God of very God, *of one essence with the Father.*"

48. Notably, Behr commends Torrance for looking at the formation of classical theology with its emphasis on Christology. See Behr, Review of *Divine Meaning*, 105.

49. Torrance, *The Christian Doctrine of God*, 7.

50. Or "the organic pattern integrating all the doctrines of the Christian faith." See Torrance, *Theology in Reconciliation*, 264. Notably, scholars at the forefront of patristics studies are approaching the Nicene Fathers along similar lines today. John Behr has initiated a project in which he contends that the way in which The Fathers did theology was through Christology. See Behr, *The Way to Nicaea Volume 1*; *The Nicene Faith: Part I*; *The Nicene Faith: Part II*; *The Mystery of Christ*. In his introduction to his recently published new translation of Athanasius' *De Incarnatione*, Behr, explaining Athana-sius' method and starting point, states, "the starting point is the one who ascended the cross, and the account then is given from this perspective. It is through this that the knowledge of God, and all that this effects, has been revealed." See Behr, "Introduc-tion" in *Saint Athanasius the Great*, 23. Though Behr does not use the exact language of Torrance, his method throughout his works on The Fathers is substantially similar to Torrance and the ὁμοούσιον. See e.g., Behr, *The Mystery of Christ*, 19 where he argues that theology must be done "through the Cross and in the manner in which the Passion is interpreted and Christ proclaimed." For this is how The Fathers did theology and how it must be done today. See also p. 87 and 174.

51. Fr. George Dion. Dragas calls this reconstruction of The Fathers on the basis of Christology and appropriation of them into his own Reformed context an "ecumenical historical reconstruction," a "synthetic approach," and a "theological reconstruction." See Dragas, "The Significance for the Church," 214–18.

accordingly, every single one of the themes which arise in *Trinitarian Faith* rests upon and arises from the ὁμοούσιον; indeed they can only be discussed because they do. The famous dictum "all roads lead to Rome" could be inverted and applied to the Torrancian-Athanasian ὁμοούσιον: all roads depart from, go through, and lead back to the ὁμοούσιον.[52]

In his discussion of the ὁμοούσιον, Torrance combines the Nicene doctrine of ὁμοούσιον with the Cyrilline doctrine of the "hypostatic union"[53] and all of their epistemological and soteriological implications. He words this in a number of ways, most often in the context of discussion about The Fathers as ὁμοούσιον but elsewhere as "realist epistemology" and the "kerygmatic" and "evangelical" proclamation of the Gospel.[54]

For Torrance the Nicene doctrine of ὁμοούσιον contains key epistemological and evangelical/soteriological implications. Primarily the ὁμοούσιον implies, "God is really like Jesus"[55] and therefore God can be known internally as he really is in himself.[56] On account of Jesus' and the Holy Spirit's ὁμοούσιον with the Father and Jesus' ὁμοούσιον with humankind God is now knowable as he is in himself. This is, according to Torrance, because it is

---

52. Chapter 1 of this book explored the historical precedence for this and Torrance's evangelical and Trinitarian approach is in line with historic Reformed Protestantism, particularly John Calvin and his emphasis on Trinity and Christology. Torrance is in line with the Reformed tradition in his approach, returning to The Fathers with an emphasis on the Christology, and by means of Christology, the Triadology of classical Christianity.

53. Cyril of Alexandria, *Third Letter to Nestorius*, 8: ὑπόστασεί μία Λογου σεσακομενή (one hypostasis of the Word incarnate). In patristic Greek ὑπόστασίς means "subject/ person." Cyril often uses the word φύσίς as well and hence his famous phrase: Μία φύσις τοῦ Λογου σεσακομενή. See McGuckin, *St. Cyril of Alexandria*, 208ff; Quasten, *Patrology: V. 3*, 139. The "hypostatic union" is the "hypostatic becoming" of the Word of God. This did not entail a change for the divine person or divine Nature, but rather an addition of human nature. In Christ the body/flesh was "hypostatically" united to the Word, that is, the hypostasis and nature of the Word. See Cyril, *Five Tomes Against Nestorius*, 1.4; 2.8; 5.5. In the hypostatic union there is a combination of a fully human nature and a fully divine nature, rooted in one "hypostasis" or subject. Therefore, there would be no person/subject of Jesus but for the incarnation of the second person of the Trinity. See also Torrance, *Incarnation*, 181–234 for Torrance's own exposition on the hypostatic union.

54. Combined intrinsically with this is Torrance's battle against dualism in theology. See Webster, "Theologies of Retrieval," 589. As shall be seen throughout this chapter and next chapter, Torrance uses The Fathers to combat dualism which was an activity prevalent across the many areas of his theological and scientific work.

55. Torrance, *Preaching Christ Today*, 55–56; Torrance, *Trinitarian Perspectives*, 86.

56. Torrance, *Theology in Reconciliation*, 241; Torrance, *Atonement*, 236; Torrance, *Trinitarian Faith*, 66–68, 72.

only through God that humankind can know God.[57] That is why, according to Torrance, Arianism and all other heresies, which are all rooted in some form of dualism, are so problematic.[58] For, the only reason that anything can be said about God is because of the ὁμοούσιον. The term also has key soteriological/evangelical meanings contained within it. A key implication is that the acts of Jesus are the acts of God and, therefore, God is really in Jesus reconciling the world to himself.[59] This means that God's οὐσία must be dynamic rather than static and his ὑπόστασεις are thus dynamic subjectifications of God internal to his very οὐσία.[60] For, to put otherwise would be to cut out the possibly of union with God in himself.

In this sense, revelation and reconciliation are inextricably connected. This is one aspect of Torrance's emphasis on the belief that "the evangelical and epistemological significance of the *homoousion* (ὁμοούσιον) is that God Himself is the actual content of his revelation and God Himself is really in Jesus Christ reconciling the world to Himself."[61] One of Torrance's favorite assertions, therefore, was "God is really like Jesus."[62] This is why, for Torrance, the Christian doctrine of God is "inescapably and essentially Christocentric."[63] Within this Torrance discusses the essential connection between revelation and reconciliation, the connection between who God is and what God does.[64] Thus, "[the ὁμοούσιον] clearly asserts, not only that

57. In his book on Athanasius, Khaled Anatolios emphasizes this similarly to Torrance. According to Anatolios, Athanasius and Irenaeus before him insisted upon the divine initiative (to use Mackintosh's word) in both salvation and revelation (Anatolios, *Athanasius*, 205–7).

58. Torrance, *Trinitarian Faith*, 119: "It is not surprising that the Nicene fathers considered Arianism as the most dangerous heresy, for it struck at the very roots of the Church's faith by calling in question the divine reality of Christ's revelation and saving activity, not to speak of their human actuality."

59. Torrance, *The Christian Doctrine of God*, 7.

60. Ibid., 129 citing Athanasius, *De Decretis*, 16ff., 22ff; *Ad Episcopos*, 17f; *Contra Arianos*, 1.16, 28; 2,33; 3.1ff; *Ad Afros*, 4f.

61. Torrance, *The Christian Doctrine of God*, 7. Elsewhere Torrance states: "the pivotal issue here . . . is the identity (the ταυτότης as Athanasius expressed it) between God and the revelation of Himself, between what he reveals of Himself and of his activity in Jesus Christ what he really is *in-himself* in his own ever-living and dynamic Being" (*The Christian Doctrine of God*, 143. He cites Athanasius, *De Synodis*, 53).

62. Torrance, *Preaching Christ Today*, 55–56; Torrance, *Trinitarian Perspectives*, 86.

63. Torrance, *The Christian Doctrine of God*, 17; Torrance, *Theological Dialogue*, 2:2.

64. Torrance, *Trinitarian Faith*, 135. As he puts it: "The *homoousion* asserts that God *is* eternally *in-himself* what he *is* in Jesus Christ, and, therefore, that there is no dark unknown God behind the back of Jesus Christ, but only he who is made known to us in Jesus Christ."

there is no division between the being of the Son and the being of the Father, but that there is no division between the acts of the Son and the acts of God."[65] This is a theme present nearly everywhere in Torrance's theology. In his intimate connection between the being of God and the acts of God Torrance also, very creatively, applies the ὁμοούσιον to grace.[66] By directly applying the term to grace Torrance uses the word in a way it had not been done before but allowed the inner meaning of the word to guide his use of it. This is possible, he feels, because of theological objectivity by allowing theological terms to dictate their own meaning. According to Torrance this is core to the patristic method of theology as he argues in his discussion of Alexandrian scientific theological method.[67]

Trinity and Pneumatology

In his Triadological emphasis on God's dynamic being of co-inhering persons, particularly in his Pneumatology, Torrance departs from the traditional Western emphasis on the *filioque*.[68] Yet, Torrance does not simply return to the Eastern view (as traditionally conceived), viewing the Father as *arche* of the Trinity. Rather, Torrance's Triadology is a Reformed version of the classical Eastern patristic viewpoint.[69]

It is only through the Nicene ὁμοούσιον that Torrance approaches Triadology proper. Torrance holds that for the Nicene Fathers, and especially Athanasius, the ὁμοούσιον, along with preserving the possibility of theology, also safeguards the key evangelical doctrine of the connection between the ontological and immanent Trinity. Torrance holds that The Fathers,

---

65. Ibid., 137.

66. Torrance, *Theology in Reconstruction*, 225. Torrance views grace as personal and connected to the person of Christ. See Torrance, *Preaching Christ Today*, 20–21.

67. Torrance, *Theology in Reconciliation*, 239–66.

68. See further Radcliff, "Thomas F. Torrance's Conception."

69. As Holmes has helpfully pointed out these traditional categories (of East vs. West) on the doctrine of the Trinity, once accepted by the scholarly consensus and known as the "de Régnon thesis," are no longer widely accepted and, as Holmes states, "neither position [on the *filioque*] does violence to the received orthodox and catholic tradition." See Holmes, *Holy Trinity*, 164. Torrance's position, arrived at by means of his creative reconstruction and dynamic combination of Greek patristic theology and Reformed evangelical theology (see particularly chapter 2 in his book *Trinitarian Perspectives* where Torrance argues for a doctrine of the Trinity based on John Calvin and Gregory Nazianzen) on the doctrine of the Trinity, is very close indeed to the position contemporary theologians and patrologists are claiming The Fathers (both Greek and Latin) themselves actually held. See the following chapter of this book for elaboration upon these ideas.

especially Athanasius, did not adhere to a general/abstract notion of οὐσία but rather, Torrance argues, as was made clear in Athanasius's conception of God's word and act intrinsic to his being, the term has "an intensely personal and concrete meaning."[70]

Torrance wants to preserve the dynamic nature of the οὐσία because he sees the term as personal as opposed to static, a view he traces back to Athanasius.[71] Here Torrance contends that Athanasius held, citing G. L. Prestige, "hypostasis lays stress on concrete independence, ousia lays stress on intrinsic constitution. Hypostasis means 'a reality *ad alios*,' ousia 'a reality *in se*; the one word denotes God as manifest, the other connotes God as being."[72] For Torrance, this means "being in internal relations."[73] Embedded within this is Torrance's discussion of περιχώρησις (*perichoresis*), which, for Torrance, means the mutual indwelling of each member of the Trinity.[74]

Torrance makes it clear that Athanasius was consistent with his scientific method and never proposed that Triadological terms be defined statically; thus, the terms remain open and dynamic. However, Torrance asserts that Athanasius adhered to the view as explicated above.[75] For, Torrance contends, if God were disconnected from his acts, their soteriological significance would fall away, a theological struggle both the Eastern Church and the Western Church have experienced.[76]

Torrance propagates the Athanasian concept of ἐνούσιος λόγος (*word intrinsic to essence*) in support of the twofold view that (a) God's οὐσία is dynamic and (b) God's λόγος is intrinsic/inherent to God's οὐσία, two concepts Torrance believes emerge from the ὁμοούσιον.[77] Herein the key doctrine that God really is like Jesus is preserved.[78] Indeed, Torrance contends

70. Torrance, *The Christian Doctrine of God*, 129 citing Athanasius, *De Decretis*, 16ff, 22ff; *Ad Episcopos*, 17f; *Contra Arianos*, 1.16, 28; 2,33; 3.1ff; *Ad Afros*, 4f. See *The Christian Doctrine of God*, 125–29 for the full discussion. In other words, "the gift and the Giver are the same" (Torrance, *Trinitarian Perspectives*, 9). See also 218–19 where Torrance cited Athanasius, *Contra Arianos*, 2:2, 38 referring to Athanasius' conception of ἐνούσιος ἐνέργεια (*energy intrinsic to essence*).

71. Torrance, *The Christian Doctrine of God*, 104.

72. Torrance, *Trinitarian Perspectives*, 15.

73. See Torrance, *Theology in Reconciliation*, 243–44.

74. Torrance, *The Christian Doctrine of God*, 102–3.

75. Torrance, *Trinitarian Perspectives*, 15 citing Athanasius, *Contra Arianos* I.II; 2.10; 3.63; *De Decretis* 22, 27; *De Synodis* 35, 41; *Ad Afros* 4.8; *Ad Serapionem* 2.5.

76. See Torrance, "Karl Barth and the Latin Heresy," 461–82 for a discussion of the Western problem.

77. Torrance, *The Christian Doctrine of God*, 125–26. See also *Theology in Reconciliation*, 226—27.

78. Torrance, *Trinitarian Perspectives*, 86.

that Athanasius asserted this doctrine because of his doctrine of revelation through Christ[79] since he emphasized the point that knowledge of God is through the Son.[80] Torrance also turns to Gregory Nazianzen in support of this point.[81]

Torrance applies the ὁμοούσιον directly to the doctrine of the Holy Spirit.[82] Torrance's Pneumatological reconstruction of the Greek Fathers is, once again, from a Reformed evangelical perspective. He approaches the Greek Fathers on their own terms and, thus, was generally opposed to the *filioque*.[83] However, perhaps because of his Protestant roots he is sympathetic to the mindset behind the *filioque*. As such, Torrance offers an ecumenical approach to the doctrine of the Trinity. Here, again, Athanasius is central, primarily his *Ad Serapionem* and *Contra Arianos*. For Torrance, Athanasius began his Pneumatology from a soteriological[84] and Christological[85] starting point because of the epistemological centrality of the Son.[86] Furthermore, for Torrance the Spirit's role is primarily to reveal the Son and therein also the Father.[87] This also means that the ὁμοούσιον of the Spirit means

---

79. Torrance, *Theological Dialogue*, 2:111.

80. Ibid., 2:2.

81. Torrance, *The Christian Doctrine of God*, 140–41. More on this below and in the following chapter.

82. See Shepherd, "Thomas F. Torrance," 108–24 for an excellent account of this.

83. Though some were more open to the procession of the Spirit from the Father and the Son than others, such as Maximus the Confessor. See Siecienski, *The Filioque* for an excellent overview of the *filioque*. See especially pp. 73–86 on Maximus. There is notable overlap in the irenic approaches of Torrance and Maximus in this debate.

84. Torrance, *Trinitarian Faith*, 209 citing Athanasius, *Ad Serapionem*, 1.23–1.27; Torrance, *Trinitarian Perspectives*, 11.

85. Torrance, *The Christian Doctrine of God*, 17; Torrance, *Theological Dialogue*, 2:2; Torrance, *Theology in Reconstruction*, 214: "This does not mean that Athanasius begins with the doctrine of the Son, merely because that has already been established, but that this is the only proper procedure because of the propriety of the Spirit to the Son, and because it is only in and through the Son or the Word that God has revealed himself."

86. Torrance, *Trinitarian Perspectives*, 8–11.

87. Torrance, *The Trinitarian Faith*, 211 citing Didymus the Blind, Epiphanius of Salamis, and Cyril of Jerusalem: "The Holy Spirit is not directly known in his own hypostasis for he remains veiled by the very revelation of the Father and the Son which he brings." Torrance sees this captured well in the saying by Gregory Nazianzen, beloved by Calvin: "No sooner do I conceive of the one than I am enlightened by the radiance of the three; no sooner do I distinguish them than I am carried back to the one. When I think of any one I think of him as the whole, and my vision is filled, and the greater part of what I conceive escapes me . . . I see by one luminary, and cannot divide or measure out the undivided light." See *Trinitarian Faith*, 213; Gregory Nazianzen *Oration* 40.41; John Calvin, *Institutes*, 1.13.17.

practically the same thing as the ὁμοούσιον of the Son, albeit with different emphases and certain nuances.

As in the ὁμοούσιον of the Son, Torrance sees epistemological significance in the ὁμοούσιον of the Holy Spirit. Torrance contends that because of the Creator-creature distinction it is only possible to know God through God and, therefore, God himself needed to unite himself to humans, which was done by means of the incarnation of the Son and the indwelling of the Holy Spirit.[88] Torrance writes, citing Athanasius, Epiphanius, Didymus, and Cyril of Jerusalem that humankind "may know the Spirit of the Father and the Son only as he dwells in [them] and brings [them] into the communion of the Holy Trinity."[89]

For Torrance God's οὐσία refers to God's "being in internal relations,"[90] which Torrance sees this flowing from the ὁμοούσιον. Owing to the ὁμοούσιον's implication that God is immediately present with humankind through Christ and in the Holy Spirit it follows that God's οὐσία is dynamically personal.[91] Using Athanasius as his support, Torrance argues a proper doctrine of the Trinity emphasizes the wholeness of the Godhead and approaches the individual persons "in terms of their coinherent and undivided wholeness, in which each person is 'whole of the whole.'"[92] Torrance believes this is rooted in Athanasius' ὁμοούσιον method and its implications for the connection between God's economy and God's ontology in both salvation and revelation.[93]

For Torrance the above means that the Spirit is enhypostatic in God's οὐσία.[94] Here Torrance relies upon The Fathers Epiphanius of Salamis[95] and Didymus the Blind,[96] though he believes the concept ultimately can

88. Ibid., 60–61; Torrance, *God and Rationality*, 165–92; Torrance, *The Christian Doctrine of God*, 13; Torrance, *Theology in Reconciliation*, 232–41.

89. Torrance, *The Trinitarian Faith*, 208–9. It is notable that Torrance's connection of Athanasius, Didymus, and Epiphanius is substantially similar to that of H. B. Swete. See Swete, *The Holy Spirit in the Ancient Church*, 211–29.

90. Torrance, *Theology in Reconciliation*, 243–44. See also *Trinitarian Faith*, 131 for one of Torrance's many references to a favorite quote by G. L. Prestige.

91 Torrance's reading of essence and person are taken from G. L. Prestige, whom he cites often in this context. See e.g., Torrance, *Theological Dialogue*, 2:10.

92. Torrance, *Trinitarian Faith*, 238 citing Athanasius, *Contra Arianos*, 1.16; 3.1ff; 4.1ff; *Ad Serapion*, 1.16, 26.

93. Torrance, *Trinitarian Faith*, 304–5.

94. Ibid., 223f; 231ff. ἐνυππόστατος: See p. 223.

95. Ibid., 208; 223 citing Epiphanius, *Haereses*, 62.3. See PG 41.1054.

96. Ibid., 223–224 citing Didymus, *De Trin.*, 1.16, 26; 2, 1ff, 8, 10; 3.19, 37; 1.9f, 11, 15f, 18f, 25, 27; 2.1, 3f, 5ff, 15, 18, 26f, 3.2, 15f, 24, 47, 55; *Con. Eun.*, Athens ed. 44, pp. 239, 253, 226ff, 246f, 255ff *De Spiritu Sanctu*, 30–39 (footnotes 158–161).

be traced back to Athanasius.[97] This means that the Spirit indwells within the οὐσία of God, giving the doctrine of the Spirit a "profound objectivity," according to Torrance[98] Torrance believes this preserves Pneumatology from any sort of subjective inwardness, whether individualistic as in liberal Protestantism or corporate as in Roman Catholic ecclesiology.[99]

According to Torrance, the enhypostatic existence of the Holy Spirit implies a procession from the οὐσία of the Father; a procession from the dynamically personal οὐσία of the Father through the Son. Here Torrance argues, referring back to Athanasius, the Spirit proceeds from the Father and receives from the Son.[100] Torrance confesses that Athanasius often used the terms οὐσία and ὑπόστασις as synonyms; however, Torrance contends that when Athanasius asserted the Holy Spirit's procession from the οὐσία of the Father this was not ὑπόστασις as he argues would later be asserted by the Cappadocians but God's dynamic οὐσία itself.[101] For Torrance this assertion is key to preserving the bond between the economic and ontological Trinity. For, without the Spirit's procession from the οὐσία of God the Spirit would not be revelation of who God really is in himself.[102]

Torrance's unique approach to the doctrine of the Trinity contributed substantially to his role in the Reformed-Orthodox Dialogue.[103] During the Dialogue Torrance continually turns to Athanasius' Triadology and his conception of the procession of the Spirit as cutting behind the divisions between East and West. For Torrance, Athanasius' Triadology cuts behind the problem entirely in its focus upon the dynamic unity of God.[104] As Torrance puts it, "Athanasius neither speaks explicitly of a double 'procession' of the Spirit nor rejects it."[105] Ultimately, Athanasius spoke of the procession of the Spirit from the Father through the Son; however, Torrance states, "Athana-

97. Ibid., 221 referring to Athanasius, *Contra Arianos*, 1.20, 33.

98. Torrance, *Theology in Reconciliation*, 234 citing Athanasius, *Ad Serapionem*, 1:19, 21, 27, 30; 3:1, 2, 5.

99. See Torrance, *Theology in Reconstruction*, 227–28.

100. Torrance, *Trinitarian Faith*, 231 citing Athanasius, *Ad Serapionem*, 1.27; 3.1; 1.2; 4.3; 1.11; 1.20; 3.1; 4.1f; 1.25; 3.1; 4.3f. See also 233–34.

101. Ibid., 236 citing Athanasius, *Ad Serapionem*, 1.10, 22, 25, 27; 2.5; 3.1. Cf. J. N. D. Kelly who sees the Cappadocians as basically Athanasian in their Triadology. See Kelly, *Early Christian Doctrines*, 263–64. However, others, such as Hanson are more in line with Torrance's distinction. See Hanson, *The Search for the Christian Doctrine of God*, 677–78.

102. Torrance, *Theological Dialogue*, 2:26.

103. Torrance, *Theological Dialogue I*; Torrance, *Theological Dialogue II*; Torrance, *Trinitarian Perspectives*.

104. Torrance, *Trinitarian Perspectives*, 13–20, especially 18–20.

105. Torrance, *Theology in Reconciliation*, 235.

sius could not have gone on to say that the Spirit proceeded from the Father *only* for it would have contradicted his basic theology."[106] Torrance sees this put forth by all the "great Eastern Fathers up to Theodoret . . . not least the well-known passages often adduced in favor of the *filioque*."[107]

The key for Torrance is to start, with Athanasius, neither from the unity nor the plurality but rather the "coinherent Trinitarian relations."[108] This is indeed a procession of the Spirit from the Father through the Son. Torrance contends that Athanasius' wording the Trinitarian relations as such was because of his basic presupposition that οὐσία did not mean "being" in the *abstract* but rather "being in internal relations."[109] Therefore, for Torrance who is here departing from the traditional Protestant insistence upon the *filioque*, the Holy Spirit proceeds from the Father. This openness on the part of Torrance and the other Reformed in the Dialogue allowed for deep agreement and rapport between the two groups.

In Torrance's papers on the Dialogue he reflects on his view that there is great significance in the fact that the agreed statement did not say "procession from the person of the Father" but rather, as it does in the Creed, simply "from the Father." The agreed statement puts it: "Since there is only one Trinity in Unity, and one Unity in Trinity, there is only one indivisible Godhead, and only one *Arche* (ἀρχή) or *Monarchia* (μοναρχία). As such, however, Gregory the Theologian reminds us, 'It is a Μοναρχία that is not limited to one Person' (Or. 29.2) . . . the μία Ἀρχή or Μοναρχία is inseparable from the Trinity, the Μονάς from the Τριάς."[110] Furthermore, the common reflection states "the perfect simplicity and the indivisibility of God in his Triune Being mean that the ἀρχή or μοναρχία cannot be limited to one Person, as Gregory the Theologian pointed out."[111] Torrance's comments concerning "the working paper on the Holy Trinity" from the dialogue are most illuminating. He feels that to limit the μοναρχία to one person would take away from the *perichoretic* Trinitarian relations.[112] Thus it is correct, in Torrance's view, to identify the μοναρχία with the Father but only if the μοναρχία is immediately connected to each person because of the inherent unity of the persons.[113]

---

106. Ibid., 218.

107. Ibid., 218–19.

108. Torrance, *Theological Dialogue*, 2:6–7.

109. Ibid., 2:20.

110. Ibid., 2:223–24.

111. Ibid., 2:231.

112. Ibid., 2:121.

113. Cf. Zizioulas who holds that the μοναρχία of the Trinity must be rooted in

The Objective Nature of Theology

In addition to being the core of theology in general and Christology, Triadology, and Pneumatology in particular, Torrance understands the doctrine of ὁμοούσιον to be a hermeneutical and theological key. As such Torrance is, once again, asserting a Reformed and evangelical Christocentrism. Torrance holds that the assertions of the Council of Nicaea were the outcome of The Fathers dissecting the inner structure of the Scriptures "by subordinating its mind (διάνοια) to the meaning of the Holy Scriptures and the apostolic mind (φρόνημα), indeed the Mind of Christ (νοῦς)."[114] Thus the concept is a theme arising from theological thinking and, in turn, guiding theological thinking. Herein it acts as a σκοπός (scope, goal, end).[115] This occurs on two levels, the scope of Scripture and the scope of faith.[116] The penultimate scope is the Nicene ὁμοούσιον[117] and therein Christ.[118] Torrance contends that the ὁμοούσιον arises out of rigid examination of Biblical statements following Athanasian scientific theology[119] and that, in turn, guides how Biblical statements are to be interpreted.[120] Here, the ὁμοούσιον also works as a hermeneutical statement in that it is the key to interpreting the Scriptures.

In this sense, the Nicene ὁμοούσιον and thus, as discussed above, a Reformed-dogmatic commitment, drives Torrance's conception of the objective nature of theology.[121] In Torrance's estimate, The Fathers solidified the core assertion that theology is scientific and dogmatic and thus objective.[122] For Torrance, because of the essential difference between creation

the person of the Father in order to preserve freedom in God. See Zizioulas, *Being as Communion*, 33–39. The following chapter of this book will examine the differences between Torrance and Zizioulas in full.

114. Torrance, *Trinitarian Faith*, 127.

115. See Lampe, *A Patristic Greek Lexicon*, 1241 for lexical information.

116. Torrance, *Reality and Evangelical Theology*, 106–7; Torrance, *Divine Meaning*, 237.

117. Torrance, *Reality and Evangelical Theology*, 112–13.

118. Torrance, *Theology in Reconstruction*, 32.

119. Torrance, *The Trinitarian Faith*, 129–30.

120. Ibid., 130 citing Athanasius *De Decretis*, 4. See also *Theology in Reconstruction*, 33.

121. Molnar states: "What attracted Torrance to history was his own quest for a scientific theology, which he found in the early fathers . . . " (Molnar, *Thomas F. Torrance*, 338). See also Radcliff, "T. F. Torrance's Trinitarian Theology," 512–13.

122. This was a topic of great interest to Torrance and he wanted to write his PhD thesis on the scientific nature of theology but was persuaded otherwise by Barth. To see this more fully unpacked in greater detail in his other work see: Torrance, *Theological*

and their Creator, it would be impossible for humankind to know God who is a completely different essence from them without God's initiative. Thus, argues Torrance, Athanasius' famous dictum: "It would be more godly and true to signify God from the Son and call him Father, than to name God from his works alone and call him Unorginate."[123] Torrance conceptualizes this as a patristic affirmation of the ultimate impossibility of any form of natural theology and, therefore, the necessity of God's self-revelation in Jesus Christ.[124]

Torrance asserts that the theme of theological and epistemological objectivity was put forth in the thought of Athanasius but also Hilary of Poitiers and Irenaeus of Lyons.[125] For Torrance, Irenaeus and, even more strongly, Hilary affirmed the aspect of Nicene theology that asserted the ultimate objective nature of Christian faith. As Torrance puts it: "Primacy in the Nicene Creed accorded to faith reflects the settled patristic view of faith,

---

Science and *Reality and Scientific Theology.*

123. Torrance, *The Trinitarian Faith*, 49 quoting Athanasius, *Contra Arianos*, 1.34.

124. Ibid., 50–64. He argues that "when we speak of God from the perspective of the Creator/creature relation, or the Unorginate/originate relation, we can only think and speak of him in vague, general and negative terms, at the infinite distance of the creature from the Creator where we cannot know God as he is *in-himself* or in accordance with his divine nature, but only in his absolute separation from us, as the eternal, unconditioned and indescribable" (50) and "any attempt to reach knowledge of God in this kind of way is self-willed" (51) but "[the scientific approach of Nicaea] in which we know things only under the constraint of their distinctive nature, applies even more forcefully to the knowledge of God, for since there is no likeness between the eternal being of God and the being of created reality, *God may be known only out of himself*" (52, italics not in the original).

125. Torrance's reconstruction of scientific theology on the basis of patristic themes is highly insightful. R. L Wilken comments that Torrance's reading of Hilary of Poitiers is fresh and unique and has much to offer contemporary scholarship. See Wilken, Review of *Divine Meaning*, 744. Indeed, there has not been significant work done on The Fathers' notion of objectivity and Torrance had deep insight into the objective nature of faith in patristic theology, due, no doubt in part, to his connection of The Fathers to Barthian theology. Primarily, however, Torrance's emphasis on the ὁμοούσιον and the inner meaning behind it regarding God's self-giving in revelation brought out this element in patristic theology and was a fresh insight. Arguably, Torrance did not actually find this notion of objectivity in The Fathers initially. See, e.g., chapter 1 of *Theological Science* where he roots his notion in James Brown, John Macmurray, and Michael Polanyi. However, his chapter on objectivity in *Trinitarian Faith* shows that, while he might not have found this concept in the Father initially, when he read The Fathers in light of current epistemological debates, a similar (and indeed complementary) notion of objectivity was there. This, once again, sheds led on Torrance's creative and reconstructive approach to The Fathers: he read them in light of the current debate and, consequently, was able to extract fresh ideas from The Fathers.

not as subjectively grounded but as an objectively grounded persuasion of the mind . . . ”[126]

κατὰ φύσιν Theology

Connected to Torrance's conception of the objectivity of theology is his use of the patristic theme of κατὰ φύσιν.[127] Torrance understands this patristic phrase to mean:

> Through faith our minds assent to the inherent intelligibility of things, yield to their self-evidencing power, and are adapted to know them in their own nature. It is upon that kind of basic contact with reality that all sure knowledge rests and all genuine understanding is established, and upon it that we continue to rely in all further inquiry and all deepening of our understanding.[128]

Torrance contends that this means objects must be studied according to their own nature. For theologians this applies directly to the object of their study, God. Torrance sees this theme put forth by Irenaeus in his discussion of early creedal and *kerygmatic* proclamations as "assertions of belief that are organized from beyond themselves by their common ground in the apostolic deposit of faith and ultimately by the self-revelation of God in Jesus Christ"[129] and Hilary's view that "God cannot be apprehended except through Himself."[130] For Torrance, these Fathers as well as Athanasius explored what it means to view theology as truly scientific and objective in nature.

For Torrance orthodox theological methodology is rooted in this "scientific theology" and "realist epistemology." Torrance adapts this patristic theme into his own theology through the Torrancian conception of "realist epistemology," which he acknowledges to be rooted in the Greek Fathers.[131] Torrance calls this method "the pure science of theology," indeed, dogmatics. Here, Torrance states,

---

126. Torrance, *The Trinitarian Faith*, 19 quoting Hilary, *De Trin.*, 1.18: "In faith a person takes his stand on the ground of God's own being."

127. From the Greek "according to nature." It essentially means "as something really is."

128. Torrance, *The Trinitarian Faith*, 20.

129. Ibid., 34.

130. Ibid., 21.

131. Torrance, *Reality and Evangelical Theology*, 103.

Theologians are engaged in the formulation of dogmatic statements in and through which [they] inquire after *the* dogma, that is, the inherent rationality of the *Logos*, the *Prima Veritas* of God, by letting him disclose Himself to [their] mind, command [their] recognition, and order and shape [their] understanding in basic ways that correspond faithfully to his words and acts.[132]

For Torrance this is κατὰ φύσιν theology. In Athanasius and the other Fathers, Torrance sees an approach to theology that arose out the Alexandrian scientific-theological method. He states that this entails "rigorous knowledge according to the inherent structure or nature (κατὰ φύσιν) of the realities investigated."[133] However, in Torrance's view, Athanasius did not blindly adopt this scientific method but rather reconstructed the method in order to work with a Biblical worldview.[134]

For Torrance the ὁμοούσιον has to do with the Gospel at its *kerygmatic* core and preserves its integrity. In Torrance's mind a number of issues are at stake here and if the ὁμοούσιον is denied there would be a number of negative implications. Primarily, Torrance holds that without the ὁμοούσιον God's revelation in Christ is not real revelation from God and therefore "theology" would not be theology but rather "mythology."[135] Thus, the ὁμοούσιον cuts out any possibility of "thinking" a way towards God; this would actually be mythology.[136] This is because it would no longer be rooted in God κατὰ φύσιν. Second, he contends that without the ὁμοούσιον Christ would not be the self-communication of God, which in turn would imply that God does not care to reveal himself.[137] Thus, the ὁμοούσιον ultimately affirms two things: That God is identical to his self-revelation in Jesus Christ and that God is eternally in himself what he is in Christ.[138]

For Torrance the only way to know God κατὰ φύσιν is through the Son, and, in turn, the only way this is possible is if the Son is ὁμοούσιον τῷ Πατρί for only through the Son who was ἐκ τῆς οὐσίας τοῦ Πατρός (*from the essence/being of the Father*) can God be known. This is because the only way

132. Torrance, *Theology in Reconstruction*, 55.

133. Torrance, *Theology in Reconciliation*, 241. See also *Atonement*, 236.

134. Torrance, *Reality and Scientific Theology*, 3–4.

135. Torrance, *Trinitarian Faith*, 133–34.

136. Torrance's discussion of mythology in Athanasius in this section of *Trinitarian Faith* often sounds substantially similar to Barth's critique of nineteenth-century liberal theology's approach to God, namely, "humanity writ large" and, indeed, Barth's approach to dogmatics in general. Cf. Karl Barth, *Church Dogmatics*, I/I; III/I. See the next chapter for a fuller examination of Torrance's connections to Barth.

137. Torrance, *Trinitarian Faith*, 134.

138. Ibid., 135.

to know God is, in fact, through the Son who is ὁμοούσιον.[139] Thus, the only way to actually do κατὰ φύσιν theology is through Christ because Christ is ὁμοούσιον τῷ Πατρί. This is because of the fact that if God is not really in Jesus, the Gospel would be empty of divine reality and validity.[140] Indeed, Torrance sees the Nicene Creed as affirming that God in his own being was present in this world.[141] In support, Torrance liked to quote a dictum of his teacher, H. R. Mackintosh, "the words of Jesus are the words of God."[142] If the Son is not ὁμοούσιον τῷ Πατρί, theology would not be κατὰ φύσιν and would therefore not be theology at all but rather mythology, which, Torrance notes, was the problem with the Arian system.[143]

Torrance elaborates on this reconstruction and explains that scientific theology means that human terms are to remain dynamic and able to be adapted to the realities that they signify, and in this way, theology is much like physics.[144] Therefore, patristic theological terminology is, in Torrance's view, "functional and not analytical language."[145] This is why, for example, Athanasius could alternate between terms in order to signify the same reality.[146] For, the terms remain open to being re-defined and changed on the basis of the realities they signify. Thus, they are "axiomatic terms."[147] This means that knowledge of new realities forced new terms to be used and old terms to be reused with different meanings in order to make them appropriate to the realities to which they refer.[148]

Herein, Torrance sees Athanasius as having developed "the basic grammar and distinctive pattern (στοιχαίωσιν καὶ χαρακτῆρα) of the faith in accordance with Christ and his divine manifestation towards us."[149] Torrance elaborates upon the dynamic nature of the axioms elsewhere in reference to the revolution in thought produced by Einstein's Relativity Theory, which he sees as similarly significant to Athanasius:

---

139. Torrance, *The Christian Doctrine of God*, 2–3 citing Athanasius, *Contra Arianos*, 2.76.

140. Torrance, *Reality and Evangelical Theology*, 14.

141. Torrance, *Space, Time and Incarnation*, 1.

142. Torrance, *The Christian Doctrine of God*, 14.

143. Torrance, *The Trinitarian Faith*, 119. More on this below.

144. Torrance, *Theology in Reconciliation*, 241.

145. Ibid., 242.

146. Torrance, *The Christian Doctrine of God*, 128–29.

147. Torrance, *Theology in Reconciliation*, 264.

148. Torrance, *The Christian Doctrine of God*, 20.

149. Torrance, *Theology in Reconciliation*, 263 citing Athanasius, *De Incarnatione* 56 and referring to *Contra Arianos* 28f.; *De Decretis* 32.

The axioms are not just a set of logical premises, antecedent to and independent of the results, but arise out of the intrinsic connections of scientific activity, and force themselves upon us as the necessary structures of thought through which the intelligible nature of things imposes itself upon our minds.[150]

Put otherwise, Torrance holds that the axioms and the scientific-theological results continuously inform one another. The prime example of how this works is Torrance's conception of the Nicene ὁμοούσιον τῷ Πατρί. For, as discussed earlier, the ὁμοούσιον and the Nicene conception of οὐσία arose out of Athanasius' reading of Scripture, but at the same time the ὁμοούσιον also governed Athanasius' reading of Scripture.[151]

Another aspect of patristic scientific theology, in Torrance's view, is that the meaning of the words in the Bible are not found nor rooted in themselves, but rather in the realities and actions they express.[152] Thus, the words always point away from themselves and to the divine reality they are expressing. This is what Torrance perceives as Athanasius' problem with the Arian method. For the Arians thought κατ᾽ἐπίνοιαν (*out of themselves/ themselves as a reference point*) whereas Athanasius, thought κατὰ διάνοιαν (*across/away/through from Himself towards God*).[153] For Torrance, this is intrinsically connected to κατὰ φύσιν for Athanasian theology was able to properly think and speak of God because it was κατὰ διάνοιαν whereas the Arians could not think of God κατὰ φύσιν because they thought κατ᾽ἐπίνοιαν and simply projected their own ideas onto God.[154]

Torrance holds that Athanasius insisted upon a dynamic view of theological terms, leaving them open to being shaped by the realities signified. However, according to Torrance, whereas Athanasius kept certain flexibility in terms, the Cappadocians made them more fixed.[155] This is seen most clearly in Torrance's conception of the Athanasian doctrine of ὁμοούσιον

150. Torrance, *God and Rationality*, 100. See also 99–103.

151. Torrance, *Divine Meaning*, 230.

152. Ibid., 232. This is also Torrance's view of Scripture. See *Reality and Evangelical Theology*. There is substantial overlap between Torrance and Barth on this subject. For Barth Scripture is a witness and points away from itself to Christ. See further Cunningham, "Karl Barth," 183–202.

153. Torrance, *Preaching Christ Today*, 52.

154. Interestingly by the time of Basil's debate with the Eunomians these terms had taken on a slightly different meaning and were employed differently than Athanasius did against the Arians. For Basil, theological thinking is actually done by ἐπίνοια, in part to preserve God's ultimate unknowability. See Ayres, *Nicaea and Its Legacy*, 191ff for a discussion of this distinction.

155. Torrance, *Theology in Reconciliation*, 245–46. See Torrance, *Theological Dialogue*, 2:117–18 for further discussion of the Athanasian view.

τῷ Πατρί. Torrance holds that Athanasius maintained a dynamic view of οὐσία and ὑπόστασις.[156] Another example is that a dynamic view of terms implied the subject of the event, Christ himself, must inform statements about himself.[157]

Apophatic Theology

Flowing from this, Torrance argues for a certain level of *apophatic*[158] reserve when doing theology.[159] In order to clarify this, Torrance distinguishes between "Athanasian *apophaticism*" and "Dionysian *apophaticism*" (named after Pseudo-Dionysius the Areopagite).[160] Torrance contends that for Athanasius, humans can only know God economically, but the key difference is that the economic God is also the ontological God. Additionally, in Torrance's Athanasian *apophaticism*, God reveals himself fully but not wholly.[161] Conversely for Pseudo-Dionysius *apophaticism* is because of "the infinite excess of God known over our knowing of him."[162] Thus, Torrance wants to preserve that Athanasian sense of *apophatic* reserve for, "precisely in apprehending him [God] we know him to be incomprehensible."[163] Torrance wants to stay far from any sort of dualism that calls the connection of God to his self-revelation into question.

---

156. Torrance, *Theology in Reconciliation*, 244–45.

157. Torrance, *Atonement*, 234.

158. ἀπόφασις. From the Greek ἀπό φασιν: *From/away from speech*. See Lampe, *A Patristic Greek Lexicon*, 219. The term basically asserts the view that any knowledge of God is always limited. However, there are different ways of understanding this.

159. Torrance, *The Christian Doctrine of God*, 158–59.

160. The fifth/sixtth-century author of the corpus attributed to Paul's convert in Athens. See Acts 17: 34.

161. Torrance, *The Christian Doctrine of God*, 81.

162. See Torrance, *Trinitarian Perspectives*, 85 especially footnote 17. See also *Theology in Reconciliation*, 221. The thrust of the argument is that the root of Athanasius' apophaticism was because of his strong distinction between God and creation whereas as the "fatal" version of apophaticism was rooted in cosmological dualism as found in Aristotelian and Stoic logic, and the statement by Basilides that "we cannot know what God is, but only what he is not." Pseudo-Dionysius, John of Damascus, and some modern Orthodox such as Vladimir Lossky took up the latter version. Note that Torrance does not lump all the Orthodox together here; for he sings high praises of Nikolas Nissiotis and his return to Athanasian theology via Karl Barth (103–9).

163. Torrance, *Trinitarian Perspectives*, 85–86.

Heresy and Mythology

Torrance notes that the Nicene Fathers saw heresy as ἀσέβεια (*impiety/ ungodliness*)[164] and usually rooted in some sort of theological or epistemological dualism.[165] Torrance references Athanasius here as stating that the Nicene Creed is "a bulwark" against them [the dualistic heresies].[166] Thus, the heretics were rooted in ἀσέβεια and did not know God κατὰ φύσιν. Torrance argues that Athanasius rejected Arianism, among other reasons, because of their dualism between God and the world.[167] For, if the Arians were right then only μυθολογία (and not knowledge of God κατὰ φύσιν) would be possible.[168] For Torrance, ἀσέβεια and therein heresy were ultimately rooted in elements of dualism, especially a dualism which separated the αἰσθητὸς κόσμος (*sensible world*) and νοητὸς κόσμος (*intelligible world*).[169] Torrance holds that this dualism was rooted in Neo-Platonic dichotomies and even appeared later in John of Damascus and his view that God is οὐσία ὑπερούσιος (*essence beyond essence*).[170] This is a dualism nowhere present in Athanasius, according to Torrance.[171]

---

164. Torrance, *Trinitarian Faith*, 42 citing Athanasius, *De Decretis*, 1–3.

165. Ibid., 111–13; Torrance says that combating the theological and epistemological dualism in which Western thought is embedded was a missionary calling for him. See The Thomas F. Torrance Manuscript Collection, Series II, Box 10: Autobiographical Writings of Thomas F. Torrance, Princeton Seminary. See also Stein, "Introduction," vi. Stein points to Robert Walker's PhD thesis written at the University of St Andrews where he points to four core elements to Torrance's though, one of which was the attack on various forms of dualism.

166. Torrance, *Trinitarian Faith*, 113 citing Athanasius, *Contra Arianos* 1.8; 2.12, 14; *De Decretis*, 12, 32; *De Synodis*, 45; *Ad Afros*, 11.

167. Torrance, *Theology in Reconciliation*, 224.

168. Ibid., 240.

169. Torrance, *Trinitarian Faith*, 114–15.

170. Often translated into English as *supra-essence*. The term is from the Greek ὑπέρ (*over/above*) and οὐσία (*being/essence*). See Torrance, *Theology in Reconciliation*, 218. Torrance does not cite what text he had in mind from the Damascene. One instance where John of Damascus used this phrase was in *De Fide Orthodoxa*, III.10 in discussion of whether the *Trisagion Hymn* refers solely to Christ or the entire Godhead. He argued that Athanasius, Basil, and Gregory all held that the hymn refers to: the three persons of the supra-essential Godhead (τὰς τρεῖς τῆς ὑπερουσίου θεότητος ὑποστάσεις). See PG 94.1020–21. The phrase also appears in Orthodox liturgical texts. See, for example, *Kontakion on the Navity of Christ*: "Today the Virgin gives birth to him who is supra-essential (ὑπερουσίον)." Torrance holds that this term is highly dualist and that dualism had made its way into the Eastern Orthodox liturgy via John Chrysostom. See *Theological Dialogue*, 1:17.

171. Torrance, *Space, Time and Incarnation*, 15. There is no doubt that the distinction between mythology and theology exists in the thought of The Fathers (Torrance's

This sort of theology, in Torrance's mind, can never be orthodox for true theology could only be done from an objective point in God.[172] Here Torrance understands himself to be significantly reliant upon Hilary, especially concerning the idea that "everything we actually think and say of God must be constrained and controlled within the bounds of the revelation of the Father in and through the incarnate Son."[173]

Creation and Natural Theology

The other side of Torrance's scientific theology is his reconstruction of "natural theology." By means of his reconstruction of The Fathers through the ὁμοούσιον Torrance provides fresh insight into patristic theology in the realm of natural science. During his time Torrance was at the forefront of those studying the relationship between science and religion and his contribution concerning The Fathers on relativity theory and natural science was truly immense.

Torrance, relying upon Irenaeus and Hilary, contends that God is absolutely free and his will to create was a free act of philanthropic love for humankind (φιλανθρωπία).[174] God's freedom was only understood by the Nicene Fathers, according to Torrance, "from the standpoint of God's incarnate self-revelation in Jesus Christ his beloved Son, the Word through whom all things were made . . . "[175] or, put otherwise, from the ὁμοούσιον. Furthermore, the knowledge that God has freely chosen to be in relation with his creation, is again a knowledge only seen through Jesus Christ.[176]

This means that creation came out of nothing and is thus completely contingent.[177] Torrance takes this concept from Athanasius, especially in *Contra Gentes* and *De Incarnatione* and also from John Philoponus and Basil the Great.[178] Basically, it means that creation cannot exist by itself for

---

many footnotes certainly document this). Torrance's context, however, might explain to a certain extent the prominence he gives to this distinction (i.e., Torrance's opposition to Bultmann's project of "demythologizing" discussed in chapter 1 of this book). Once again, this is, in part, the genius to his approach to The Fathers: Torrance reconstructs The Fathers in light of Reformed theology and brings them into play in contemporary debates.

172. Torrance, *Trinitarian Faith*, 51.

173. Ibid., 81–82 citing Hilary, *De Trinitate*, 1.13–19.

174. See Lampe, *A Patristic Greek Lexicon*, 1475 for lexical information.

175. Torrance, *Trinitarian Faith*, 91.

176. Ibid., 92–95.

177. Ibid., 95–102.

178. Ibid., 98–100.

it is entirely dependent upon God for its very being.[179] The contingency of creation means, for Torrance, that it can be studied in itself, although this will not lead to theological knowledge of God himself, but rather only about his creation.[180] Torrance's commentators have hailed Torrance's re-situation of natural theology under the auspices of revelation as a positive development.[181]

Christological-Pneumatological View of the Church and Sacraments

Torrance also approaches his ecclesiology from the point of view of the ὁμοούσιον. Torrance roots his ecclesiology directly in "the internal relation of the Son to the Father" (the ὁμοούσιον)[182] because it was clear "to the catholic fathers that there was a profound interconnection between ecclesiology and Christology as well pneumatology, the key to which, as in the doctrine of the Holy Trinity, was the Nicene *homoousion*."[183] Torrance expands this by stating:

> The doctrine of the Church must be expounded in terms of its *internal relations*, and not some external relation, to Jesus Christ, for it is in Christ and his inherent relation to the Father and the Holy Spirit that the essential nature of the Church is to be found.[184]

Torrance understands this conception to have come directly from Athanasius, who had an ecclesiology that was also directly rooted in an understanding of the Church's participation in the Son who is ὁμοούσιον τῷ Πατρί.[185] Torrance argues that it was only in Western ecclesiology that there

179. Ibid., 100–101. Torrance refers to Basil, *De Spiritu Sancto* and Aristedes, *Ad Autolycus*: "If [God] were to withdraw [his] presence from the creation it would vanish into nothing." See p. 101. Interestingly this is an idea substantially similar to the one put forth by Jonathan Edwards. See Edwards, *The Great Christian Doctrine*, 4.3.

180. Torrance, *Trinitarian Faith*, 102–4. Hence Torrance's massive amount of scholarship done in the field of the natural sciences. See Torrance, *Divine and Contingent Order*; Torrance, *Space, Time and Incarnation*; Torrance, *Space, Time and Resurrection*. Here, the influence of Barth is certainly evident. Cf. Barth, *Church Dogmatics*, II/1 135–36.

181. See e.g., McGrath's discussion in *T. F. Torrance*, 190–92.

182. Torrance, *Trinitarian Faith*, 264.

183. Ibid., 277.

184. Ibid., 264.

185. Ibid., 264–265 citing Athanasius, *In Ps.*, 21.22.

began to develop a distinction between the external fellowship of believers in the Church and the Church as the mystical Body of Christ, which
Torrance roots in traces of dualistic Origenism.[186] Indeed, Torrance sees a
direct correlation between theology, especially Christology and Triadology,
and ecclesiology. For example, Torrance sees in Arianism a Christology that
only allowed for a moral union between Christ and God and thus Arian
ecclesiology was a community of like-minded believers. Contrast this to
Torrance's view of Nicene ecclesiology: a real ontological union of believers
with Christ and one another.[187]

Connected to this is the notion of *kerygma*. For Torrance, Irenaeus of
Lyons developed the concept of the apostolic *kerygma*. For Irenaeus, as Torrance puts it, "the incarnation of the Lord and the message of salvation, fact
and meaning, the Word and the word, the Truth and truths, were all intrinsically integrated and might not be torn apart without serious distortion of
the faith."[188] This means, for Torrance, that salvation and the message about
salvation are inseparable. Therefore, because the church is the place wherein
God has united humankind to himself in Christ, the church also embodies
the *kerygma* and the deposit of faith.[189] Torrance contrasts this Irenaean
and "realist" conception of the church, centered on the ὁμοούσιον, with with
Tertullian's significantly more legalist, dualist, and static conception of the
church being bound together by discipline and his rigid conception of the
"rule of faith."[190]

For Torrance the church is one, holy, catholic, and apostolic on the
basis laid out above, namely, the ὁμοούσιον and *kerygma*. The church, according to Torrance, is one because Christ is one.[191] The church is holy
on the basis of the holiness of the Trinity.[192] Finally, the church is catholic
and apostolic because of her rootedness in the apostolic mind, faith, and
preaching.[193] Thus, there is one baptism into Christ's body containing the
encapsulation of the apostolic *kerygma*.[194]

Torrance contrasts this realist and ὁμοούσιον-centered view of the
church with what he sees as dualism in the Roman Catholic and liberal

186. Ibid., 270.
187. Ibid., 277–78.
188. Ibid., 260.
189. Ibid., 261.
190. Ibid., 270–71.
191. Ibid., 279–80.
192. Ibid., 280–82.
193. Ibid., 282–89.
194. Ibid., 289–301.

protestant wings of the church. For Torrance, both of these churches had left behind any sort of objective notion of the church by replacing the objectivity of the Holy Spirit as enhypostatic in God with either the human Spirit, as in liberal Protestantism, or with the church herself, as in Roman Catholicism.[195] Torrance argues that the patristic view, as explicated by Athanasius and Irenaeus, was significantly more objectively focused. Torrance appropriates this thinking imaginatively into his own Reformed context in his discussion of the corporate episcopate and sharing in the ministry of Christ primarily by asserting the vicarious priesthood and ministry of Christ and the church's sharing in this ministry.[196]

Torrance roots his view of the sacraments entirely in the person of Christ. For him, the vicarious humanity of Christ[197] in patristic theology means that Christ was a vicarious priest on behalf of humankind.[198] Torrance elaborates upon this further and explicates the vicarious role of the ascended Christ in worship, a view he takes from Athanasius and Cyril.[199] Connected to this, Torrance puts forward the view that the primary sacrament of the church is Jesus Christ himself[200] and holds that this means that the sacraments must be understood as participating in the mystery of Christ through the Spirit.[201] This means that the act of baptism looks beyond itself

195. Torrance, "Karl Barth and the Latin Heresy," 471. See also Torrance, *Theology in Reconciliation*, 234.

196. See Torrance, *Royal Priesthood*, especially the last chapter and also Torrance, *Conflict and Agreement 1*; Thomas F. Torrance, *Conflict and Agreement 2*.

197. See below for more on the vicarious humanity of Christ.

198. See Torrance, *Theology in Reconciliation*, 110–111 citing Athanasius, *Contra Arianos*, IV:6.

199. Ibid., 139–214. See especially 156ff. David Fergusson states: "Torrance's commitment to a strong Christological view of worship and the sacraments determines his doctrine of the ascension" (Fergusson, "The Ascension of Christ," 103). Notably, Torrance's eschatology is also rooted in Torrance's Christology. See Stanley S. MacLean's recently published PhD dissertation for an exploration of this aspect of Torrance's eschatology: *Resurrection, Apocalypse, and the Kingdom of Christ*. MacLean argues that Torrance's eschatology is "an imaginative attempt at recapturing the eschatological orientation of the early church" (xvi). Notably, Torrance connects Athanasius to Calvin in the realm of eschatology. In his discussion about the difference between Eastern and Western eschatology, Torrance propagates that Calvin was basically Athanasian in his eschatology because of the affirmation of a "world-affirming" character, distinct from the Western view that was "world-denying." See Torrance, *Space, Time and Resurrection*, 155. Torrance references Athanasius, *De Incarnatione*, 29ff., and Maximus, *Capita Gnostica*, M.P.G. 90, 1108.

200. Torrance, *Theology in Reconciliation*, 82. Compare this to Barth who holds that Christ is the one true sacrament. See Barth, *Church Dogmatics*, IV/2, p. 55. Torrance's view arises, in part, from his "realist" epistemology, as discussed above.

201. Torrance, *Theology in Reconciliation*, 82.

to the baptism of Christ in the Jordan, a view rooted in Athanasius.[202] In his article *The One Baptism Common to Christ and His Church*[203] and various articles in *Conflict and Agreement* 2[204] Torrance elaborates upon his Christologically conditioned view of the sacraments of baptism and communion rooting them entirely in the person of Christ, and, in particular, the humanity of Christ which he calls the "matter or substance" of the sacraments.[205]

Piety, Godliness, and Asceticism

Torrance understands two words to be inextricably connected to scientific theology and orthodoxy: εὐσέβεια (*piety*) and θεοσέβεια (*godliness*). The dual concepts of piety and godliness, which Torrance feels are core to The Fathers and the ὁμοούσιον, are central to his notion of the *Consensus Patrum* and play a major role in Torrance's creative reconstruction of The Fathers. Essentially, he understands this theme to be concerned with living a life in accordance with the nature of God. The scientific nature of theology has to do with the epistemological side of this. Piety and godliness have to do with what might be labeled the spiritual, physical, and even ascetical side of knowing God in accordance with who he is in himself. Torrance's approach to asceticism has set the stage for further Reformed and evangelical explorations of this important Greek patristic theme.[206]

---

202. Ibid., 83–89. Cf. Athanasius, *Contra Arianos*, 1.47: "For when the Lord, as man, was washed in Jordan, it was we who were washed in Him and by Him. And when He received the Spirit, it was we who by Him were made recipients of It."

203. Torrance, *Theology in Reconciliation*, 83–105.

204. Torrance, *Conflict and Agreement 2*. See especially 93–202.

205. See e.g., Torrance, *Conflict and Agreement*, 2:142. Torrance sees himself as following Calvin in this emphasis who, according to Torrance, followed the patristic tradition. Torrance sees the evangelical Scottish tradition adhering to this approach as well. See e.g., Torrance, *Scottish Theology*, 40 for his discussion of John Knox's similarity to the liturgies of St. Mark and St. James. Torrance's high view of the sacraments is further notable as part of the return to the patristic tradition explored in the previous chapters. Chapter 2 argued that many Protestant evangelicals are attracted to the rich sacramental life of the patristic tradition which they find in Roman Catholicism and Eastern Orthodoxy. Torrance is also attracted to this high view of the sacraments but he finds it in his own Reformed tradition.

206. See further Radcliff, "A Reformed Asceticism," 43–56 for one such attempt in the Scottish Reformed context and also Radcliff, "The Vicarious Humanity of Christ as the Basis of Christian Spirituality" (forthcoming 2016) for a constructive attempt at approaching Christian spirituality in general from the basis of the vicarious humanity of Christ.

Torrance feels that Origen excellently captured the patristic connection of piety and real theology.[207] For Torrance, Origen combined the objective and scientific approach asserted by Irenaeus and Hilary with spiritual training.[208] Put otherwise, this is "asceticism" or, in Torrance's words, "ascetic theology." As he puts it:

> To know God and to be holy, to know God and worship, to know God and to be cleaned in mind and soul from anything that may come between people and God, to know God and be committed to him in consecration, love and obedience, go inseparably together.[209]

Torrance contends that, according to Origen (as well as Clement, and Athanasius) only through a leaping forward of the awakened mind could truth be known, a leaping forward gained by corporate pious living (κατ'εὐσέβειαν).[210] For Torrance, this ascetical aspect of theology is essential. Indeed, the "transformation and reconciliation of the mind" as he puts it is more important than academic theological knowledge.[211] Ultimately, for Torrance, this is a transformation to the "mind of Christ."[212] Torrance contends it is a lifelong process, the outcome of which is a "theological instinct."[213]

207. Though one wonders what Torrance thought of the story of Origen's certain extremity in ascetical zeal. Eusebius of Caesarea, the ancient Christian historian and also great admirer of Origen, preserved the account that Origen castrated himself, taking the words of Christ "absurdly literal" concerning some becoming eunuchs for the Kingdom of Heaven's sake. See Eusebius, *Ecclesiastical History* 6.8 referring to Matthew 19:12.

208. Torrance, *Trinitarian Faith*, 36, 41.

209. Torrance, *The Mediation of Christ*, 26. This is a common theme among The Fathers as can be seen in the plethora of monastic texts, especially those of the Desert Fathers. Torrance surely had these in mind as well the ascetic theology of Athanasius in *De Incarnatione*, 57: "But for the searching of the Scriptures and true knowledge (γνῶσιν ἀληθῆ) a honorable life (βίου καλοῦ), a clean soul (ψυχῆς καθαρᾶς), and virtue according to Christ (τῆς κατὰ χριστὸν ἀρετῆς) are necessary . . . for without a clean mind (καθαρᾶς διανοίας) and an imitation of the life of the saints (τῆς πρὸς τοὺς ἁγίους τοῦ βίου μιμήσεως), one would not be able to comprehend (καταλαβεῖν) the words of the saints." See PG 25b.196–97 for the full text. Asceticism is a term not often used in Protestant circles but absolutely central to Eastern Orthodoxy. It is best captured by the classic compilation of Nicodemus of the Holy Mountain and Makarios of Corinth, *The Philokalia*. An English translation exists translated by Palmer, Sherrard, and Ware.

210. Torrance, *Reality and Scientific Theology*, 84. See also *The Christian Doctrine of God*, 74.

211. See Torrance, *Atonement*, 437–47.

212. Torrance, *Trinitarian Faith*, 127.

213. Torrance, *Atonement*, 437–47.

For Torrance, asceticism and all aspects of sanctification are rooted in Christ.[214] The human side of the process occurs through participation in the mind of Christ, through Christ's vicarious intercession as High Priest and human participation through "incessant prayer in offering [oneself] daily to God through the reconciling and atoning mediation of Christ."[215] Torrance retrieved this from The Fathers, especially Cyril of Alexandria, particularly his emphasis upon the continuing intercession of Christ. According to Torrance, as Christ intercedes for humankind they are continually conformed to his own mind.[216] Torrance argues that for Cyril humankind is sanctified "as [they] are enabled to share with [Christ's] mind" and "[their] human mind which has been sanctified and healed in him, that [they] may be associated with him in his priestly presentation of himself and of [them] through himself to the Father."[217] Torrance argues that through this *noetic* union humankind is presented to the Father in Christ. Whilst this union is already complete in the incarnate Christ himself, according to Torrance, it is applied to humankind through participation accomplished by the indwelling of the Holy Spirit.[218] As Torrance states:

> It is then in pneumatological terms that Cyril understands the intimate union between us and Christ: the presence of the Mind of Christ in us and his offering of our mind to the Father, for the Spirit, he reminds us, is the Mind of Christ, and it is in the same Spirit that our mind is sanctified and lifted up through Christ into God.[219]

As the bond of connection between humankind and God,[220] the Holy Spirit, by the grace of God, incorporates humankind into *noetic* (νοητός)[221] and herein personal union with Christ and therein God *in se*. This discussion of the possibility of knowledge of God only through and by God is of course

214. See further Alexandra Radcliff's excellent article: "Sanctification: Words for the Weary" for a constructive examination of the Torrance brothers on this subject. She argues that, with the Torrance brothers, sanctification must be objectively rooted in Christ; otherwise it becomes a work and Christians are forced to attempt to "sanctify themselves." Christians can rather rest in God for their sanctification and no longer be "weary."

215. Torrance, *Atonement*, 446.

216. See in particular Cyril's *Commentary on the Gospel of John* and *De Adoratione*.

217. Torrance, *Theology in Reconciliation*, 180.

218. Ibid., 180–81.

219. Ibid., 182.

220. Ibid., 183.

221. Lampe, *A Patristic Greek Lexicon*, 917: "Intelligible, falling within the sphere of νοῦς, apprehended by the intellect."

central to Reformed theology[222] and emphasized by Torrance's beloved teachers Karl Barth and H. R. Mackintosh.[223]

As Christ intercedes for his church and she participates in this worship, the church is continuously sanctified and renewed: "That is why [people] cannot be theologians without incessant prayer in offering [themselves] daily to God through the reconciling and atoning mediation of Christ."[224] As Torrance states:

> Through study of the holy scriptures, through meditation and prayer [theologians] tune into the mind of God incarnate in Jesus Christ, the source of all rationality until [their] own minds, healed, renewed, and sanctified in him, are instinct with his truth."[225]

So, through prayer and worship Christ continually allows his church to more fully realize their union with himself.[226] This is on account of the vicarious humanity of Christ, which will be explored in full below.

---

222. See e.g., Calvin, *Institutes*, I, particularly, I.7.5.

223. e.g., Karl Barth, *Evangelical Theology*, 15–26. See Mackintosh, *The Divine Initiative*, 39–70.

224. Torrance, *Atonement*, 446.

225. Ibid., 447.

226. It should be noted that Torrance's conception of asceticism and soteriology, while rooted in The Fathers, is significantly different from others also reliant upon the patristic witness. Contemporary Orthodox views of soteriology and sanctification, while certainly assuming much from the earlier Fathers, focused more substantially upon the later ascetical tradition as found in the Byzantine tradition, especially Maximus the Confessor and Gregory Palamas. For example, Isaac the Syrian emphasizes the three stages of prayer: Penitence, purification, and perfection. See Makarios, *Early Fathers from the Philokalia*; Lossky, *The Mystical Theology of the Eastern Church*, 204. Also, the ultimate end of the Christian life as stated by a later Russian ascetic Seraphim of Sarov is the "attainment of the Holy Spirit." See Serafim, *A Conversation of Saint Seraphim*; Lossky, *The Mystical Theology of the Eastern Church*, 196–97. Ultimately, the focus of this stream is on the final stage of this ladder of spiritual development towards God: *Hesychasm* or perfect silence and union with God. See Lossky, *The Mystical Theology of the Eastern Church*, 207–9. As such these figures typically root spiritual practices and, ultimately, *theosis* subjectively in (a subjective version of) sanctification rather than objectively in Christ's redemption work and an objective version of sanctification rooted in Christ. Gregory Palamas discusses this perfect union of God in great detail in his defense of the *hesychastic* tradition on Mt. Athos. He argues that in prayer it is possible and indeed the goal to have a *noetic* vision of God's uncreated light. See Lossky, *The Mystical Theology of the Eastern Church*, 215–16. See below for elaboration on this point.

The Vicarious Humanity of Christ

As discussed, Torrance holds that only God can save; however only God as a man.[227] Thus, the ὁμοούσιον has to be preserved on both the human and divine sides. The theme of the vicarious humanity is perhaps Torrance's greatest contribution to patristic and theological scholarship. This theme arises directly from his imaginative reconstruction of The Fathers on the basis of the ὁμοούσιον. Owing to the fact that Christ is ὁμοούσιον with God and with humankind Christ's work was truly vicarious and eternally saving. This is a major reformulation of the Reformed doctrine of election and, more deeply, *sola fide* (salvation by faith alone) and *sola gratia* (salvation by grace alone).[228] Torrance pushes for a Christologically-rooted doctrine of election in departure from Federal theology's decree-rooted version which propagates "double predestination."[229] In Torrance's combination of Greek patristic and Reformed theology Torrance creatively restates the patristic notion of the humanity of Christ and the Reformed notion of election, dynamically combining the two concepts into one: the vicarious humanity.

In order to connect the person and work of Christ, a major theme in Torrance's greater theology, utilizing Irenaeus, Torrance upholds the centrality of the person of Christ for both salvation and sanctification:

> It was that Jesus had taken what Irenaeus spoke of as our leprous humanity upon himself, but that instead of becoming a leper himself, he healed and transformed our 'leprous' human nature and restored it to be like the flesh of a newborn child.[230]

For Torrance this means that the entirety of Christ's life was saving and he saw this pointing to a deep connection between the person and the work of Christ, making all of Christ's salvific activity internal to his very person.[231]

227. Torrance, *Trinitarian Faith*, 149–50. See also 159.

228. Torrance argues that the centrality of the vicarious humanity of Christ was captured by the Reformer John Calvin. See Torrance, *Scottish Theology*, 45.

229. *Westminster Confession of Faith*, 3. See Torrance, Introduction to *The School of Faith*. See further his brother, James B. Torrance: "Strengths and Weaknesses of Westminster Theology," 45–53 for a similarly-minded critique of Westminster theology. He is particularly critical of the place accorded to God's decrees. See also Torrance's friend and fellow founding editor of the *Scottish Journal of Theology* J. K. S. Reid's critique of the Calvinist tradition's rooting of election in God's eternal decrees rather than in Christ: Reid, "The Office of Christ in Predestination," 5–19.

230. Torrance, *Atonement*, 441.

231. See Torrance, "Karl Barth and the Latin Heresy," 461–82. As Irenaeus puts it: [Christ] therefore passed through every age, becoming an infant for infants, thus sanctifying infants; a child for children, thus sanctifying those who are of this age . . . a youth for youths . . . and thus sanctifying them for the Lord" (Irenaeus of Lyons, *Against*

Torrance sees a focus on the unity of incarnation and atonement in The Fathers. Any separation of this, argues Torrance, separates the person and work of Christ, which is entirely against the ὁμοούσιον. Indeed, Torrance sees atonement falling within the life, especially the person, of the mediator.[232] The overarching implication of this is that salvation must be understood to have occurred within the person of Christ. Torrance sees this assertion explicated in Athanasius, Cyril, and Leontius of Byzantium, among others, by means of the patristic doctrine of the hypostatic union.[233]

The key aspect to Torrance's doctrine of the vicarious humanity of Christ consists of his use of the patristic terms "anhypostasis" and "enhypostasis," meaning the assumption of common humanity by one specific divine person.[234] This is a patristic concept[235] attributed to Leontius of Byzantium[236] and also Epiphanius and Didymus in another sense, as discussed earlier, and finally adopted and used by the Reformers.[237] The terms preserve the belief that the human nature of Christ had no person other than the person of the divine Word. For Torrance this doctrine can be traced back to Cyril of Alexandria in *Contra Theodoretum*.[238] Additionally, Cyril developed this theology contra Nestorianism surrounding the Council of Ephesus in 431 C.E. Torrance argues that both Severus of Antioch and John of Damascus developed the doctrine further.[239] For him, the doctrine of anhypostasis affirms the notion that the humanity taken by Christ is the common humanity of mankind, for it had no human hypostasis of its own. Rather, Christ's

---

Heresies, 2.22).

232. Torrance, *Trinitarian Faith*, 155–58; Torrance, *The Mediation of Christ*, 64–65.

233. By applying this Christological concept directly to Soteriology Torrance is using it very imaginatively. See his dogmatics lectures, e.g., Torrance, *Incarnation*, 85. Similar to Torrance, John Meyendorff sees a strong connection between the Christological doctrine of the hypostatic union in Christ and the soteriological doctrine of *theosis*. See Meyendorff, *Byzantine Theology*, 163–64.

234. Torrance, *Incarnation*, 85.

235. Torrance, *Trinitarian Faith*, 131.

236. Torrance, *Theological Science*, 217ff, 269; Torrance, *Space, Time and Resurrection*, 51; Torrance, *The Christian Doctrine of God*, 144, 160.

237. Torrance, *Incarnation*, 197, for example. Torrance sees these as brought together by the Scottish theologian Robert Boyd. See also Torrance, *Scottish Theology*, 70–71.

238. Torrance, *Incarnation*, 84; Torrance, *The Christian Doctrine of God*, 160 citing *Apologia contra Theodoretum*, PG, 76, 397C and *Thesaurus de Trinitate*, PG 75, 8, 101D–104B.

239. Torrance, *The Christian Doctrine of God*, 160 citing Severus of Antioch, *Collected Letters*, tr. E. W. Brooks, *Patrologia Orientalis*, 1, 14, pp. 186–94 and Iain R. Torrance, *Christology After Chalcedon* pp. 114–16, 125f. as well as John of Damascus, *De Fide Orthodoxa*, 3.3–9.

humanity is enhypostasized in the Logos. Therefore, he argues, the flesh of Christ is in fact God's election of humankind for a relationship with God,[240] meaning that it was an act from the side of God on behalf of all humankind. For Torrance this means that humanity is personalized and humanized in the person of Christ.[241] Torrance sees these dual doctrines as ruling out both the Apollinarian and Monophysite heresies.[242] Finally, in Torrance's estimate this doctrine was brought to fruition in the thought of Leontius of Byzantium and the theology of the fourth, fifth, and sixth ecumenical councils in 451 C.E., 553 C.E. and 681 C.E., respectively.

Key to Torrance's understanding of the vicarious humanity is his conception that the Lord came *as* man not *in* man. This is a concept Torrance found in Athanasius.[243] Torrance contends that for The Fathers this included the reality that in the incarnation the Son of God assumed the whole man. Key to Torrance's theology is the view that in becoming man, Christ took humanity and converted it back to God. For Torrance this entails two elements: (1) The assumption of the whole man and subsequently (2) the assumption of fallen humanity.

Torrance sees in The Fathers, especially Athanasius, the assertion that Christ assumed the whole man.[244] He sees this as being put forth primarily by Athanasius in texts such as *Ad Epictetus* and *De Incarnatione*. Torrance contends that this was the impetus of Athanasius' entire doctrine of the humanity of Christ. Thus, Torrance feels strongly that for Athanasius Christ's humanity was not merely instrumental but rather that his doctrine of the incarnation must be understood as a real "becoming" on the part of God; God coming "as" man.[245] He sees Athanasius articulating Christ's assumption of "the whole man" vicariously, for the sake of mankind.[246] As Torrance sees it, this was one of the central aspects of Athanasius in *Contra Arianos*[247] thus extricating the Greek Fathers (especially Athanasius and Cyril and those

240. Torrance, *The Christian Doctrine of God*, 146.

241. Ibid., 160–61.

242. Ibid., 160.

243. Torrance, *Trinitarian Faith*, 149ff. See also *Theology in Reconciliation*, 227ff.

244. Torrance, *Trinitarian Faith*, 151–52.

245. Ibid., 150–52 citing Athanasius, *De Incarnatione*, 2.30; 3.31,35, 53 as well as *Contra Apollinarem*, 1.2, 15; *Contra Arianos*, 1.41, 45; 2.35, 52, 71; 3.2ff, 31ff, 35, 37ff, 40, 43ff, 48, 51ff, 57ff, 63; 4.6ff; Gregory Nazianzen, *Epistle 102*; Cyril of Alexandria, *Epistle ad Nestorius*, MPG 77.3, 116BC; *Adversus Nestorius*, MPG 76.1, 17B; 20D; 21 AB; 28C; 35A; *Quod unus sit Christus*, MPG 75, 1257A; 1272B; 1277C.

246. Torrance, *Theology in Reconciliation*, 228.

247. Ibid., 228ff.

following them) from the accusation that they were semi-Apollinarian,[248] an accusation put forward by, for example in R. P. C. Hanson[249] and J. N. D. Kelly.[250] Torrance did not adhere to the distinction between Alexandrian and Antiochene theology driving these critiques nor did he see Athanasius as a semi-Apollinarian. He argues that "to omit such a major ingredient in Athanasius' doctrine of Christ is seriously to distort it and to import into it false problems for which false solutions are then sought."[251] Torrance did much to recover this key aspect of Athanasius' thought and his former student George Dragas successfully continued this battle in his scholarship on Athanasius.[252] In fact, contemporary patristic scholarship no longer assumes the *Logos-Sarx/Logos-Anthropos* framework used for so long and Torrance's role in this cannot be overstated.[253]

For Torrance the assumption of the whole man means that Christ assumed the human mind and turned it back to God. Torrance saw this doctrine explicated clearly in Cyril of Alexandria, as well as by Athanasius and Gregory Nazianzen contra the Apollinarians. This is key for Torrance because without the assumption of the human mind, only man's bodily

248. The traditional view of Torrance's time was that of Alois Grillmeier who argues Athanasius was semi-Apollinarian because he did not believe there was a human soul in Christ. See Grillmeier, *Christ in Christian Tradition*, 193–219. Connected to this, Grillmeier distinguishes between the *Logos-Sarx* Christology of the Alexandrians and the *Logos-Anthropos* Christology of the Antiochenes. See ibid., 175ff. Grillmeier places Athanasius on the *Logos-Sarx* side and thus with an "instrumental" view of the human nature of Christ. See p. 205. See also Rankin, "Carnal Union with Christ i," 162; Hanson, *The Search for the Christian Doctrine of God*, 351–53.

249. Hanson understands Athanasius to have been a semi-Apollinarian holding to a "space-suit" Christology. See Hanson, *The Search for the Christian Doctrine of God*, 448–53.

250. Kelly, *Early Christian Doctrines*, 280f, 284ff.

251. Torrance, *Theology in Reconciliation*, 229.

252. See Dragas' monumental PhD thesis which, by a comprehensive comparison of the language in *Contra Apollinarem* and accepted Athanasian texts, argues that the former text is without a doubt Athanasian in authorship. See Dragas, "St. Athanasius Contra Apollinarem." See also Dragas, *Saint Athanasius of Alexandria*, 1–24 for a much shorter summary of some of his key discoveries, highlighting the linguistic arguments. Notably, Torrance wrote a glowing introduction to Dragas' thesis.

253. Statements from Athanasius such as "the savior having in very truth become man, the salvation of the whole man was brought about . . . the whole man, body and soul alike, has truly obtained salvation in the Word himself" (*Ad Epictetus 7*, PG 26.1061) are now better understood. Torrance's work here also makes better sense of Cyril. For Cyril, the term "flesh" designated the whole man, as can be seen, for example, in his exposition of Deuteronomy 10:22: "seventy-five souls out of Egypt," namely, that it meant the whole person, not just the soul. Therefore, Cyril could state that the Word made flesh meant the whole human being, including the soul. See e.g., Cyril of Alexandria, *Scholia 25; Festal Letter 8.5*.

existence could be saved. However, the "directive principle," namely the human mind, was what most needed to be saved.[254] For, without a human mind Christ's atoning work could no longer be truly vicarious.[255] The view that Christ assumed the whole man, including and especially the human mind, was basic to the theology of Athanasius who asserted that Christ took humanity and redeemed, sanctified, and renewed it within his own person.[256] This is a theological assertion Torrance sees put forth even more clearly by Gregory Nazianzen and Basil of Caesarea.[257]

When Torrance looks back to the fourth century and the outbreak of the Apollinarian heresy, which denied a human mind in Christ, he sees Gregory Nazianzen as preserving the fact that Christ assumed the whole fallen[258] man,[259] body and mind.[260] Without this assertion, the full redemption of humankind cannot be preserved. Here, Torrance holds that Athanasius, as well as many other classical patristic authors, asserted that in the incarnation the *Word* (λόγος) assumed fallen humanity.[261] Torrance was fond of Gregory Nazianzen's dictum, "the un–assumed (ἀπρόσληπτον) is the unhealed (ἀθεράπευτον)."[262] In Torrance's view it is absolutely necessary to affirm that Christ assumed fallen humanity in all its guilt and corruption,[263] for to assert otherwise would call into question the salvation of humankind, especially the transformation of the human mind and its redirection

254. Torrance, *Theology in Reconciliation*, 112.

255. Ibid., 112–13, 150–51.

256. Ibid., 153.

257. Ibid., 154.

258. Torrance does not appear to explicitly distinguish in a definitive manner between "fallen humanity" and "sinful humanity" in the theology of the Greek Fathers. This distinction appears to have been in the background of his discussion, (i.e., he seems to have held that Christ assumed fallen humanity while remaining sinless) but he does not explicitly set these two elements apart. In his discussion of the Greek Fathers on the notion of Christ's assumption of fallen humanity, Noble provides elaboration upon Torrance's view (though, not in reference to Torrance) and argues that the Greek Fathers indeed distinguished between "fallenness" and "sinfulness" and held that Christ assumed "fallen" humanity yet remained "sinless." See Noble, *Holy Trinity: Holy People*, 166–68.

259. In *Trinitarian Faith* Torrance does not make much of Christ's assumption of fallen humanity. However, elsewhere this is central to his theology and his reading of The Fathers. See Torrance, *Trinitarian Faith*, 153–54 where he discusses the *kenotic* aspect of the incarnation (from κένωσις). See also ibid., 161–68.

260. Torrance, *The Mediation of Christ*, 39–40; Torrance, *The Christian Frame of Mind*, 6–9.

261. Torrance, *Incarnation*, 61–65; see also 200–201.

262. Gregory Nazianzen, *Letter 101: To Cledonius the Priest*. PG 37.181.

263. Torrance, *The Mediation of Christ*, 39.

towards God.[264] This means that, in Jesus, man finally knows God. Torrance asserts that The Fathers believed that Christ assumed fallen humanity in all its guilt; diseased in mind and soul[265] and transformed the human mind.[266] This is a development in Torrance's thought for in his early lectures Torrance holds that Christ did not possess a fallen will.[267]

The Atonement

Intricately connected to the vicarious humanity in the Torrancian *Consensus Patrum* is the atonement. Torrance distinguishes between the Latin and Greek views of the atonement. For Torrance the ὁμοούσιον upholds the ontological aspect of the atonement, which is key for him.[268] Torrance points out that this is why the Western Fathers often split the ontological and forensic elements of the atonement, whereas the Eastern Fathers did not.[269] At this point Torrance refers to the patristic doctrine of θέωσις/θεοποίησις (*theosis*)[270] which he understands to be a way of expressing "this consubstantial self-giving of God to mankind through Christ and in his Spirit."[271] Torrance appropriates the Greek patristic notion of θέωσις and reconstructs it into a truly Reformed version of this classic patristic doctrine. As such Torrance departs from the typical Western (Roman Catholic and Reformed evangelical) emphasis on the forensic/juridical elements of the atonement.[272]

Torrance sees Athanasius as putting forth a view concerning the mediation of Christ consisting of Christ mediating the things of God to man and the things of man to God.[273] For Torrance this includes the interces-

264. Torrance, *Atonement*, 437–47, 139–214; Torrance, *The Mediation of Christ*, 78.

265. Torrance, *The Mediation of Christ*, 39.

266. Torrance, *Atonement*, 437–47.

267. Dawson, *An Introduction to Torrance Theology*, 55–74; Torrance, *The Doctrine of Jesus Christ*, 122–23; Baker, "The Place of St. Irenaeus," 23–24.

268. Torrance, *Trinitarian Faith*, 160–61.

269. Ibid., 161. See also Torrance, "Karl Barth and the Latin Heresy" for a fuller version of this critique

270. Ibid., 139–45, 188–90.

271. Ibid., 139. See also Torrance, *Theology in Reconstruction*, 217. Torrance uses the term "deification" but does not like the implications it contains. Elsewhere he prefers "theosis" and even "mediation" (*Trinitarian Faith*, 188ff and *The Mediation of Christ*, 71). See also Habets, *Theosis in the Theology*. Though, Habets' net is cast fairly wide regarding what Torrancian themes he considers to be contained under the umbrella of *theosis*.

272. See Torrance, "Karl Barth and the Latin Heresy."

273. Torrance, *Trinitarian Faith*, 149; Torrance, *The Mediation of Christ*, 73;

sory role Christ played as priest as well as his role in θέωσις. In Torrance's estimate, θέωσις must not be understood as an impersonal absorption into the divine nature. The contrary is in fact the case. For him, θέωσις necessarily needs to be viewed as occurring within the person of Christ. He argues that θέωσις occurred first to the humanity of Christ by the indwelling of the Holy Spirit and is applied to humanity.[274] Therefore, it is for him a very personal relationship.[275] Accordingly, Torrance views θέωσις as the obverse of the incarnation and sees this as occurring with the help of the Spirit, thus being intensely personal. He sees this explicated in patristic figures such as Irenaeus and Athanasius.[276] In Irenaeus Torrance sees θέωσις in the saint's discussion of the indwelling of the Holy Spirit within humanity.[277] It is in Athanasius, however, that Torrance sees this soteriological perspective discussed most fully. Torrance contends that for Athanasius θέωσις occurred within the person of Christ, to the humanity of Christ, and therefore to the common humanity of all.[278] Thus, this is a very personal act of God in Christ.[279]

Torrance contends that because of both the ὁμοούσιον and the vicarious humanity, it is impossible to think of the atonement other than having taken place in the person of Christ, and thus in the being and life of God himself.[280] Furthermore, because of this, salvation is necessarily universal in range.[281] Here Torrance sees in Athanasius a wonderful connection between the personal and ontological aspects of the atonement.[282] Herein, he sees the atonement to have been a "wonderful exchange"[283] that is boundless and for all without qualification[284] wherein God remained impassible[285] and

---

Torrance, *The Christian Doctrine of God*, 144.

274. Torrance, *Trinitarian Faith*, 189–90 citing Athanasius, *Contra Arianos* 1.46 f.

275. Ibid., 188ff.

276. Ibid., 189; Torrance, *The Mediation of Christ*, 71.

277. Ibid., 189–90.

278. Ibid., 138.

279. Torrance, *Theology in Reconciliation*, 228–31.

280. Torrance, *Trinitarian Faith*, 155.

281. Ibid., 155. Torrance sees a notion of the limited atonement to imply elements of Nestorianism dividing God from Christ and God's being from God's acts. See Torrance, *Scottish Theology*, 19.

282. Torrance, *Trinitarian Faith*, 157.

283. ἀνταλλαγή: See ibid., 179ff.

284. Ibid., 181.

285. Ibid., 184–88.

humankind is united to God in θέωσις.[286] This is then applied to individual humans by means of the Holy Spirit.

Torrance holds that if salvation is not viewed in such terms it becomes an external juridical/forensic exchange, a divergence which he calls the "Latin Heresy."[287] Torrance believes that the traditional Greek patristic doctrine of atonement preserved the fact that the atonement, though having external aspects, was something which occurred internally to the life of the incarnate Son and therefore moved back through the ὁμοούσιον to the very being of God. Without this the atonement does not have reference to who God is in his own being. Thus, for Torrance, Christ went through each part of human life sanctifying it.[288] This means that the humanity of Christ has soteriological significance itself because of the hypostatic union[289] and that Christ died for all on the cross for Christ took the humanity of all upon himself.[290]

The view that salvation must be viewed in personal/ontological terms as opposed to external/forensic terms is a typical Torrancian theme and he devotes much time to it in his dogmatics lectures.[291] However, his use of this theme in *Trinitarian Faith* and elsewhere when his *Consensus Patrum* is more explicitly present has some nuances inasmuch his use of the patristic concept of θέωσις has to do directly with The Fathers whereas in his lectures, for example, the discussion is less explicitly patristic.

In Torrance's early theology, he was uncomfortable with the doctrine of θέωσις. The dominant view during Torrance's time was that of Harnack, that the Greek Fathers' soteriology was entirely focused on absorption into God and therefore the end of corruption and death. Harnack saw this as "Hellenistic."[292] Initially Torrance as well adhered to this view as can be seen in a brief discussion of Athanasius in his thesis written under Karl Barth in the 1950s: *The Doctrine of Grace in the Apostolic Fathers*, one of Torrance's earliest works.[293] In a footnote discussing the doctrine of θέωσις in the early Fathers such as Irenaeus and Athanasius, Torrance states "nothing could be

---

286. Ibid., 188–90.

287. Torrance, *The Mediation of Christ*, 40–41; Torrance, "Karl Barth and the Latin Heresy," 461–82.

288. Torrance, *The Mediation of Christ*, 41.

289. Torrance, *Incarnation*, 198; 210.

290. Torrance, *Atonement*, 125–29.

291. Ibid., 97–114. Torrance's view, though very much patristic, contains elements of John McLeod Cambell's insistence on the "filial" aspect of the atonement over the "forensic/judicial" aspect. See Campbell, *The Nature of the Atonement*, 151–91.

292. Harnack, *History of Dogma*, 5:22.

293. Torrance, *The Doctrine of Grace in the Apostolic Fathers*.

Hellenistic,"[294] taking the traditional view following Harnack. Though Torrance initially had trouble with the patristic doctrine of θέωσις, eventually he came to view the doctrine not as Hellenistic but as orthodox, standing alongside Georges Florovsky and his view of "Christian Hellenism."[295] By the 1970s, Torrance viewed θέωσις as the "epistemological relevance of the Holy Spirit."[296] Throughout the *Trinitarian Faith*, published in the 1980s, Torrance calls θέωσις a Christological and Pneumatological doctrine of great import and, as argued, Torrance sees θέωσις happening within the person of Christ thus connecting his person and work and recovering the patristic doctrine from the accusations of impersonal absorption into God. Torrance's focus on the connection between person and work enables Torrance to depart from the traditional Western tendency towards a dualistic theory of the atonement.

Furthermore, in his reformulation of θέωσις Torrance departs from the traditional Eastern Orthodox view as preserved by Lossky and reconstructs the Greek patristic doctrine into a Reformed evangelical version. Lossky, relying upon Gregory Palamas, asserts that in θέωσις humankind is united to God's energy (ἐνέργεια) but not God's essence (οὐσία).[297] Additionally, for Lossky θέωσις is rooted in sanctification and, as explored earlier in this chapter, is the outcome of a life of perfect prayer. For Torrance, to separate God's ἐνέργεια from God's οὐσία cuts away the possibility of real union with God in Christ and herein God's full presence in Christ, thus denying the ὁμοούσιον. With this insight Torrance recenters θέωσις upon the humanity of Christ and emphasizes the indwelling of the Holy Spirit.[298] As such, Torrance departs from Lossky and neopalamism.[299]

Torrance locates θέωσις in his doctrine of Christ and the atonement rather than in sanctification.[300] Habets brings out this centeredness of θέωσις in Torrance in his book. He argues througout that Torrance's doctrine of θέωσις "illuminates his incarnational view of the atonement."[301] Torrance is critical of views of θέωσις along the lines of Lossky which consider

294. Ibid., 140.

295. Torrance, *The Christian Doctrine of God*, 96.

296. Torrance, *Theology in Reconciliation*, 248.

297. Lossky, *The Mystical Theology of the Eastern Church*, 213.

298. See Torrance, *Trinitarian Faith*, 188–90.

299. See the following chapter for expansion of this point.

300. See his discussion of it in *Trinitarian Faith*, 188–90. It is the "third form of atoning exchange" which he discusses.

301. Habets, *Theosis in the Theology*, 1. See throughout the rest of the book, however.

it to entail some sort of impersonal absorbtion into the divine nature[302] and of any separation of God's essence God's energies which is inherent to the Losskian version of θέωσις.[303] In order to avoid any sort of subjectivism or division of God's being from God's acts, Torrance roots the doctrine of θέωσις in the person and, more particularly, the humanity of Christ. This gives θέωσις an objective centeredness in Christ, and therein God and, indeed, the ὁμοούσιον, the center of the Torrancian *Consensus Patrum*. This is, in many ways, a departure from the traditional reading of Athanasius and the Greek Fathers' view of θέωσις. Typically the Greek Fathers are considered to have held to an entirely metaphysical conception of redemption whilst the West was more focused upon the forensic and faith based aspect.[304] Yet Torrance's rooting of θέωσις in atonement (thus departing from the Losskian reading) portrays the Greek approach to redemption and justification less in metaphysical categories and more in personal categories. It is, as such, very much a Reformed approach and reconstruction of this classical Greek patristic doctrine.

The emphasis upon union with Christ and the indwelling of the Holy Spirit is central to Reformed theology and John Calvin in particular.[305] Reformed theologians, often directly influenced by Torrance, are not only recovering the theme of union with Christ but the doctrine of θέωσις. While this is still very fresh in Reformed theology and theologians debate which elements of θέωσις are compatible with Reformed theology and which are not, many are recovering this doctrine into the Reformed tradition following the Reformed evangelical reading offered by Torrance discussing what is now being labelled a "Reformed doctrine of *theosis*."[306]

302. Torrance, *The Christian Doctrine of God*, 95–96.

303. See ibid., 187.

304. See e.g., Denney, *The Christian Doctrine of Reconciliation*, 37–44. He says that Athanasius' view was "metaphysical rather than moral" because it was entirely in "physical categories" and thus sin and reconciliation have nothing to do with it. See p. 37 and p. 42, respectively.

305. See e.g., Calvin, *Institutes*, 3.11.23. Though hyper-Calvinism often emphasizes the juridical/forensic elements of the atonement as found in Calvin, recent scholarship on Calvin has been arguing that union with Christ is absolutely central to Calvin's theory of the atonement. See e.g., Canlis, *Calvin's Ladder*. Accordingly, Reformed theology has been following suit and emphasizing union with Christ as central to Reformed thought. See e.g., Billings, *Union with Christ*.

306. See Murphy, "Reformed *Theosis?*" 191–212 and Habets, "'Reformed *Theosis?*,'" 489–98. Whereas Murphy calls for a recovery of *theosis* including the Eastern Orthodox distinction of God's essence and God's energies, Habets wants to appropriate the theme in a more Torrancian fashion leaving behind this element and re-centering the doctrine on Christ and in atonement. Accordingly Habets roots *theosis* in the vicarious humanity of Christ and in soteriology (rather than God's uncreated energies and

Though many still follow Harnack, it is becoming more common to view θέωσις along Torrance's lines rather than Harnack's. Notable theologians who are in agreement with Torrance are Georges Florovsky,[307] Trevor Hart,[308] and Donald Fairbairn.[309] The consensus of these scholars and Torrance is that though some of The Fathers, such as those following in extreme Origenism, indeed assumed much from Hellenistic philosophy in their theology, there was a strong biblical strain of thought, namely the Irenaeus-Athanasius-Cyril stream consisting of Fathers who held to an intensely personal/Christological/Pneumatological conception of *theosis*. Torrance's role in recovering The Fathers from this accusation is highly significant.

CONCLUSION

This chapter has argued, by using Torrance's *Trinitarian Faith* with regular reference to his many other works, that Torrance's reading, use, and appropriation of The Fathers is an imaginative reconstruction of patristic theology into a Torrancian *Consensus Patrum* which is a Reformed evangelical version of classical Greek patristic themes. Torrance imaginatively reconstructs Greek patristic themes by (a) centering them upon the Nicene ὁμοούσιον (and, the best proponent, Athanasius) and by (b) reading and using them theologically as opposed to patrologically or historically. Herein, Torrance uses The Fathers thematically and in a Christocentric way. This chapter has labeled Torrance's imaginative reconstruction "the Torrancian *Consensus Patrum*" and this chapter has explored the two primary ways in which Torrance has reconstructed Greek patristic theology into this Reformed evangelical *Consensus Patrum*: (1) By re-organizing The Fathers into theological streams of thought centered upon Christ and (2) by extracting the "inner logic/connections" behind patristic theology, which Torrance sees

---

sanctification). Bruce McCormack, on the other hand, is highly critical of any attempt to appropriate *theosis* into the Reformed tradition seeing the Penal Substitution as central and *theosis* as detracting from this defining Protestant doctrine. See McCormack, "The End of Reformed Theology?" 46–64.

307. Florovsky, *Bible, Church, Tradition*, 115.

308. Hart, *Christ in Our Place*, 152–82.

309. See Donald Fairbairn, "Patristic Soteriology," 289–310 for an outstanding discussion on the different views of *theosis* among The Fathers and his argument for a personal view along Torrance's lines. It is noteworthy that Fairbairn asked Torrance to read chapter 4 of his PhD thesis which has been subsequently published as *Grace and Christology in the Early Church* on *theosis* and grace. Torrance kept this document until his death and it is preserved in the manuscript collection at Princeton Theological Seminary. See The Thomas F. Torrance Manuscript Collection. Special Collections, Princeton Theological Seminary Library. Box 187.

as theological and "catholic" themes. Finally, this chapter has argued that the driving force behind the Torrancian *Consensus Patrum* is Torrance's Reformed evangelical approach centered upon the Nicene ὁμοούσιον and that this emphasis has great merit inasmuch as it allowed Torrance truly fresh insight into The Fathers. Overall, Torrance's *Consensus Patrum* provides new insight into these Greek patristic themes and is an excellent reconstruction of theology on the basis of catholic themes. Torrance's emphasis on the close identity between God's being and God's acts (God's economy and ontology) is insightful and helpful by drawing out the patristic emphasis on divine initiative in salvation and revelation.[310] Furthermore, some of Torrance's contemporaries share this commitment in addition to Torrance's hope for a departure from the more Augustinian and Western approach.[311] Ultimately, Torrance's Christocentric/Trinitarian and evangelical reading of The Fathers provides fresh insight into many elements of both patristic and Reformed theology, particularly asceticism, the vicarious humanity, and an ontological version of the atonement.

By returning to the Athanasius-Cyril axis of classical theology on sanctification and asceticism, Torrance bypasses the distinction between God's essence and energies, at least as it was expressed in the Losskian interpretation of the later ascetical tradition, and returns to the classical emphasis on a Christologically-centered asceticism.[312] This is done by means

310. As aforementioned, this is a Torrancian concept but is not a Torrancian way of putting it. Rather it is a name garnered from H. R. Mackintosh. See Mackintosh, *The Divine Initiative* for a classic discussion which undoubtedly influenced Torrance.

311. For example the Roman Catholic theologian, Karl Rahner, whose approach in this regard is substantially similar to Torrance. See, for example, Rahner, *The Trinity.* In this groundbreaking book, Rahner propagates a number of items akin to Torrance such as a Trinitarian reading of creation (see page 13). Most notably, Rahner proposes a departure from the Augustinian Trinitarian approach of his own Catholic tradition for he argued that, following Augustine and Aquinas, Western theology has separated the one God *(De Deo Uno)* from the Triune God *(De Deo Trino)* (see pages 9–48). Rahner proposes a return to the pre-Augustinian conception adopted by the Greek Fathers for, he says, "otherwise it is impossible to reach a doctrine of grace and of Christology" (see page 17). Rahner contends that, essentially, the traditional Western separation disconnects God in himself from God to us. Torrance and Rahner have shown how this deeply rooted theological problem causes serious problems both epistemologically and soteriologically. Torrance is actually very appreciative of Rahner's approach in *Trinitarian Perspectives* calling him in line in basic Trinitarian theology with both Barth and Athanasius. See Torrance, *Trinitarian Perspectives,* 81–84. Furthermore, Torrance is similarly critical of Aquinas. See Torrance, *Scottish Theology,* 4. Another Protestant example is Colin Gunton. See Gunton, *Promise of Trinitarian Theology;* Gunton, *Father, Son, and Holy Spirit.* The following chapter will discuss Torrance's departure from Augustine in full.

312. E.g., Lossky, *The Mystical Theology of the Eastern Church,* 213. This is hugely

of Torrance's reconstruction of The Fathers on the means of the ὁμοούσιον centered reading of The Fathers' theology. This sheds fresh light on asceticism and sanctification.

Torrance's Reformed evangelical take on asceticism roots this classic practice in his Christology and soteriology instead of as a human work to be accomplished. As such, Torrance offers a huge contribution to asceticism in the Protestant tradition. Though Protestantism has inherited a great ascetical tradition from the Greek Fathers, owing to a potential temptation to understanding asceticism as a form of works based righteousness, the Protestant tradition has tended to stray away from using this word and discussing the concept.[313] Torrance returns to this theme and brings it back into his own Reformed tradition, with the Reformed emphasis on the finished work of Christ and salvation by grace. Here Torrance's combination of Greek patristic theology (asceticism) and Reformed theology (salvation entirely by grace) produces great fruits (asceticism by grace).[314] This can be of great service to the evangelical tradition of theology and his contribution herein cannot be overstated. This method can be applied further and one wonders whether Torrance's method could be applied further to a reading of the Byzantine ascetic tradition in light of the evangelical perspective of the Reformation with similar fruitfulness.[315] Perhaps the great Byzantine ascetical tradition as encapsulated in the *Philokalia*[316] could be better understood

---

important. On account of a multitude of misinterpretations (such as Lossky or those who view asceticism more as a work to be done), Protestants have typically been fearful of this classic practice. The classical version of asceticism, however, roots the practice objectively in God's gracious self-giving in Christ. As such, it flows from salvation rather than playing any role in it. There are many figures who are within this classical line (e.g., Athanasius, Calvin, Scougal, Torrance) and it is to this classical line that Protestants wishing to retrieve asceticism should return. See further Radcliff, "A Reformed Asceticism."

313. Though it should be noted that many are returning to this important practice. See, for example, Foster, *Celebration of Discipline*; Jones, *The Sacred Way*. It is often called "spiritual discipline/exercise" now.

314. See Noble, *Holy Trinity* for a similarly-minded combination of classic patristic theology and (in Noble's case) the Wesleyan tradition. In this publication of his 2012 Didsbury Lectures, Noble seeks to extricate the Wesleyan doctrine of Christian perfection from any form of subjectivism and root it objectively in the doctrine of the Trinity and Christology (person and work). Noble argues that this was Wesley's view and it is in line with The Fathers.

315. Torrance himself likely avoids the Byzantine ascetic tradition on account of perceived dualism.

316. Palmer, Sherrard, and Ware, *The Philokalia*. See also Colliander, *Way of the Ascetics*.

in light of the evangelical perspective of the Reformation. Here, Torrance's method could be applied further.[317]

Torrance's notion of the vicarious humanity has rooted salvation, sanctification, and *theosis* more fully in the person of Christ than traditionally has been done. The Torrancian vicarious humanity indeed recovers The Fathers from accusations of Apollinarianism, Monophysitism, and other heresies that deny the full integrity of Christ's humanity. Furthermore, it is a creative exploration of the Reformed notion of election rooted in Christ. There is debate where Calvin stood on the issue but later Reformed theology rooted election in God's eternal decrees.[318] However, Karl Barth reformulated this doctrine by rooting God's election in Christ.[319] Torrance picks this up and reformulates the concept further by means of the patristic concept of the humanity of Christ, the outcome being the Torrancian vicarious humanity.[320]

However, it is notable that there is substantial disagreement with Torrance on the patristic rootedness of his view that Christ assumed fallen humanity.[321] Athanasius, for example, does speak of Christ's assumption of

317. See Radcliff, "A Reformed Asceticism," for further exploration of this idea.

318. See e.g., *The Westminster Confession of Faith*, 3. See Torrance's Introduction to *School of Faith* and also Torrance, *Scottish Theology*, 125–53 for critiques of Federal theology's rooting of election in God's decrees rather than in Christ.

319. See McCormack, "Grace and Being," 94.

320. Notably, Torrance sees the Christologically conditioned version of election affirmed in the evangelical Scottish tradition by figures such as John Knox and Robert Bruce. See Torrance, *Scottish Theology*, 14 and 57, respectively.

321. Demetius Bathrellos, argues that other than Nestorianism and divergent forms of divisive Christology in the early church, the unfallenness of Christ's assumed humanity was taken for granted. See Bathrellos, "The Sinlessness of Jesus," 113, 124 n. 2. His contention is that in the incarnation Christ assumed unfallen humanity and redeemed humanity by its union with God (118–19). His conclusion is that for Christ to have been true man, he needed to assume unfallen humanity because fallenness is not an essential part of what it means to truly be human. Georges Florovsky (relying upon Maximus the Confessor) argues that the Son assumed unfallen humanity (he calls it "the first formed human nature") and voluntarily submitted it to the fallen condition of humanity. See Florovsky, *Creation and Redemption*, 97–98. He argues that sin is not an essential part of human nature but is rather a "parasitic and abnormal growth." Typically the Orthodox adhere to this view. See e.g., Lossky, *The Mystical Theology of the Eastern Church*, 142. Though, there is also agreement with Torrance. Scholars such as Thomas Weinandy, concur with Torrance on this matter. See Weinandy, *In the Likeness of Sinful Flesh*, 23–38. The majority of Weinandy's conclusions are akin to Torrance's; the impetus of the argument being twofold: (1) By the incarnation sinful humanity was redeemed and (2) by the incarnation corrupt humanity was deified. Luminaries such as John Meyendorff and John Zizioulas also agree with Torrance and Weinandy. See further Baker, "The Place of St. Irenaeus," 27. Again, part of the issue here seems to be that contemporary theologians seem to not work with the strict distinction between

the whole man and in places he spoke as if Christ's body was entirely liable to death being mortal like any other human body. However, when he states this he immediately nuances it, arguing, "the indwelling of the Word loosed it from this natural liability"[322] and would not have died any sort of natural death[323] and when discussing the uniqueness of the God–man Jesus, Athanasius states, "he took [his body] from a spotless, stainless virgin, without the agency of human father—a pure body, untainted by intercourse with man."[324] Irenaeus as well speaks of Christ's humanity itself as unique because of his virgin birth.[325] Torrance often cites Gregory Nazianzen's *Letter 101: To Cledonius*: "the unassumed is the unhealed." Contextually, Gregory was speaking about Christ's assumption of the human mind, which Torrance understands to include the assumption of fallen humanity because the mind is the directive principle of the human person (and thus the directive principle of the fallen human person).

An element missing from Torrance's discussion of Christ's assumption of fallen humanity which may add to the discussion and shed light on the disagreement with Torrance is Maximus the Confessor's notion of "will." For Maximus, whom those asserting Christ's assumption of unfallen humanity typically reference in support of their view, there are two types of will, "natural will" (θέλημα φυσικόν) and "gnomic" will (θέλημα γνωμικόν).[326] The gnomic will is a part of a human hypostasis whereas the natural will is a part of the human nature. The gnomic will is the seat of sin and enslaved to sin whereas the natural will is entirely free. Therefore, for Maximus the

---

"fallen humanity" (which Christ assumed according to the Greek Fathers) and "sinful humanity" (which Christ did not assume according to the Greek Fathers).

322. Athanasius, *De Incarnatione*, 4.20, PG 25b.129–32.

323. Ibid., 4.21, PG 25b.132–33.

324. Ibid., 1.8, PG 25b.109.

325. Irenaeus, *Adversus Haereses* 3.21.10, PG 7a.0955–0056.

326. See Maximus *Quaestiones ad Thalassium*, 21, PG 91.312–16; *Disputation with Pyrrhus*, PG 91.313D–316A, 337B. Maximus distinguishes between the two stating that the natural will is a desire for things according to nature (κατὰ φύσιν) whereas the gnomic will is willful movement of reason (λογισμοῦ) towards something." See PG 91.153A. See also John of Damascus, *De Fide Orthodoxa*, 3.14ff, PG 94.1034ff for a summary of the patristic view. The basic idea is that if Christ has a full divine nature and a full human nature he must have both a human and a divine will but since, contra Nestorianism, it must be asserted that Christ did not have a human hypostasis he only had a natural human will but not a hypostatic human will, the element of the human will which had fallen in Adam. That is, the gnomic will is connected to the will of the individual person. Thus, there is not a gnomic will in Christ because Christ's individual person (hypostasis) is divine not human. See also Gregory of Nyssa, *On the Making of the Man* for a related distinction (he distinguishes between the "vegetative soul" and "rational soul").

incarnate Christ had a natural human will but not a human gnomic will. Therefore Christ assumed an unfallen will and kept this in addition to his divine will.[327] Thus, for Maximus the assumption of a fallen gnomic will implies Nestorianism because it meant the assumption of two hypostases for Christ did not assume a fallen hypostasis because he did not have a human hypostasis at all; rather only one divine hypostasis. It is this view to which Orthodox theologians such as Florovsky and Lossky are referring. Thus, when they explain what they mean by "unfallen humanity" they clarified that it was Maximus and the concept of gnomic will to which they are referring.[328]

Torrance may well have been aware of this nuance but simply did not find it helpful for his purposes. As Matthew Baker points out, in at least one early work Torrance states that Christ did not assume a fallen will.[329] However elsewhere the assumption of a fallen will seems integral to his theology.[330] It is furthermore notable that Torrance does not use many Eastern Fathers post-Cyril other than Severus of Antioch and John Philoponus, both of whom have traditionally been accused of having Monophyistic leanings.[331] Often the Monophysites emphasized the assumption of fallen humanity and its subsequent transformation by deification.[332] Regardless, Torrance does not employ this nuance as captured by Maximus, perhaps on account of his bypassing of Byzantine theology and returning to the Nicene tradition.[333]

327. Meyendorff, *Christ in Eastern Christian Thought*, 112ff. See Maximus *Quaestiones ad Thalassium*, 21, PG 9.312–16.

328. Related to this, the Eastern Fathers tend to view each individual soul as created by God whereas the Western Fathers often view the soul as inherited from one's parents. See e.g., Gregory of Nyssa, *On the Soul and the Resurrection*. He argues that each soul is created by God and because God is free from the necessity of sin so each soul created by God is free from the necessity of sin, that is, until it wills to sin by choice. Augustine seems to waver but tends towards viewing the soul as inherited in order to defend his doctrine of original sin against Pelagianism. See e.g., *Epistle* 166.27. Cf. Jerome, *Epistle* 126.

329. Baker, "The Place of St. Irenaeus," 23–24.

330. Torrance, *Atonement*, 437–47.

331. Baker, "The Place of St. Irenaeus," 25.

332. Though Iain Torrance successfully locates Severus less in the "Monophysite" camp (as traditionally understood) and more in line with classical Nicene and Cyrilline theology. See Iain R. Torrance, *Christology After Chalcedon*. Here Iain Torrance argues that Severus distanced himself from both Nestorianism and Eutychianism and evades critiques of Monophysitism in the traditional sense, building upon certain recent trajectories of readings of so-called Monophysitism. See e.g., 14–19 for his location of the project within the recent trends.

333. More on this in the following chapter.

Another element missing from Torrance in his discussion of Christ's assumption of fallen humanity which, again, might add to the discussion and shed light on the disagreement is a precise definition of "inherited sin." In the Augustinian tradition there is inherited corruption as well as inherited guilt, however, in the Eastern tradition the focus is solely on being born into a situation of corruption.[334] Thus it is likely that the Greek Fathers asserted Christ's assumption of the whole corrupted man because, as Noble states, for the Greek Fathers, "'fallenness' is more of an *ontological* than a *moral* category."[335]

For the Latin Fathers "fallenness" also included moral guilt. In argument against Pelagius, Augustine asserts humanity's inheritance of Adam's guilt.[336] According to the version of "fallenness" and redemption of the Greek Fathers, Christ's assumption of the "whole man" means body and soul and when the Greek Fathers discuss Christ being born into fallen humanity they mean being born into a state of mortality. This would mean that Christ assumed humanity that was in the same situation and state as the rest of humanity, namely, humanity corrupted and dying. However, this would not necessarily mean Christ assumed humanity tainted by guilt. Torrance himself seems to hold to a concept of inherited sin including inherited guilt.[337] Torrance's emphasis here may furthermore be because of his focus on the noetic effects of the Fall, which was so central to his theology of the vicarious humanity of Christ.[338]

---

334. See Romanides, *The Ancestral Sin*. This text is Romanides doctoral dissertation. He argues that the Latin tradition, due primarily to Augustine, focuses too heavily on the forensic elements of the Fall, the Cross, and "inherited sin." His conclusion is that the Greek tradition has preserved a much more robust and biblical conception of the Fall, the Cross, and "inherited sin," namely, being born into a situation of sin and the consequences of sin, namely death, but not inheriting the guilt of sin.

335. Noble, *Holy Trinity*, 164.

336. *On merit and the forgiveness of sins and the baptism of infants*. PL 44:109–200. Contrast this with Athanasius who asserts being born into a state of corruption and death. See Athanasius, *Contra Apollinaris* 1.7 PG 26.1104–5. See further Romanides, *The Ancestral Sin*. Romanides articulates the now traditional Eastern Orthodox view that the Fall consisted of death (ontological) rather than a punishment (forensic) from God. Humanity inherits mortality from their parents but not guilt or punishment from God. Christ, being born of a virgin, was born outside this cycle and therefore able to free humankind from it (155–69).

337. See Torrance, "Karl Barth and the Latin Heresy," 477.

338. See the epilogue to Torrance, *Atonement*, 437–47: "The Reconciliation of the Mind." The Torrance archives at Princeton Seminary contains a handwritten note by Torrance which states: "Sin is existential severance from the truth but in order to understand that properly we must be in the truth." See The Thomas F. Torrance Manuscript Collection. Special Collections, Princeton Theological Seminary Library. Box 52.

So, in light of the disagreement with Torrance on this subject, the question then arises: where did Torrance learn this reading of the Greek Fathers? Torrance may have learned his reading of the Greek Fathers on this subject from his beloved teacher H. R. Mackintosh. Torrance states:

> I recall [Mackintosh] directing of us to Gregory Nazianzen's principle that 'the unassumed is the unhealed,' with special reference to the fact that in becoming incarnate the Holy Son of God assumed our flesh of sin, thereby condemning sin the flesh in order to sanctify, heal and redeem us.[339]

None of this is meant to question the theological legitimacy of Torrance's view that Christ assumed fallen humanity; this may very well be a legitimate theological point to assert. Furthermore, The Fathers do assert Christ's assumption of fallen humanity.[340] Rather, this is meant to offer an attempt at making some sense of the wide-ranging disagreement with Torrance on this issue, noting potentially missing nuances in Torrance's discussion which might help to bring the theological conversation forward. Perhaps Torrance's concept of the fallen humanity of Christ is best called a patristic "principle," as Robert Walker helpfully puts it in discussion of Torrance's theology.[341]

Torrance's Christologically centered soteriology, particularly his theology of the vicarious humanity of Christ offers not only an imaginative reconstruction of Irenaeus' doctrine of recapitulation[342] but also an evangelical and Christocentric approach to asceticism, piety, and godliness via the vicarious humanity. Torrance provides fresh insight into not only patristic Christology in general but also the vicarious humanity of Christ in particular. Patristics scholars had not discussed this theme and Torrance draws it out of Athanasius and the other Fathers very insightfully and imaginatively.

---

339. See *Itinerarium Mentis in Deum: T. F. Torrance—My Theological Development.* The Thomas F. Torrance Manuscript Collection. Special Collections, Princeton Theological Seminary Library, Series II, Box 10. Interestingly, in contrast to these lectures which Torrance remembers, Mackintosh's language is somewhat different in the appendix to his book *The Person of Jesus Christ:* "[Christ's humanity] is a new humanity, unique in perfectness of initial constitution" (533).

340. See Noble, *Holy Trinity,* 163–75 for an overview of the notion of "fallenness" in the Greek Fathers. As explored above, what they meant by fallenness is the real question.

341. Walker, "Incarnation and Atonement," 32–34. That is, a principle that Torrance develops from The Fathers.

342. Baker, "The Place of St. Irenaeus," 42: "Torrance's notion of the vicarious humanity of Christ . . . must be regarded as a major restatement of the Irenaean doctrine of recapitulation."

Indeed by situating the patristic theological themes of *theosis*, asceticism, and more generally reading The Fathers via a perspective focused upon grace and the vicarious humanity Torrance draws out elements from The Fathers not appreciated by patristics scholars to date.[343]

Intrinsically connected to Torrance's departure from the Augustinian tradition and return to the Greek patristic tradition and his departure from later Reformed confessions (especially the Westminster Standards) and return to the ὁμοούσιον is his departure from Federal theology and the *ordo salutis* and return to the doctrine of union with Christ and focus on the person of Christ.[344] This is clear from his emphasis on the ὁμοούσιον and Greek patristic themes such as *theosis*. This chapter discussed Torrance's activity in this regard and how Torrance proposes a more Greek, personal, and incarnational soteriology as opposed to the more Latin, functional, and atonement centered soteriology traditional in Reformed theology.

Torrance's emphasis on Greek patristic soteriology is a fresh perspective in light of ongoing debates, particularly in North America, over such things as "double imputation."[345] Torrance, relying upon the Greek patristic tradition, takes the emphasis away from such things as double imputation and returns it to the person of Jesus Christ.[346] His return to a Greek patristic approach over and against a more Western approach could provide a helpful lens for dissatisfied Protestants. Many Reformed and evangelical theologians have been following Torrance in this regard such as Donald Fairbairn in patristics,[347] Andrew Purves in pastoral theology,[348] Myk Habets and Bobby Grow in regards to reading Calvin and Calvinism,[349] and

343. Baker states that his fellow Eastern Orthodox theologians have much to learn from Torrance in this regard. See Baker, "The Place of St. Irenaeus," 42.

344. Torrance is highly critical of the *ordo salutis* in Federal Calvinism because he thinks it operates with a medieval conception that "reversed the teaching of Calvin that it is through union with Christ *first* that we participate in all his benefits" (i.e., as opposed to participating in Christ's benefits and then in Christ himself). See Torrance, *Scottish Theology*, 128.

345. The debate between John Piper and N. T. Wright for example.

346. This is not an argument for Torrance's disagreement with double imputation. Rather, the soteriology of Torrance and the Greek Fathers would likely include double imputation but this would not be their emphasis.

347. Fairbairn, *Grace and Christology*; Fairbairn, "Patristic Soteriology," 289–310. Fairbairn's project reviewed patristic doctrines such as *theosis* in light of a personal and Christocentric notion of grace which he sees as patristic (Cyril of Alexandria and John Cassian in his book).

348. Purves, *Reconstructing Pastoral Theology*.

349. Habets and Grow, *Evangelical Calvinism*.

J. Todd Billings in theology and ministry.[350] These theologians are adopting Torrance's approach[351] and imaginatively reconstructing their various theological specializations on the basis of an emphasis on union with Christ reminiscent of Torrance.

The Torrancian *Consensus Patrum* also consists of catholic figures and streams which Torrance constructs around the themes discussed in this chapter. The following chapter will explore the streams that Torrance saw in theological history and explore the way in which Torrance constructs them around the catholic themes particularly the Nicene ὁμοούσιον. So, it is the catholic figures and themes of the Torrancian *Consensus Patrum* which this thesis shall next explore.

---

350. Billings, *Union with Christ*. Though Billings' book is not without certain problems. See further Radcliff, Review of *Union with Christ*, 81–83.

351. Often directly from Torrance. Habets wrote a PhD dissertation on Torrance and Purves was Torrance's student.

CHAPTER 4

T. F. Torrance's *Consensus Patrum*

CATHOLIC STREAMS

It is only when Greek Patristic Theology is studied and interpreted in the strong Biblical perspective restored through the Reformation of the Church in the West that its permanent place in the founda- tions of Evangelical Theology may be appreciated in a new way . . . [and] when Reformed Theology is reassessed and interpreted in light of its ancient roots in the evangelical theology of the early centuries that its essential catholicity and its unifying force are to be understood.

Thomas F. Torrance, *Trinitarian Perspectives*, 21–22.

INTRODUCTION

Chapter 1 of this book explored the notion of the *Consensus Patrum* in historical Roman Catholicism, Eastern Orthodoxy, and Protestantism. This chapter argued that despite a brief respite in the nineteenth and early twentieth centuries, classic Protestantism has long contended for a *consensus*. Though there have been differing views as to what the *consensus* looks like and consists of, classic Protestantism has consistently looked to it. Chapter 2 of this book argued that, due to the abovementioned respite, twentieth-century evangelical Protestantism has seen a "discovery" of The Fathers. Suggesting that T. F. Torrance offers an helpful example of a Protestant (Reformed and evangelical) approach to The Fathers, chapter 3 of this book explored the catholic themes that comprise the Torrancian *Consensus Patrum*. This chapter also examined how Torrance extracts these themes from patristic theology and imaginatively reconstructs them in light of Reformed and evangelical theology. The argument that Torrance reconstructs these themes around the central theme of the ὁμοούσιον τῷ Πατρί ran throughout and the chapter explored the way in which this key Nicene theme affects the rest of the the Torrancian *consensus* serving as its lynchpin.

Torrance not only imaginatively reconstructs catholic themes but also catholic figures and streams or threads.[1] This chapter shall constructively discuss Torrance's grand vision of the patristic era as well as the creative connections he makes to it. Torrance's reconstruction of The Fathers into these streams is his most creative and constructive contribution to patristics and, indeed, offers a plausible and helpful template of patristic theology for Reformed and evangelical theologians wishing to read The Fathers from within their own tradition. Torrance had a panoply of sources he was working with and certain pieces simply did not fit into the vision he had of the inner connections lying behind church history and the different streams of theology.[2] This vision drives his method and the Torrancian *Consensus Patrum* emerges out of it in full force. Torrance understands there to have been a number of figures and streams of thought in the patristic era, some more pious and orthodox than others. In this chapter the different figures and streams comprising the Torrancian *Consensus Patrum* as well as their

1. Torrance himself does not seem to use the term "stream" or "thread." This chapter and the discussion of Torrance's "streams" and "threads" is a constructive examination of theological history (in particular early theological history) as seen through the eyes of Torrance in the hopes of gaining deeper understanding concerning Torrance's conclusions and what he saw when he looked at the theological history of the church. Andrew Purves very helpfully pointed out the concept of "threads" and "streams" in Torrance's theology in a personal conversation in 2009.

2. A quick glance at any of his books reveals that Torrance was extremely widely read. His brother David Torrance remembers of his brother's university days: "The university librarian apparently had never met a student who borrowed so many books. He often returned home with an entire rucksack full. He read far beyond the books prescribed for his particular study." Apparently one of his professors even called him a "mine of learning." See David Torrance, "Recollections and Reflections," 29. His nephew, Robert Walker, ruminates, "He read voluminously and would absorb and retain ideas. In both church and university he soon became recognized as something of a polymath, at home in several fields, not only in theology itself but in philosophy and science, particularly in the field of science and theology for which he later became so well known." See Walker, "Recollections and Reflections," 39.

relationships shall be explored. In Torrance's connections of these figures and reconstruction of them into streams, the Torrancian *Consensus Patrum* palate emerges in all its fullness.

This chapter will argue that Torrance reconstructs[3] theological history into "streams," namely the evangelical stream whose fulcrum is the "Athanasius-Cyril axis," the Cappadocian distinction which led to the dualist Byzantine stream, and the dualist Western/Latin stream. The Nicene-evangelical stream is the core to the Torrancian *Consensus Patrum* because of its Christological centeredness on the ὁμοούσιον and the evangelical perspective it preserves; the other streams are departures from the *consensus* typically rooted in some sort of dualism. Torrance, though Reformed and evangelical, does not solely emphasize the Protestant Reformers or the Reformed Scholastics (though he is appreciative of many of them) but returns to classical theological figures from church history. He also departs from the typical Western emphasis on Augustine and returns rather to the Greek Fathers. Some of Torrance's connections are more traditional and some are extremely creative. These streams are an imaginative reconstruction of The Fathers in themselves and are driven by the themes discussed in chapter 3 of this book, primarily the Reformed, dogmatic, and evangelical commitment to the Nicene ὁμοούσιον. This chapter will explore the different figures, streams, and connections in the Torrancian *Consensus Patrum* emerging on the basis of the themes.

THE EVANGELICAL STREAM

In Torrance's grand vision of the patristic era there is one overarching stream running throughout the church's history: the evangelical stream. Torrance understands the *consensus* to be connected on the basis of a common mindset rather than a truly numerical agreement (as in the Vincentian method discussed in chapter 1). He believes that certain eras of theological history best captured the inner structure of the Gospel.[4] For Torrance, these eras are connected to one another in one interconnected stream running

---

3. Robert Walker states: "TF's theology is highly original, which does not mean first and foremost that he developed new concepts, although he did, but that he made new connections between known theological ideas and concepts. For him, originality was not necessarily thinking new thoughts but making new connections." See Walker, "Recollections and Reflections," 43.

4. See further Colyer, *How to Read T. F. Torrance*, 360.

consistently throughout theological history; a sort of "golden-thread" running throughout the church's history.[5]

In Torrance's vision, the three instances that best captured this inner structure are Nicaea (particularly Athanasius), the Reformation (particularly Calvin), and contemporary evangelical theology (particularly Karl Barth).[6] Here Torrance sees the Reformers' emphasis on grace as complementary to the Nicene Fathers' emphasis on the ὁμοούσιον,[7] creatively connecting Nicene theology and his Reformed evangelical tradition.[8] This is entirely

5. Though peripheral to the present study, it is interesting that Torrance connects a number of non-theological figures to this stream as well on account of their realist epistemological perspective. The four main figures are John Philoponus, Michael Polanyi, James Clerk Maxwell, and Albert Einstein. In turn, Torrance uses the non-theological figures to shed light on the theological figures and *vice versa*. For example, John Philoponus (490–570 C.E.) is one of Torrance's favorite insights into Athanasius. Torrance sees Philoponus as carrying the relational view of space and time from patristic theology into the realm of physics. By doing so, Torrance contends, Philoponus preserves three key points: (1) The doctrine of one God, (2) the doctrine of the goodness of creation, and (3) that God conferred rationality upon nature. See *Reality and Scientific Theology*, 5–6. Torrance contends that James Clerk Maxwell (1831–1879 C.E.), Michael Polanyi (1891–1976 C.E.), and Albert Einstein (1879–1955 C.E.) all shared in the basic κατὰ φύσιν method of scientific inquiry. See Torrance, *Preaching Christ Today*, 45. Torrance sees Einstein as a propagator of a similar view of space and time to the Nicene Fathers, chiefly Athanasius. See ibid., 16. For Torrance the doctrine of the ὁμοούσιον propagates Einstein's *theory of relativity*, at its core, before Einstein. Torrance argues that Einstein combated the dualism latent in the thought of his time, because of Cartesian and Newtonian assumptions, much the same way Athanasius combated the dualism latent in his culture, because of Hellenistic and Arian thought. See Torrance, *Theology in Reconciliation*, 74–75. Torrance argues that The Fathers, prior to Einstein, put forth the core of the Relativity Theory, for they realized that the Biblical view of God's relation to mankind would not work with a "container notion" of space and time, but only with a "relational notion." See Torrance, *Incarnation*, 218.

6. Torrance, *Reality and Evangelical Theology*, 14–15. See also, *Preaching Christ Today*, 20 and *Theology in Reconciliation*, 235–37 and *Theology in Reconciliation*, 285. See also Torrance, *Theology in Reconstruction*, 267.

7. Torrance, *Theology in Reconstruction*, 225. Torrance considers grace to be intrinsically personal as it was connected to the person of Jesus Christ. See Torrance, *Preaching Christ Today*, 20–21. See also his PhD thesis written under Barth: *The Doctrine of Grace in the Apostolic Fathers*.

8. More specifically, Torrance connects John Calvin to the Greek Fathers via Calvin's theology of *pietas* and *religio*. Torrance argues that this was the same as Greek patristic *eusebia*. Inherently connected to this, in Torrance's thought, is also the "realist epistemology" of Athanasius. Additionally, Torrance argues that for Calvin this meant that terms must, therefore, remain open to being defined by the realities they signify. See *Trinitarian Perspectives*, 41–47. See also *The Christian Doctrine of God*, 10. In an interesting discussion on the relation to Calvin's hermeneutical method to that of his context, Torrance argues that despite the fact that his medieval context had forgotten the patristic conception of words as images pointing to a reality, Calvin returned to

consistent with his immense stress upon the shared identity between the giver of grace and the gift of grace and his assertion of the intensely personal nature of grace, discussed in the previous chapter.

Torrance sees Karl Barth as inheriting the Nicene tradition and the Reformation tradition, bringing them together.[9] Regarding the intrinsic connection of Reformed and Nicene theology Torrance states:

> When Greek Patristic Theology is studied and interpreted in the strong Biblical perspective restored through the Reformation of the Church in the West that its permanent place in the foundations of Evangelical Theology may be appreciated in a new way . . . [and] when Reformed Theology is reassessed and interpreted in light of its ancient roots in the evangelical theology of the early centuries that its essential catholicity and its unifying force are to be understood.[10]

This quote illuminates Torrance's evangelical stream and his understanding of the connection between patristic theology, best exhibited by

___

this method and in doing followed the Athanasian conception of words pointing to realities in a dynamic way. See Torrance, *The Hermeneutics of John Calvin*, 91. See also 164–65 where he describes Calvin's theological methodology in nearly identical terms to the way he conceived of Athanasian theological methodology. Torrance finds Calvin's view of accommodation to be substantially similar to the Greek Fathers as well. Torrance contends Calvin returned to the concept of "realist epistemology" and a dynamic conception of the Word. Herein, Calvin returned to the Nicene doctrine of ὁμοούσιον τῷ Πατρί and tied the doctrine into the realm of epistemology, thereby returning to Athanasius-Hilary and departing from Origen-Augustine. See Torrance, *Theology in Reconciliation*, 83–88.

    9. There is certain precedent for such a connection. See Roldanus, *Le Christ Et L'homme Dans La Théologie d'Athanase d'Alexandrie*. See in particular pp. 2, 4, 218–19, 359, and 373. In his book, Roldanus examines Athanasius' theological anthropology, arguing that Athanasius asserts a strict distinction between God and creation. Though Anatolios is critical of Roldanus on this point (see Anatolios, *Athanasius*, 228). Anatolios calls Roldanus' reading of Athanasius a "Barthian eisegesis" at times. Anatolios sees a more dynamic interaction between God and humanity in the thought of Athanasius (as opposed to the strict dichotomy he sees drawn in Barth and Roldanus' reading of Athanasius). Sometimes Torrance's emphasis on salvation entirely from the side of God and his attack on any form of traditional natural theology does (in a way similar to Roldanus) make Athanasius look like a strict Barthian and the ὁμοούσιον sound like a Barthian theology of revelation and salvation but, overall, he simply sees overlap in their shared commitment to a theology driven by the incarnation and God's presence with humankind and imaginatively reconstructs each in light of the other. Thus, Torrance might say: Athanasius was a Barthian and Barth was an Athanasian. Furthermore, Torrance's emphasis on the vicarious humanity of Christ acts somewhat as a balance to this inasmuch as, for Torrance, God's interacts directly with the world via the humanity of Christ.

    10. Torrance, *Trinitarian Perspectives*, 21–22.

Athanasius; and Reformed theology, best exhibited by John Calvin; and preserved and re-presented in modern times by Karl Barth. Torrance also asserts that there were three stages/instances of theology that affirmed the notion that divine revelation is God revealing his οὐσία to humankind: patristic (ὁμοούσιον), Reformation ("the immediate act of God in the presence of his Being as revealed"), and Karl Barth (bringing the two together; being-in-act and act-in-being).[11] Torrance clarifies that The Fathers emphasized the being of God in his acts and the Reformers emphasized the acts of God in his being,[12] arguing that although The Fathers of Nicaea preserved the teaching that Jesus is God, this core concept did not find its way into the rest of the life of the church, especially in the West, and thus "many aspects of the Church were allowed luxuriant growth that was unchecked and uncriticized by the central dogma of Christ."[13] The Reformers, argues Torrance, attempted carry this into every aspect of the church. He states, "it was an attempt to put Christ and his Gospel once again into the very centre and to carry through extensive reform by bringing everything into conformity to him and his Gospel."[14] Ultimately then, according to Torrance, the Reformation is "not contrary to but complementary to that of Nicaea, Ephesus, Chalcedon, etc."[15]

Torrance sees Barth as inheriting these two traditions and combining them dynamically, viewing him as a sort of "funnel" through which the Nicene theology of the ὁμοούσιον of Christ and the Reformation theology of the ὁμοούσιον of grace are dynamically combined and filtered into contemporary Western theology. As such, Torrance sees Barth as a modern Athanasius, or to put it another way, Athanasius as an ancient Barth. Torrance connects Barth and Athanasius directly on a number of levels, but primarily in his Triadology and the emphasis on the dynamic nature of the being of God,[16] understanding Barth as the theologian who brought the Trinity back to the forefront of theology and in doing so returning modern theology to classical theology.[17] Torrance consistently maintains that both Barth and

---

11. Torrance, *Reality and Evangelical Theology*, 14–15. See also, *Preaching Christ Today*, 20 and *Theology in Reconciliation*, 235–37 and 285.

12. Torrance, *Theology in Reconstruction*, 230.

13. Ibid., 265.

14. Ibid.

15. Ibid. See also, Torrance, "Karl Barth and the Latin Heresy," 462–63.

16. Torrance also claims that Barth's "realist view" of the Bible was similar if not identical to the Athanasian and Greek patristic notion of σκοπός. See Torrance, *Reality and Evangelical Theology*, 101. See also *Divine Meaning*, 130–78 for Torrance's view of Athanasius' hermeneutics.

17. Torrance, *The Christian Doctrine of God*, 7–10; Torrance, "Karl Barth and the

Athanasius asserted a doctrine of the Trinity preserving the connection between the economic and immanent Trinity. Torrance believes Barth was doing this in order to preserve the conception that the gift of grace and the giver of grace as identical.[18] Torrance puts this in various manners, for example, stating that God is "Being in Person."[19] Elsewhere, Torrance elaborates upon this in more detail when he connects the Athanasian concepts of ἐνούσιος λόγος and ἐνούσιος ἐνέργια[20] directly to the Barthian conception of "Being-in-Act and Act-in-Being."[21] Torrance sees these two concepts as not only mutually informing but as asserting the same basic theology: that there is no disconnection between God to us and God in himself.[22]

Latin Heresy," 462.

18. Torrance, *Karl Barth: An Introduction to His Early Theology*, 146. Torrance also points to overlap between Calvin and Gregory Nazianzen in Triadology. He says that they both held that the Ἀρχή of the Godhead is rooted in the being of God. See Torrance, *Trinitarian Perspectives*, 62–63.

19. Torrance, *The Christian Doctrine of God*, 4. While not entirely dismissive of connecting Athanasius to Barth, Anatolios argues whereas for Barth the emphasis is entirely on divine otherness, for Athanasius and Irenaeus the focus on divine otherness is inextricably connected with divine condescension. Anatolios argues that the polemic against the *analogia entis* found in Barth is not at all a part of the Athanasian system. For Barth revelation and salvation are entirely from the side of God and not at all intrinsic to humanity. See Anatolios, *Athanasius*, 207–8. Anatolios argues that for Athanasius, while still completely from the side of God who is always ὁ ποιῶν (*the one doing*), salvation is by cooperation with God's grace. Thus, while for both Athanasius and Barth salvation and revelation are entirely from the side of God who was the effecter, for Barth this is something entirely extrinsic to creation whereas for Athanasius this is something intrinsic to creation by grace (ibid., 177–87). Though surely this is an over-simplification of Barth's theology. Anatolios' picture of Barth as distinct from Athanasius sounds like the *Der Römerbrief* era Barth. See Barth, *The Epistle to the Romans*. Yet, in Barth's essays on the humanity of God, the kinship between Barth and Athanasius is more along the lines of Torrance's depiction. See Barth, *Humanity of God*.

20. See Torrance, *The Trinitarian Faith*, 72 citing *Theology in Reconciliation* 222f, 226ff, 235ff.

21. Torrance, *The Christian Doctrine of God*, 149. See also *The Mediation of Christ*, 40.

22. See Torrance, *The Christian Doctrine of God*, 28 citing Barth, *Church Dogmatics* I.1, p. 380.

Torrance understands this evangelical stream to have run from Athanasius and Cyril through Anselm,[23] Kierkegaard,[24] certain figures in Scottish theology, and finally to its climax in Barth (and H. R. Mackintosh who was a sort of conduit of Barth's theology into Scotland). Furthermore, Torrance argues that there is an evangelical stream within the Scottish Reformed theological tradition which preserved Greek patristic theology.[25] Torrance's book *Scottish Theology: From John Knox to John McLeod Campbell* is an account of the Scottish theological tradition's recurring struggle with varying levels of dualism, legalism, and logicalized scholastic thought and the evangelical stream running through it back to the Nicene era.[26]

23. Torrance connects Anselm (c. 1033–1109 C.E.) to the Nicene stream most significantly in regards to his theological method. Torrance sees Anselm as sharing an "axiomatic" method with Athanasius. See *God and Rationality*, 100–101. Torrance sees Anselm as approaching theology in a similar if not the same way as Athanasius. Thus for Torrance, there was an element of Athanasian thought in the medieval west preserved by Anselm; though, Torrance has certain problem with Anselm's doctrine of the atonement which he believes was more of an external and forensic exchange. See "Karl Barth and the Latin Heresy," 477.

24. Torrance connects Athanasius, Anselm, and Søren Kirkegaard (1813–1855 C.E.) as realists in their "axiomatic thinking." See *Reality and Scientific Theology*, 86–93. Interestingly, Torrance included both Anselm's *Epistle on the Incarnation* and *On the Procession of the Spirit* and Kierkegaard's *Philosophical Fragments* in the reading for his Dogmatics courses at New College. Additionally, for his dogmatics seminars he assigned Anselm's *Cur Deus Homo* combined with Hilary's *On the Trinity* and Athanasius' *Contra Arianos* and *Letters on the Spirit*. See Torrance's Dogmatics Syllabus in The Thomas F. Torrance Manuscript Collection. Special Collections, Princeton Theological Seminary Library. Box 51.

25. Torrance argues that pagan dualism infiltrated theology via Augustine, and despite Thomas Aquinas' attempt to eradicate this from theology by means of Aristotelian metaphysics, by the time of the Reformation there existed a dualism between Scripture and the Word of God. Torrance argues that John Reuchlin (a German theologian who lived from 1455–1522 C.E.) challenged this view and the Scot John Major affirmed the challenge (1467–1550 C.E.) with the argument that with Nicaea it must be propagated that the Word of God who came to mankind in the Scriptures is ὁμοούσιον with God. See Torrance, *Preaching Christ Today*, 18–19. Thus, Torrance sees the evangelical stream running into parts of Scottish Reformed theology. However, see Torrance, *Scottish Theology*, 125–158 and Torrance, *The School of Faith*, xvi–xxi for Torrance's critique of non-evangelical Reformed theology. See also Torrance, *Karl Barth: Biblical and Evangelical Theologian*, 213–40 for Torrance's account of dualism pervasive in Western theology.

26. Torrance, *Scottish Theology*. Torrance sees the older Scottish tradition as steeped in Greek patristic theology (see 49–90), John Knox as essentially evangelical but struggling with notions of limited atonement and double predestination (1–45), and Federal theology (epitomized in Westminster Calvinism) as "logicalized Calvinism" which separated God from Christ in a Nestorian fashion and God's being from God's acts in a medieval scholastic way (93, 125–53).

Torrance sees the evangelical stream in the Scottish church preserved in such figures as Robert Boyd, John Forbes of Corse, and John McLeod Campbell. For Torrance, Robert Boyd was indebted to the Greek Fathers, particularly Basil, Gregory Nazianzen, and John Chrysostom[27] and John Forbes of Corse was indebted to Athanasius, Gregory Nazianzen, John Chrysostom, and Cyril of Alexandria.[28] McLeod Campbell's emphasis upon the personal nature of the atonement was inherently evangelical as well, according to Torrance.[29] Torrance understands the later figures to have developed the ideas of the earlier figures and indeed to complement one another.[30]

The fount of this evangelical stream is the Nicene stream (and its best exponent, Athanasius) and the themes (especially the ὁμοούσιον). Torrance sees other, diverging, streams of theological history: the Augustinian stream (leading into Latin Scholasticism) and the Cappadocian distinction (leading into the Byzantine trajectory), both of which were problematically rooted in some form of dualism.[31] Torrance is, as a western and as a Protestant uniquely returning to the Greek tradition of Athanasius and Cyril over and against the Augustinian tradition.

THE AUGUSTINIAN STREAM

Perhaps the clearest example of Torrance's departure from the typically Western and typically Reformed reading of The Fathers is his emphasis on the Greek Fathers, particularly Athanasius and Cyril, and his less positive reception of Augustine.[32] Typically Protestants see their doctrines of justification, especially grace and election, as traceable in some form back to Augustine; however, they have not traditionally located any version of these doctrines in the Greek Fathers in a substantial way.[33] This is likely because of the Protestant evangelical emphasis upon the doctrine of justification, particularly penal substitution, over all other doctrines and, therefore, the

27. See Torrance, *Scottish Theology*, 66–74.

28. Ibid., 80.

29. Ibid., 287–315.

30. Such as Anselm who deepened the church's understanding of the *homoousion*. See Torrance, *Theology in Reconstruction*, 265.

31. See below.

32. It should be noted that Torrance's critique is typically more of "Augustinian thought" than Augustine himself. See, e.g., Torrance, *Gospel, Church, and Ministry*, 209 and Torrance, *Theological Dialogue*, 1:12. Perhaps Augustine was not really an "Augustinian."

33. Hence the many "discoveries" discussed in chapter 2.

perceived lack of relevance of The Fathers prior to Augustine on justification.[34] Regardless of the reason, however, Protestant evangelicals (especially Torrance's own Reformed tradition) have often avoided the Greek Fathers.[35] The previous chapter explored the way in which Torrance emphasizes Greek patristic themes such as *theosis* as opposed to typically Reformed evangelical themes such as penal substitution (albeit, holding them together). Accordingly, Torrance's emphasis is on the Greek Fathers and not Augustine. As such, Torrance magnifies the ways in which the Protestant, particularly evangelical, tradition is truly in line with the Greek patristic tradition.

Torrance departs from Augustinian thought because he considers it "inherently dualistic."[36] In *Trinitarian Faith* Torrance cites Augustine a mere ten times[37] and throughout the rest of his many writings on The Fathers his general approach to Augustine, especially regarding his soteriology, is negative. Torrance considers Augustine somewhat dualist in certain areas[38] and sees elements of a Nestorian-type separation of God in himself from God to us found in Augustine's theology.[39] According to Torrance this dualism in

34. See e.g McCormack, "The End of Reformed Theology?" 46–64. McCormack here (and elsewhere) argues for the centrality of Penal Substitution for Reformed theology.

35. See e.g., McGrath, *Iustitia Dei* who spends (a meager) seven pages on the pre-Augustinian tradition. Of course, McGrath's book is excellent on the Western tradition and has become the standard text on this subject. So, this is not to critique McGrath on what he does; rather it is simply to say that his approach is illustrative of the greater Protestant assumption (a) that justification is central and (b) that the Greek Fathers do not have much to say on the doctrine.

36. Torrance, *Theology in Reconciliation*, 285. Though, notably, Torrance refers to Augustine's Triadology positively: "Augustine was said not to know Greek but there is no doubt that his *De Trinitate* is steeped in the teaching of the Greek Fathers . . ." Torrance thinks Augustine received this theology from Hilary of Poitiers. See Torrance, *Trinitarian Perspectives*, 22. Furthermore, Torrance was clearly influenced by Augustine in his emphasis on grace and through the Reformed elements in his own thought (such as election) which surely had at least some rootedness in Augustine. Therefore, the Augustinian stream must not be mistaken for an "Augustine stream." Torrance is critical of later Augustin*ian* thought (and its roots in Augustine himself) but is also deeply appreciative of Augustine on many levels.

37. See the appendix of this book. Gerald Bonner states: "More than most authors Augustine has been the object of unjustified denunciation by those who have not read him." See the quotation in Barnes, "Rereading Augustine's," 145. This is not to imply that Torrance did not read Augustine. However, it is a plausible inference from the lack of references to him in *Trinitarian Faith* that Torrance does not indwell Augustine in the same way he does Athanasius nor accord him the same level of detailed study he offers the Nicene stream in *Trinitarian Faith*.

38. Both cosmological and epistemological dualism. See Torrance, *Theological Dialogue*, 1:11–12.

39. Torrance, *Theological Dialogue*, 1:13–14. Torrance contends that Byzantine

Augustinian theology pervaded even to Western (really, starting with Ter-tullian) and Augustinian theology of the sacraments, dividing the work of God and the work of man in the sacraments, emphasizing the latter rather than the former.[40]

Torrance argues that certain dualist elements of Reformed thought were inherited from Augustinian thought.[41] He is particularly critical of dualist views of the atonement and election that separate God from Christ which he sees as stemming from Augustinian convictions and being deeply rooted in Western theology.[42] Torrance ultimately sees the perversions to which the Reformers protested against as rooted in Augustinian theology.[43]

Torrance as western, Protestant, Reformed, and, in many ways, follow-ing Calvin in his reading of church history and tradition was, therefore, ab-solutely unique in his critique of Augustine and return to the Greek patristic tradition. Chapter 1 of this book examined how both the Roman Catholic and Protestant (especially Reformed) branches of Western Christianity have traditionally emphasized Augustine over the Greek tradition.[44] Yet, as ar-gued, Torrance sees himself most in line with the Scottish evangelical tradi-tion, more reliant upon the Greek Fathers.[45] Here Torrance has shown that the Reformed evangelical tradition is indeed in line with the Greek patristic tradition (and not solely the Latin patristic tradition).[46] This is ecumenically

---

dualism (Gregory Palamas, John of Damascus, etc.) was basically similar to Augustin-ian dualism in their division of God from Christ.

40. Torrance, *Theology in Reconciliation*, 95–99. Torrance is actually fond of Au-gustine's view, however; he is, again, simply critical of *Augustinian* thought (97–98). He sees the Augustinian stream emphasizing the "inward grace" part of Augustine's theology of the sacraments and not Augustine's view of God acting in the sacraments. He sees both of these present in Augustine but thinks the Augustinian stream wrongly emphasized the human side rather than the divine side.

41. Torrance, *Theological Dialogue*, 1:13. Here, Torrance is particularly critical of Calvin's view of election, presumably the disconnection of this from his the person of Christ. See Torrance's friend J. K. S. Reid's magisterial article on this: Reid, "The Office of Christ in Predestination," 5–19.

42. See e.g., Torrance, "Karl Barth and the Latin Heresy."

43. Torrance, *Conflict and Agreement*, 1:76.

44. With notable exceptions. See Rahner, *The Trinity*.

45. See Torrance, *Scottish Theology*, particularly his discussion of John Forbes of Corse. See also Torrance, "Introduction" in *The Mystery of the Lord's Supper*. Torrance sees Bruce as following the Greek Fathers over Augustine. See also Torrance, "Introduc-tion" in *The School of Faith*. Torrance sees the Scottish Reformed tradition having a more Christological emphasis and lens.

46. Chapter 1 of this book explored how the Western tradition (Protestant and Catholic) has generally followed Augustine over the other Fathers. For example, Calvin cited Augustine more than any other Father. See Oort, "John Calvin," 689. In systematic

relevant for it has not only portrayed how the Reformed evangelical tradition is in line with the Greek patristic tradition but also has, herein, opened the door for Reformed dialogue with both eastern[47] and western churches.[48]

It is notable that Torrance's critique of Augustine in particular and Augustinian-Latin theology in general is substantially similar to his critique of contemporary Roman Catholicism and Federal Calvinism. Torrance critiques Augustine for dividing God from his Word and the Latin tradition for emphasizing the juridical aspect of the atonement dividing God from Christ.[49] Torrance also critiques Roman Catholicism and Federal Calvinism for doing the very same.[50] The overlap is substantial.[51] The previous chapter of this book explored Torrance's departure from forensic notions of the atonement and a return to the Greek conception of *theosis* and union with Christ. Torrance's critique of Augustine may well be in line with his

---

theology, if The Fathers are utilized at all, Augustine is typically referenced the most. See e.g., Berkhof, *Systematic Theology,* who utilizes Augustine and Cyprian.

47. Torrance, *Theological Dialogue* 1; *Theological Dialogue* 2. The ecumenical point of contact between Torrance and the Orthodox might be more than a theological connection. Orthodox scholars also tend to be strongly allergic to Augustine. See, for example, Romanides, *The Ancestral Sin*; Romanides, *Franks, Romans, Feudalism, and Doctrine*; Yannaras, *Elements of Faith*; Yannaras, *Orthodox and the West*. These Orthodox theologians hold Augustine responsible for "most of what went wrong with the west in the middle ages . . ." (Papanikolaou and Demacopoulos, "Augustine and the Orthodox," 33). Romanides accuses Augustine of having a distorted view of the Fall/inherited sin and Yannaras faults him for not holding to the essence/energies distinction. Illustrative of this view, Hart states: "The theology of grace of the late Augustine, his increasingly intransigent extremism regarding the creature's 'merit,' his hideous theology of predestination and original guilt, his conviction that genuine trust in the purity and priority of grace obliged him to affirm the eternal damnation of infants who died unbaptized—in short, the entire range of his catastrophic misreading of Paul's theology (attributable only in part to bad Latin translations)—is all very far from what a modern Orthodox Christian is likely to recognize as the Church's faith" (Hart, "The Hidden and Manifest," 194). Despite this particularly scathing critique of Augustine in the first pages, Hart is relatively more gracious to Augustine throughout the remainder of his paper.

48. See his very appreciative discussion of Karl Rahner's Trinitarian theology and departure from Augustine and return to the Greek tradition. Torrance, *Trinitarian Perspectives,* 77–102. Though Torrance does have his hesitations about the extremely intimate ontological identification between the economic and immanent Trinity in Rahner.

49. See e.g., Torrance, "Karl Barth and the Latin Heresy," 470–79.

50. See e.g., Torrance, *Theology in Reconciliation,* 9–10 and "Introduction" in *The School of Faith,* xvi–xxi.

51. Here, perhaps, Torrance may be falling into the temptation of Newman before him to amalgamate contemporary debate with ancient theology. Newman saw the liberals of his day as contemporary Arians. See Daley, "The Church Fathers," 31.

critique of forensic notions of the atonement in Roman Catholicism and Federal Calvinism.[52]

THE NICENE STREAM

Emphasizing Augustine and the Augustinian tradition far less than traditionally done in his Reformed and evangelical tradition, Torrance returns rather to the Greek Fathers. Accordingly, in the Torrancian *Consensus Patrum* the Nicene stream of theology, which is the fulcrum of the overarching evangelical stream, is central and indeed the core of the evangelical stream discussed earlier in this chapter. Driving this stream is a shared mindset and methodology consisting of (a) an assumption of the unapproachability of God, (b) the view that it is only by God that God is known, and (c) a view of the dynamic nature of theological terms.[53] All of these arise out of the Nicene ὁμοούσιον and the epistemological and soteriological implications therein discussed in chapter 3.

Torrance contends that the Council of Nicaea "has a unique place in the history of the Christian Church as 'the Great and Holy Synod.'"[54] Furthermore, he holds that subsequent Ecumenical Councils[55] looked back to

52. Torrance was clearly in support of the Reformation and Reformation theology, however Luther probably would have stood within the Augustinian stream. Torrance's comments concerning Luther are often largely negative accusing him of some sort of dualism (in e.g., *Space, Time, and Incarnation*) in similar tones to his critiques of Augustinian and Federalist thought.

53. Torrance, *Theology in Reconstruction*, 30.

54. Torrance, *Trinitarian Faith*, 13.

55. Generally the "Ecumenical Councils" refer to Nicaea (325 C.E.), Constantinople (381 C.E.), Ephesus (429 C.E.), Chalcedon (451 C.E.), Constantinople II (553 C.E.), Constantinople III (681 C.E.), and Nicaea II (787 C.E. The first four Ecumenical Councils laid out the foundations of Orthodox Christology. The First Council (Nicaea, 325 C.E.) affirmed Christ's full divinity. The Second Council (Constantinople I, 381 C.E.) affirmed Christ's full humanity. The Third Council (Ephesus, 431 C.E.) affirmed the oneness of Christ's person. The Fourth Council (Chalcedon, 451 C.E.) affirmed the duality of Christ's natures. These first four councils laid out the basis of orthodox Christology. The Fifth and Sixth Ecumenical Councils essentially clarified the Third and Fourth Ecumenical Councils. The Fifth Council (Constantinople II, 553 C.E.) affirmed the duality of Christ's natures and clarified precisely what this did not mean and what it did mean. The Sixth Council (Constantinople III, 680 C.E.) clarified the theology of the duality of Christ's natures even further. Essentially, the Fifth and Sixth Councils clarified the earlier councils, especially the third and fourth. The Seventh Council (Nicaea II, 787 C.E.) was a very practical council. Here, the proper use of images was affirmed. The Seventh Council clarified what the earlier six councils affirmed by affirming the use of icons. Basically, this council argued that because of the theology that had been propagated at the first six councils, icons were therefore acceptable

Nicaea as their "normative basis."[56] Torrance does not explicitly limit the councils to the first four but rather holds to the ecumenicity of the full seven of the Eastern and Western churches; and though he is clearly primarily informed by the councils of Nicaea I, Constantinople I, Ephesus, and Chalcedon in his theology he does positively cite figures working contemporary to the later of the Seven Ecumenical Councils.[57]

However, Torrance never explicitly argues for a chronologically driven "golden-age" like the Reformers before him did and Torrance does cite Fathers after the fifth century and thus Florovsky's critique of Protestants assuming a "pattern of decay" in their reading of church history[58] cannot be directed at Torrance; as such he breaks free from this traditional Protestant perspective. Furthermore, Torrance's emphasis on the first four ecumenical councils in general and the Council of Nicaea in particular is not because of chronology but rather the emphasis on the ὁμοούσιον.[59] The councils and Fathers that were driven by the Word-focused theology were simply more in tune with God and how to speak about God. Thus, Torrance does not emphasize the first four councils for chronologically driven reasons; rather, these figures simply happened to be more in line with the evangelical stream. As noted, other, much later theologians, (e.g., Anselm, Calvin, Kierkegaard, Barth) fit in the stream (albeit only in certain ways).

THE ATHANASIUS-CYRIL AXIS OF CLASSICAL THEOLOGY

For Torrance, even more so than Nicaea, the flowering of the *Consensus Patrum* is the "Athanasius-Cyril axis of classical theology,"[60] especially

---

and good. Thus, the Seventh Council portrayed the practical implications of the earlier six Ecumenical Councils. See Davis, *The First Seven Ecumenical Councils* for further information. Roman Catholics have fourteen more councils which are considered Ecumenical. Traditionally Protestants consider only the first four councils Ecumenical. In the *Institutes,* Calvin considered the Seventh Ecumenical Council to have fallen into idolatry. See *Institutes,* 1.11. Calvin considered the first four councils to be ecumenical but that soon after the church began a gradual decline from her "golden-age." See Lane, *John Calvin,* 39–40, 46.

56. Torrance, *The Trinitarian Faith,* 13.

57. For example, Severus of Antioch and John Philoponus. See the previous chapter. See further Baker, "The Place of St. Irenaeus," 25.

58. Florovsky, *Bible, Church, Tradition,* 110

59. See e.g., his article "Athanasius: A Study in the Foundations of Classical Theology" in *Theology in Reconciliation.*

60. Torrance, *Theology in Reconciliation,* 9.

Athanasius "the foundation of classical theology."[61] Athanasius and Cyril serve as the fulcrum of both Torrance's Nicene stream and his evangelical stream. Torrance sees Athanasius as an absolutely pivotal theologian here who preserved and propagated a Biblical worldview in a culture that strongly denied all aspects of it.[62] Torrance is for the most part consistent in his use of Athanasius in that throughout his published work the same themes are discussed in relation to Athanasius and he consistently turns to Athanasius; however, Torrance certainly developed and deepened his understanding of those themes throughout his career.[63] In an early text, *Conflict and Agreement*, Torrance already had begun to use Athanasius in support of his view of the sacraments[64] and his view that Christ assumed fallen and sinful humanity,[65] both of which are constant themes in Torrance's later texts, as discussed in the previous chapter.

A number of nineteenth-century scholars stand with Torrance and view Athanasius in a positive light. As Behr puts it, they are "effusive in their praise for Athanasius" such as Moehler, Newman, Neale, Gwatkin, Bright, and Robertson[66] and a number of twentieth-century scholars such as Florovsky, Dragas, Moutsoulas, Twomey, and Person.[67]

The Torrancian Athanasius stands in the center of classical biblically based theology. Herein, Athanasius stands in a distinct thread of thought, which is rooted in a certain theological method, exegetical method, and positive theology. At his core, the Torrancian Athanasius is a theologian who sought to:

---

61. Ibid., 215–56.

62. Torrance's situating of Athanasius in such a positive light stands out against a generally critical assessment of Athanasius' character popular during his era. These scholars' accusation is that Athanasius' theology was mere propaganda, as his primary intention was the assertion of as much political power as possible. Indeed, for them Athanasius was simply a political thug like many other leaders in late antiquity. Thus, they do not spend much, if any, time in discussion of the saint's theology. Rather, the focus is typically on his character and actions. Arnold provides an excellent summary of the historical critiques of Athanasius in modern times: forgery, invalid consecration as bishop, and/or use of brutal violence to suppress schism. These critical approaches to Athanasius include: Seeck, Schwartz, Caspar, Setton, Opitz, Schneemelcher, and, to some extent, Hanson. See Arnold, *The Early Episcopal Career*, 11–13, 181–186.

63. The only actual change was in regards to Torrance's view of *theosis*, as discussed in the previous chapter.

64. Torrance, *Conflict and Agreement*, 1:74.

65. Ibid., 1:149.

66. Behr, *The Nicene Faith*, 1:165. See also Arnold, *The Early Episcopal Career*, 11–23.

67. Arnold, *The Early Episcopal Career*, 21.

Develop an organic structure in theological understanding of God through discerning the coordination between the concrete pattern taken by the divine condescension in the Incarnation of the Son, and the inherent order of Trinitarian relations in the Godhead, linking them together through the pattern of God's interaction with us described in terms of *from (or to) the Father, through the Son, and in the Spirit.*[68]

At first glance, it may seem that Torrance orchestrates his notion of the *Consensus Patrum* based upon Athanasius himself; however, it is more deeply rooted than this, for, Torrance's reliance upon Athanasius is because of his view of what is the "core" of the *consensus,* namely the ὁμοούσιον. Based upon this, Athanasius is the theologian who most properly fits in the *consensus* and thus was the exemplar thinker in Torrance's system. Nevertheless, others fit into this system, not based upon how they lined up with Athanasius, but rather how they lined up with this core orthodoxy.

The first aspect of the significance of the Torrancian Athanasius is that he was a highly significant figure because of the theological assertions he affirmed and, conversely, those he denounced. Torrance holds that Athanasius did three main things. First, he rejected dualism, primarily the Origenist and Alexandrian dichotomy of the κόσμός αἰσθητός (*sensible world*) and the κόσμος νοητός (*intelligible world*).[69] This accusation of Origen of dualism, oft stated by Torrance, was put forward earlier by Gwatkin in the connection of the Arians to Origen in their conception of the δεύτερον θεὸν, or "second God."[70] Second, he rejected the Arian notion of thinking, which was not κατὰ φύσιν (*according to nature*) nor κατὰ διάνοιαν (*across from themselves to God*) but rather κατ' ἐπίνοιαν (*out of themselves*) and restored the proper of way of doing theology, reading the Bible, and using theological terms, allowing the σκοπός (*mark, goal, end*) to govern.[71] Third, for Torrance, Athanasius rejected the Stoic doctrine of λόγοι σπερματικοί (*spermatic words*).[72]

68. Torrance, *Theology in Reconciliation,* 251.

69. Harnack had already articulated the view that Athanasius distanced himself from Origen and some scholars, such as R. L. Wilkin, argue that Torrance assumes Harnack's reading of Athanasius and Origen. See Wilken, Review of *Divine Meaning* 744; Ernest, *The Bible in Athanasius of Alexandria,* 13.

70. Gwatkin, *Studies of Arianism,* 38. For an example of Origen's use of this concept see Origen, *Contra Celsus* 5.39 (PG 11.1244). Torrance does, however, offer a fairly positive appraisal of Origen in chapter 2 of *Trinitarian Faith.* See *The Trinitarian Faith,* 35–41.

71. Torrance, *Theology in Reconstruction,* 48; Torrance, *Preaching Christ Today,* 52. See also *Reality and Scientific Theology,* 5.

72. Torrance, *Theology in Reconciliation,* 217 citing Athanasius, *Contra Gentes*

Torrance perceives Athanasius as being a distinct thread of thought and theology. Indeed, he sees Athanasius as unique in respects to the culture around him and the general trend of extreme Alexandrian theology, and therein as the foundational thread of orthodox theology.[73] He sees two extreme camps in the early church, Antioch and Alexandria, which were the root of heretical tendencies, but the "middle stream," as Torrance sees it, was "Irenaeus to Athanasius to Cyril."[74] It is this stream that preserved orthodox Christology.[75] Elsewhere, Torrance emphasizes the "Athanasius-Cyril axis" as central for theological agreement and therein reunification between split denominations.[76]

Torrance also places Athanasius in the "Episcopal tradition," which stood alongside but was distinct from the "Catechetical School tradition" of Origen (c.185 C.E.–232 C.E.) and Clement of Alexandria (died c. 215 C.E.). Torrance locates Athanasius as falling in line with the tradition of "the Biblical-theological understanding of the Gospel" of Irenaeus of Lyons (c. 115/125 C.E.–130/142 C.E.), Melito of Sardis (died c. 180 C.E), Alexander (died c. 326 C.E.), Peter (died c. 311 C.E.), Dionysius of Alexandria (c. 190 C.E.–265 C.E.), and Demetrius (died c. 126 C.E.), all of whom were bound together by their common Hebraic/Biblical worldview.[77] Torrance distinguishes this from the traditional Alexandrian Catechetical school of Origen and Clement, especially in the realm of Biblical interpretation.[78] Torrance argues that what fastens all these theologians together is a specific theological methodology, a worldview; therefore, a distinct system of theology which arose.[79]

---

40 where Athanasius clarified concerning his view of the Word that he "spoke not of the seminal [word] (σπερματικόν), which is soulless, reasonless, and without intellect (ἄψυχον ὄντα καί μηδὲν λογιζόμενον μήτε νοοῦντα) but rather spoke of the living and powerful self-Word of the good God, the God of the universe (τὸν τοῦ ἀγαθοῦ καὶ θεοῦ τῶν ὅλων ζῶντα καὶ ἐνεργῆ θεὸν αὐτολόγον)." See PG 25b.80–81 for the full text.

73. See especially the chapter entitled "Athanasius: A Study in the Foundations of Classical Theology" in Torrance, *Theology in Reconciliation*, 215–66.

74. Torrance connects Irenaeus on a variety of levels. Chapter 3 of this book discussed the connection in "scientific theology." See further Torrance, *Incarnation*, 198. As an aside, Torrance did not adhere to the traditional distinction between Antiochene and Alexandrian theology (as mentioned in chapter 3 of this book). See Torrance, *Theology in Reconciliation*, 229.

75. Torrance, *Incarnation*, 198.

76. Torrance, *Theology in Reconciliation*, 9–10.

77. Ibid., 215.

78. Torrance, *Divine Meaning*, 229.

79. Cf. Newman's view of the episcopal tradition, which was similar. King argues this was exemplified by Newman in his early period. See Newman, *The Arians of the*

Combined with Athanasius' place in the Alexandrian Episcopal tradition is his adoption of Alexandrian scientific method. Torrance holds that Athanasius, following Origen and Clement of Alexandria, adapted the Alexandrian tradition of science into theology and followed the method of the Alexandrian scientific tradition, ἡ μέθοδος τῆς εὑρέσεως (*heuristic method*).[80] Therefore, Athanasius had an explicit method of Biblical interpretation and methodology, which in turn affected his entire theology.[81] Torrance maintains that Athanasius believed that theological language and terms are pointers to the reality they signified for a term "is essentially an operational term in which some image, idea or relation is taken from our this-worldly experience to point beyond itself to what is quite new and so to help us get some kind of grasp upon it."[82] In this sense terms are παράδειγμα (*models*) that point "beyond its creaturely form and content to the intended reality (πρὸς ἄλλο τι βλέποντα)," and they provide an "analogic account."[83]

Theologically, Torrance argues that Athanasian Triadology focuses on the wholeness of the Godhead and viewed each person of the Trinity "in terms of their coinherent and undivided wholeness, in which each person is 'whole of the whole.'"[84] Torrance believes this is rooted in Athanasius' method and starting point, namely the doctrine of ὁμοούσιον:

> Athanasius' approach to the doctrine of the Holy Trinity took its start and controlling norm from the revealing and saving acts of God in the 'incarnate παρουσία' of his only begotten Son in Jesus Christ, and moved through the ὁμοούσιος τῷ Πατρί to its ultimate ground in the eternal Godhead. The Nicene formulation gave exact expression to the supreme truth of the Gospel that God himself is the content of his revelation and that the Gift which God bestows upon us in his Grace is identical with himself the Giver of the Gift—the point to which Athanasius gave such attention in his doctrine of θεοποίησις.[85]

Fourth Century; Newman, *Lectures on the Prophetical Office*. See also King, *Newman and the Alexandrian Fathers*, 38–46

80. Torrance, *Theology in Reconciliation*, 216. This is a term that Torrance notices initially in Clement but sees as a part of the Alexandrian scientific-theological tradition in general. See Torrance, *Theology in Reconciliation, 241*.

81. Torrance, *Divine Meaning*, 235–37.

82. Torrance, *Space, Time and Incarnation*, 16.

83. See ibid., 16–17.

84. Torrance, *Trinitarian Faith*, 238 citing Athanasius, *Contra Arianos*, 1.16; 3.1ff; 4.1ff; *Ad Serapion*, 1.16, 26.

85. Ibid., 304–5.

Thus, Torrance views Athanasius as rooting his Triadology in the one-ness of the Godhead, rather than the threeness of the divine persons. This is why Torrance says: "Athanasius actually preferred to speak of God as Μονάς rather than as Ἀρχή, since his understanding of the Μονάς was essentially as the Τριάς."[86] For Torrance this came out the clearest in Athanasius' under-standing of the procession of the Spirit: ἐκ τῆς οὐσίας τοῦ Πατρός.[87] As such, Torrance sees Athanasius' Triadology, with the Son and Spirit rooted in the Father's οὐσια not in his ὑπόστασις.[88]

Athanasius did not hold centrality by himself according to Torrance, however, and Torrance connects Cyril to Athanasius as the "axis" of clas-sical theology.[89] In Torrance's mind Cyril of Alexandria (c. 376–444 C.E.) faithfully followed Athanasius in his Triadology. Torrance states: "Upon the Athanasian-Epiphanian basis classical Christian theology developed into its flowering in the great work of Cyril of Alexandria."[90] This is further evident for Torrance in the sense that Cyril strongly established that God to us is the same as God in himself.[91]

For this reason Torrance holds that Cyril believed the Spirit proceeds from the Father and the Son ("ἐκ Πατρός καὶ Υἱοῦ").[92] However, Torrance asserts that this does not mean Cyril held to the *filioque* but rather that he bypassed this doctrine entirely.[93] Torrance feels that Cyril and Athanasius together asserted that the Spirit, rather than proceeding from the person of the Father, proceeds from the being of the Father.[94] For Torrance, Cyril of

86. Ibid., 313.

87. Ibid., 236.

88. Gregg and Groh agree inasmuch as they believe Athanasius emphasized God's nature over God's will, both in creation and in the begetting of the Son (*Early Arianism*, 171–76). They see the Arian position, on the other hand, focusing on God's will and the voluntary aspect of creation and begetting (171–76). For Gregg and Groh, Athanasius' soteriology focused on union of God and man whereas the Arian's focus was on the imitation of Christ, the perfect disciple, by other disciples (161–83). Harnack's view of Arianism is also similar to Torrance's in some senses. Harnack considers Arius to have been a Neo-Platonist *par excellence* (see See Anatolios, *Athanasius*, 93–96). Further-more, Harnack sees Arianism as having arisen out of Antiochene theology (see Har-nack, *History of Dogma*, 4:3) and, more mildly, Origen (ibid., 4:20–21), a view similar to that of Newman as well (see Anatolios, *Athanasius*, 93–96). For Rowan Williams, on the other hand, Arius, rather than being an extreme Antiochene in theology, was more Alexandrian see ibid., 93–96).

89. Torrance, *Theology in Reconstruction*, xiv.

90. Torrance, *The Christian Doctrine of God*, 185.

91. Torrance, *Trinitarian Faith*, 339.

92. See ibid., 338–339 citing Cyril, *MPG* 75.577, 580f & 585; 575–617.

93. Ibid., 340.

94. Torrance, *The Christian Doctrine of God*, 192.

Alexandria was a faithful Athanasian in this sense. The way in which this is evident to Torrance is in Cyril's understanding of the Athanasian concepts of ἐνούσιος λόγος and ἐνούσιος ἐνέργια,[95] namely, that God's Word and God's activity are both intrinsic to the οὐσία of God.

EPIPHANIUS OF SALAMIS, DIDYMUS THE BLIND, GREGORY NAZIANZEN, AND HILARY OF POITIERS

Torrance connects Gregory Nazianzen (c. 329–390 C.E.), Epiphanius of Salamis (c. 310–403 C.E.), Didymus the Blind (c. 313–398 C.E.), and Hilary of Poitiers (c. 300–368 C.E.) to his Nicene stream of theology. Though others, such as Hanson,[96] and J. N. D. Kelly[97] note some similar connections, for example, Irenaeus, Didymus, and Epiphanius, Torrance's connection to Hilary is a fresh perspective.[98] These figures are connected on the basis of the Triadology that arose from their shared methodological and theological commitment. Torrance sees in this stream a focus on the dynamic nature of God's ὀυσία meaning emphasis on neither unity nor Trinity but unity in Trinity. Torrance garners this Triadological emphasis from an emphasis on the ὁμοούσιον which he sees in the Nicene stream. Torrance connects Cyril to Athanasius via the conception that the Spirit proceeds from the Father and the Son ("ἐκ Πατρός καὶ Υἱοῦ").[99]

Torrance considers Epiphanius of Salamis and Didymus the Blind to be within the *consensus* inasmuch as they followed the basic convictions surrounding the Athanasian-Cyrilline ὁμοούσιον. He connect them primarily through their view that the Son and the Spirit are ἐνυπόστατος (*substantiated/subjectified*) in God,[100] which he thinks preserve the dynamism of God's οὐσία. Torrance notes that Epiphanius spoke of the Son and the Spirit as ἐνυπόστατος in God, "that is, as having real, objective personal being in

95. Torrance, *Trinitarian Faith*, 72 citing *Theology in Reconciliation* 222f, 226ff, 235ff.

96. Hanson, *The Search for the Christian Doctrine of God*, 633–67.

97. Though Kelly also connects the Cappadocians. See Kelly, *Early Christian Doctrines*, 263–64. Kelly also connects Hilary to this group (269).

98. Though Hanson makes a similar connection (*The Search for the Christian Doctrine of God*, 459–507).

99. See Torrance, *The Trinitarian Faith*, 338–39 citing Cyril, *MPG* 75.577, 580f & 585; 575–617.

100. Ibid., 221 citing Epiphanius, *Anc.*, 5–10, 67, 72, 74, 81; *Haer.*, 57.4f, 62.1ff, 6, 65.1ff. See also *The Trinitarian Faith*, 210 citing Basil, *Epistle.*, 234.1; cf 235.2; 236.1ff; *Con. Eun.*, 2.32. See also *The Christian Doctrine of God*, 189. More on this below.

God and as coinhering hypostatically in him."[101] Furthermore, Torrance points out that Epiphanius spoke of the Holy Spirit as "ἐν μέσω (*in the midst*) of the Father and the Son" and as the "σύνδεσμος τῆς Τριάδος (*the bond of the Trinity*)."[102] The significance that Torrance sees in Epiphanius however lies primarily in the fact that he, like Gregory Nazianzen, understood the Son and the Spirit's "being of the Father and with the Father is beyond beginning and beyond time (ἀνάρχως καὶ ἀχρόνως)"[103] and, as such, not limiting the Μοναρχία to the person of the Father.[104] Indeed, Torrance understands Epiphanius to be Athanasian in that he held that the Spirit comes from the "inner being and life and light of the Holy Trinity."[105] Furthermore, he was Athanasian in that "he abhorred any partitive thinking of God either as he is in himself or as he is toward us."[106] Torrance holds that this was tied to Epiphanius' Spirit-rooted epistemology:

> We may know the Spirit of the Father and the Son only as he dwells in us and brings us into the communion of the Holy Trinity. That is to say, our approach to the doctrine of the Holy Spirit must be from his inner '*enhypostatic*' relation to the triune being of God.[107]

Torrance argues that Didymus, like Epiphanius, held to the concept of ἐνυπόστατος.[108] Thus Torrance understands Didymus to be arguing for a thread similar to that of Epiphanius and therein Athanasius. Torrance roots this in Didymus' view that God's actions to mankind are inherently connected to his being, for "Didymus was clearly critical of a distinction between the energies or operations of God and the immediate activity of his being, such as was put forward by Basil."[109] For Didymus, as for Epiphanius, the Holy Spirit is ἐνυπόστατος in God "in such a way that in him the Gift and the Giver are identical."[110] Torrance notes that while Didymus usually spoke

---

101. Torrance, *Trinitarian Faith*, 221 citing Epiphanius, *Anc.*, 5–10, 67, 72, 74, 81; *Haer.*, 57.4f, 62.1ff, 6, 65.1ff.

102. Ibid., 328; 222 citing Epiphanius *Anc.*, 4, 7f, 10; *Haer.* 62.4; 74.11.

103. Ibid., 222 citing Epiphanius, *Anc.*, 46; *Haer.* 57.4; 62.3; 69.36; 70.8, 73.36; 74.1; 76.6, 21.

104. Ibid., 329.

105. Ibid., 222.

106. Ibid.

107. Ibid., 208 citing Epiphanius, *Haer.*, 57.4f; 62.1f, 6; 74.9ff; 72.22; *Anc.*, 5, 10f, 67f, 72, 81.

108. Ibid., 223 citing Didymus, *De Trinitatae*, 1.16, 26; 26; 2, 1ff, 8, 10; 3.19, 37.

109. Ibid., 210 citing Basil, *Epistle.*, 234.1; cf 235.2; 236.1ff; *Con. Eun.*, 2.32.

110. Ibid., 324 citing Didymus, *De Trinitatae*, 2.1–3; *De Sp. St.*, 3ff, 16–25; 32–40,

of the Spirit as proceeding ἐκ τῆς ὑπόστασεως of the Father, he also spoke of the Spirit as proceeding ἐκ τῆς ὑπόστασεως of the Son[111] but, Torrance argues, despite that fact that Didymus here diverged from the Athanasian ἐκ τῆς οὐσίας τοῦ Πατρός he qualified it by stating that this is to be understood according to the oneness of the Godhead and that Didymus even combined the two concepts.[112]

When Torrance looks to Gregory Nazianzen he sees a theologian who was much closer to Athanasius than Basil and Gregory of Nyssa. In Torrance's words:

> Gregory Nazianzen was clearly rather worried about the element of Origenist subordinationism that had cropped up in the Cappadocian doctrine of the Holy Trinity in which he shared with the others in speaking of the Father as 'greater' than the Son and the Spirit, while nevertheless trying to do justice to the unity and equality of the three divine persons.[113]

Torrance holds that Gregory tried to get around Basil's method by using Athanasian language[114] and that starting point was the ὁμοούσιον, as it was with Athanasius.[115] As such, Torrance sees Gregory Nazianzen as following in this stream of thought more than his fellow Cappadocians.[116] Torrance argues that the Council of Constantinople (381 C.E.), though without doubt indebted to the Cappadocians, was actually more Athanasian in its content inasmuch as it asserted that the Son and the Spirit proceed from the Father's οὐσια, rather than ὑπόστασις.[117] Here, Torrance argues that Gregory of Nazianzus was not pleased with the Council of Constantinople I in 381 C.E. and played a role in the creedal language of "from the Father," which Torrance sees as not meaning "from the ὑπόστασις of the Father," but rather "from the οὐσία of the Father."[118] Torrance interprets Gregory as a *via media* between Basil and Athanasius; whose views implied an Athanasian way of viewing the Trinity, asserting that Gregory upheld the unity of God on the

---

57–61. See also Torrance, *Trinitarian Faith,* 326. See also Torrance, *Trinitarian Faith,* 199.

   111. Ibid., citing Didymus, *De Trinitatae,* 1.15, 18, 26, 36; 2.1ff, 5; 3.3, 5, 38; *De Sp. St.,* 26, 37.

   112. Ibid., 325 citing Didymus, *De Trinitatae,* 2.2; 2.5.

   113. Ibid., 320.

   114. Ibid., 316.

   115. Ibid., 320.

   116. Torrance, *The Christian Doctrine of God,* 112–13.

   117. Ibid., 182. More on this below.

   118. Torrance, *Trinitarian Faith,* 245–46.

basis of the ἀρχή of the Father, but with an important nuance, the ἀρχή and αἰτία are causes and relations happening beyond time and eternally.[119] Torrance understands this as a divergence from the traditional Cappadocian view, as propagated by Basil. Indeed, for Torrance this is more along the lines of Athanasius' focus on the οὐσία and starting from the ὁμοούσιον.

Torrance also includes Hilary in this stream. Torrance connects Hilary to the Nicene and Athanasian stream in a variety of aspects in addition to the objectivity of theology discussed in the previous chapter. First, Torrance sees Hilary as a propagator of the Irenaean view that God can only be known through himself.[120] In Torrance's mind this is a necessary epistemological and theological assertion and was a primary reason why Athanasius felt inclined to define the Nicene doctrine of ὁμοούσιον τῷ Πατρί. Another connection Torrance makes is via Augustine. Torrance asserts that Calvin adopted the Triadology of Augustine, who despite a lack of knowledge of the Greek language, was steeped in Greek patristic theology because of the influence of Hilary on his theology.[121] Thus, according to Torrance, Hilary acted as a conduit bringing Greek patristic theology to the west.

THE CAPPADOCIAN DISTINCTION

Torrance does not return to the Greek Fathers without distinction, however. He finds a divergence from the *consensus* in certain aspects of the Cappadocian tradition; a divergence Torrance sees magnified in the later Byzantine and Eastern Orthodox tradition. Any divergence, however, means for Torrance a subtraction from the patristic assertion that because of the ὁμοούσιον humankind has knowledge of God in himself and is truly united to God and saved. In general, Torrance sees these divergences as falling into some sort of theological dualism which cuts off knowledge of and union with God in himself and thus is unfaithful to the meaning of the Nicene ὁμοούσιον.

Torrance's main problem with the Cappadocians concerns their emphasis on οὐσία as general and ὑπόστασις as particular in God and their securing of the monarchy of the Trinity in the ὑπόστασις. The problem is that this implies some level of subordination in the Trinity, according to Torrance. Torrance additionally takes issue with what he sees as inherent theological dualism imbedded in the move. For Torrance this move severs God's economy from God's ontology, which would imply that humankind

119. Ibid., 239.

120. Torrance, *The Christian Doctrine of God*, 10. See also Torrance, *Theological Science*, 20 for Hilary's view of terminology.

121. Torrance, *Trinitarian Perspectives*, 22.

cannot really know God as he is in himself and cannot really be united to God; two assertions that are for Torrance core assertions of orthodoxy and the patristic tradition flowing from the inner meaning of the ὁμοούσιον. Torrance states:

> The Cappadocian redefinition of *ousia* as a generic concept, with the loss of its concrete sense as being with internal relations, meant that it would be difficult if not impossible for faith to move from the Self-revelation of God in his evangelical acts to what he is inherently *in-himself*.[122]

Elsewhere, he states:

> What is at stake here is the need not to surrender the Transcendence and ultimate incomprehensibility of God's eternal Being, and the need to affirm the oneness between the so-called 'economic Trinity' and the 'immanent Trinity,' what Eastern theology speaks of as the relation between the 'divine essence' and the 'divine energies.'[123]

It is important to note Torrance does not amalgamate the Cappadocians here.[124] Torrance does see important nuances between each of the Cappadocians. Torrance appreciated many elements of Basil's Pneumatology[125] and notes overlap between Basil and Athanasius on Pneumatology.[126] Torrance argues that Basil did in fact agree with the Athanasian concept of coinherence, however, he believes that Basil's view is distinct from Athanasius inasmuch as he equated οὐσία with φύσις, taking away its dynamic meaning and giving it a more abstract one.[127]

Torrance argues that in their rooting of the unity of God in the ἀρχή and αἰτία, though, the Cappadocians understood the Son and the Spirit to be eternally caused without any separation between cause and effect.[128] Torrance notes that Athanasius and Dionysius of Alexandria had earlier propagated a similar idea. However, the difference is that the Cappadocians'

---

122. Torrance, *Theological Dialogue*, 2:32.

123. Ibid., 2:119.

124. Indeed Torrance cites Basil frequently and refers to him positively often throughout *Trinitarian Faith*; *Theology in Reconciliation*; and *Theology in Reconstruction*.

125. Torrance, *Trinitarian Faith*, 218.

126. Torrance, *Theology in Reconstruction*, 217. Though, there was development in Torrance's view on this point. See below.

127. Torrance, *Trinitarian Faith*, 316–17. Athanasius held to a more dynamic view of οὐσία according to Torrance.

128. Ibid., 317 citing Gregory/Basil, *Contra Eunomius*, 1.25; 2.12; 3.1; *Homily* 24.4.

generic view of οὐσία led them "to say that the Son and the Spirit owe their being (τό εἶναι) to the *Person* (ὑπόστασις) or (πρόσοπον) of the Father."[129] Thus for Basil the Spirit proceeds from the ὑπόστασις τοῦ Πατρός rather than ἐκ τῆς οὐσίας τοῦ Πατρός as for Athanasius and Cyril. Indeed, in Torrance's words, "the main thrust of the Cappadocian teaching . . . was to make the first Person of the Trinity or the ὑπόστασις of the Father the sole Principle or Cause or Source of Deity (ἀρχή, αἰτια, πηγή Θεότητος)."[130]

Torrance takes issue with the fact that the Cappadocians distinguished between οὐσια as a generic and ὑπόστασις as particular because this changed the earlier approach from "ὁμοούσιον as the key to the identity of the Holy Trinity, to an emphasis on the ὑποστάσεις."[131] Torrance also critiques the Cappadocian view that the Father is the sole ἀρχη, αἰτία, or πηγή Θεότητος. For, he argues, Athanasius held that this concept was actually Arian.[132] Torrance argues that the Athanasian concept of the Son as "ὅλος Θεός" necessarily implies that the Son, and not solely the Father, must be ἀρχή of the Trinity.[133] However, Torrance's main issue with the Cappadocian development in Triadological terminology is, if they were right, it would be impossible to know God in himself, which would be a direct contradiction to the ὁμοούσιον.[134]

Torrance understands this distinction from Athanasius to be rooted in Basil's difference in approach, namely from Origenistic "spiritual and moral convictions" as opposed to the Athanasian soteriological and ontological approach.[135] Basil's basic approach, then, contrasts with that of Athanasius for Torrance holds that Athanasius believed the Son and Spirit both come forth ἐκ τῆς οὐσίας τοῦ Πατρός.

According to Torrance, the "Cappadocian distinction" opened the door to a trajectory that divided the essence and energies of God. This trajectory, argues Torrance citing Didymus, damages the reality of God's immediate

---

129. Ibid., 318.

130. Ibid., 241.

131. Ibid., 241.

132. Ibid., 241 citing Athanasius, *De Synodis,* 16.

133. Ibid., 80 citing Athanasius, *Contra Arianos,* 3.6; 4.1. Torrance puts it: "The Cappadocian's attempt to redefine οὐσια as a generic concept, with the loss of its concrete sense as being with internal relations, meant that it would be difficult if not impossible for theology to move from the self-revelation of God in his evangelical acts to what he is inherently *in-himself.* If God's Word and act are not inherent (ἐνούσιοι) in his being or οὐσια, as Athanasius insisted, then we cannot relate what God is toward us in his saving revelation and activity to what he is *in-himself,* or vice versa."

134. Ibid., 246.

135. Ibid., 313.

presence with humankind.[136] It is a basic theological dualism that Torrance sees in much of later Byzantine and Eastern Orthodox theology; in reaction to this Torrance wants to preserve a more Athanasian conception.

Notably, there is certain development in Torrance's view of the Cappadocians. Whilst in the 1960s Torrance voices hesitation about the ascetical slant of Basil's pneumatology,[137] at this early stage Torrance does not discuss what would become his emphasis on the procession of the Holy Spirit from the οὐσια of the Father nor does he mention the "Cappadocian distinction" as such. In the following decade Torrance begins to discuss what he sees as a division between God's essence and energies in the Cappadocian Fathers and later Byzantine theology, particularly John of Damascus,[138] but it is only by the 1980s that Torrance's critique of the Cappadocian distinction emerges in its full force. There are a plethora of reasons why Torrance's view may have developed as such. Most likely it is perhaps because Torrance's aversion to the Cappadocian distinction is really more about the 1980s than the 380s. By the time of the publication of *Trinitarian Faith* Torrance was deep in an ongoing heated debate with his former assistant at New College, John Zizioulas, who is now the Metropolitan of Pergamon. Zizioulas believes that in order to preserve God's freedom to be, God's being must be rooted in a specific person, which he sees as occurring in the person of the Father[139] and Zizioulas accordingly insists upon the Father as ἀρχή of the Son and the Spirit (otherwise, for Zizioulas, God would not have freedom to be). Zizioulas takes serious issue with any theology that views God's being in the abstract and moving to his persons. For Zizioulas, Torrance's view of God's being as dynamic does not get around the problem of an impersonal being of God; rather this exacerbates the problem making relations the primary being.[140]

Other Orthodox scholars, such as Lossky, see the procession of the Spirit from the person of the Father as a core theological assertion found in incipient forms in Athanasius.[141] Meyendorff, for example, traces this view back to Athanasius as well, holding that Athanasius believed in a sharp distinction between essence and energy in God. In Meyendorff's words:

> The notion of creation, as expressed by Athanasius, leads to a distinction in God between his transcendent essence and his

136. Ibid., 210.

137. Torrance, *Theology in Reconstruction*, 219, 224.

138. Torrance, *Theology in Reconciliation*, 252.

139. Zizioulas, *Being as Communion*, 33–49, especially 34.

140. Zizioulas, *Communion and Otherness*, 134–37, especially 134 and 136.

141. Lossky, *The Mystical Theology of the Eastern Church*, 57–58, 62.

properties such as "power" or "goodness," which expresses his
existence and action *ad extra*, not his essence.[142]

Meyendorff explicates the division of essence and energies, a view that what
would later be called "Palamism," is in fact precisely the theology Athanasius espoused concerning the distinction between γεννάω (*begetting*) and
γενάω (*creating*).[143] Thus, Torrance's oft quoted Athanasian phrase "it would
be more pious (εὐσεβέτερον) and true (ἀλεθὲς) to signify (σημμαίνειν) God
from the Son (ἐκ τοῦ Ὑιοῦ) and call him Father, than to name (ὀνομάζειν)
God from his works alone and call him unoriginate (ἀγένητον)"[144] was
used by Meyendorff to portray Athanasius' distinction between ὀυσία and
ἐνέργεια (*energy*). Meyendorff sees this distinction as being especially important in the context of deification.[145] Thus, Palamas' formulation of what
Meyendorff holds to be an Athanasian distinction of the three elements of
God: essence, energy, and the three hypostases.[146]

For Torrance, to assert with Zizioulas et al. the procession of the Spirit
from the person of the Father is to cut behind the economic and immanent
Trinity. Torrance does not, however, hold that Athanasius spoke explicitly
about the procession of the Spirit. However, the implications of Zizioulas,
Gregory Palamas, and the Cappadocians on this implies a denial of the trajectory of Athanasius' theology and, even more so, the Nicene ὁμοούσιον as
Torrance sees it. Torrance does not critique Zizioulas explicitly in his many
writings.[147] However, by reading in between the lines it is clear that Tor-

142. Meyendorff, *Byzantine Theology*, 130.

143. Ibid., 131–32.

144. Torrance, *The Trinitarian Faith*, 49 citing Athanasius, *Contra Arianos* I.34 and
referencing *Contra Arianos*, I.16, 33; *De Dectretis*, 31, and Hilary *De Trinitate*, I.17;
3.22; 2.6–8.

145. Meyendorff, *Byzantine Theology*, 186.

146. Ibid., 186 citing PG, 151.1173B. See also Meyendorff, *Byzantine Theology*, 187
for further elaboration on the Palamite viewpoint of a threefold distinction between
energy, hypostases, and essence. However, see the section on the "Byzantine trajectory" in this chapter and also further comment on this in the concluding section of this
chapter: this Palamite threefold tier in God does not necessarily mean what its critics
(even Torrance) think.

147. Despite deep theological disagreement, Torrance seems to have respected
Zizioulas as a theologian. In correspondence Torrance states of Zizioulas: "Some of us
may have differences over the way in which he interprets The Fathers in the doctrine of
the Holy Trinity but any disagreement is one that is matched with great respect for his
outstanding theological ability and the unusual freshness of his mind which had such
a stimulating effect upon his students and academic colleagues in Scotland." See The
Thomas F. Torrance Manuscript Collection. Special Collections, Princeton Theological
Seminary Library. Box 172. Though, there was much controversy "behind the scenes."
See a draft of a letter later sent His All-Holiness Demetrius I, Ecumenical Patriarch

rance's critique of the "Cappadocian distinction" is rather a wholehearted critique of John Zizioulas' reading of the Cappadocians.[148] Thus, when Torrance presents the "Cappadocians vs. Athanasius" he reveals a significant amount about the debate which was going on between Torrance and Zizioulas; the amount it actually reveals about the fourth century is less certain; as such, perhaps "the Cappadocians vs. Athanasius" might be better delineated "John Zizioulas vs. T. F. Torrance."

At least, the Cappadocian and Athanasian/Nicene streams are unlikely to be as clear-cut as Torrance presents them. Perhaps here, as Morrison argues, Torrance falls too much into the "good guys/bad guys schematization."[149] Many scholars, though perhaps not as strongly as the Metropolitan of Pergamon himself, hold to Zizioulas' viewpoint that the Cappadocians were faithful Athanasians. For example, Meijering holds a connected viewpoint and believes that Athanasius held that the Father was the origin of the Son, in ὑπόστασις not in οὐσια.[150] Additionally, J. N. D. Kelly holds that the notion of general and particular, which Torrance sees in the Cappadocians and not Athanasius, was present in both camps of theology.[151] Lossky also holds that the ἀρχή of the Trinity is located in the ὑπόστασις of the Father[152] and sees the general/particular distinction to have come from Athanasius.[153] Here, some also accuse Torrance of assuming Harnackian patrology to a certain extent.[154] Harnack and other Protestant, mostly Ger-

---

written in 1988, where Torrance states: "It was I who brought John Zizioulas to Edinburgh and thus introduced him to our Church and theological life in Great Britain, and have supported him in every way I could. However, when, due I presume to his rather existentialising interpretation of the Greek Fathers, he came to put forward the idea that it is the Person of the Father who is the source of the Divine Being, I felt I could not support him as a proper representative of Orthodox Theology." See The Thomas F. Torrance Manuscript Collection. Special Collections, Princeton Theological Seminary Library. Box 170 for this and further critique of Zizioulas.

148. Torrance's nephew, Alan Torrance, takes up elements of Torrance's argument and engages Zizioulas directly. See Alan Torrance, *Persons in Communion*.

149. Morrison, Review of *The Trinitarian Faith* 119.

150. Meijering, *God Being History*, 95–99.

151. Kelly, *Early Christian Doctrines*, 265.

152. Lossky, *The Mystical Theology of the Eastern Church*, 57–58, 62.

153. Ibid., 51.

154. "Harnack read through Hanson." See Wilken, Review of *Divine Meaning* 744; Ernest, *The Bible in Athanasius of Alexandria*, 13. See also Baker, "The Place of St. Irenaeus," 43. Though, as Baker notes, it is "unacknowledged" by Torrance. The main problem with the accusation put forward by Torrance's critics that he assumes the Harnack thesis, though it does have some merit (i.e., Torrance's reading of Athanasius and the Cappadocians does look something like Harnack's reading), is that Torrance's texts provide no basis for this. Torrance nowhere cites Harnack in his distinction between

man liberal, scholars, contended for a view of the fourth century consisting of the "Old Nicenes" and "New Nicenes"[155] that was, to use Parvis' words, "ineluctably Hegelian."[156] The Old Nicenes emphasized the fluidity of theological terms and focused on God's presence with humankind. The New Nicenes became more theologically rigid and dogmatic. Protestants tend to see themselves arising from the Old Nicenes who were more in tune with the West in their doctrine of the Trinity. Though this view was once a widely accepted scholarly consensus, this is no longer the case and most contend that the fourth century was significantly less simply categorized than this. Most patrological scholarship today considers the Harnackian "Old Nicene vs. New Nicene" division as far too simplistic. Indeed, many not hailing from the Eastern Orthodox tradition conceive of the Cappadocians as faithful Athanasians.[157] The current trend tends to depart from these categories and view Nicene theology in a more synthetic fashion that Torrance's distinctions.[158]

---

the Cappadocian stream and the Nicene/Athanasian stream. Therefore, Torrance's distinction between Athanasius and the Cappadocians may sound like Harnack but there is no empirical textual evidence to point to the possibility that Torrance reached his conclusions on the basis of Harnack; indeed the two do have substantial differences. Torrance, for example, never accuses the Cappadocians of Arianism and he sees significant differences among the Cappadocians themselves. The only existing evidence points to the fact that Torrance arrives at his conclusions on the basis of an indwelling of the primary texts. Once again, his reading of Athanasius and the Cappadocians consists of a reconstruction of their theology around the Nicene doctrine of ὁμοούσιον and thus it is through this that he arrives at his Cappadocian/Athanasius division. His problem with the Cappadocian distinction, then, is substantially different from Harnack's. For, as argued, Torrance's problem is that the Cappadocians, though orthodox, strayed from the inner meaning of the ὁμοούσιον. Therefore, Torrance's view merits some consideration. Indeed, Torrance's severing of Athanasius from the Cappadocians may very well have allowed him to see the Alexandrian saint in a fresh perspective.

155. Harnack, *History of Dogma*, 4:80–107.

156. Parvis, *Marcellus of Ancyra*, 3. Parvis argues that this view was prevalent across 20th century patristic scholarship, however it still affects readings today inasmuch as figures such as Marcellus are brushed over in the focus on Athanasius and Arius (3–5).

157. For example, Kelly, *Early Christian Doctrines*, 263–65. However, there are also some who are similar to Torrance. See e.g., Behr, *The Nicene Faith*, 1:27–28. Behr contends Harnack's conception too simplistic and the Cappadocians were not subordinationist but that there is merit to his distinction between the two camps.

158. See e.g., Ayres, *Nicaea and Its Legacy*; Anatolios, *Retrieving Nicaea*. Ayres says "recent Trinitarian thought has engaged the legacy of Nicaea at the fairly shallow level frequently relying on assumptions about Nicene theology that are historically indefensible and overlooking the wider theological matrices within which particular theologians are situated" (*Nicaea and Its Legacy*, 1).

THE BYZANTINE TRAJECTORY

Torrance argues that the Cappadocian distinction developed into the Byzantine trajectory and sees elements of Basil's pneumatology opening the door to a trajectory later taken up by Byzantine theologians and modern Eastern Orthodox theology, namely, the distinction between God's essence and energies.[159] According to Torrance's reading, the Cappadocians developed the "one οὐσία, three ὑπόστασεις" conception of the Trinity, which he sees as a positive development. However, because of the subsequent charge of tri-theism they developed the concept of the ὑπόστασις of the Father as the ἀρχή of the Trinity; Torrance sees this, however, as a non-Athanasian development taking away from the Spirit as God's full presence to humankind.[160] Torrance argues that the Cappadocian Fathers' emphasis on the distinction between essence and energies in God paved the way for Gregory Palamas to separate God's being and God's acts and thereby making God unknowable in himself in some form of dualism.[161]

Torrance argues that the Cappadocian-Palamite essence/energies distinction is inherently dualist and un-Athanasian. However, many scholars, such as Georges Florovsky, who portray Athanasius as asserting this distinction, read Athanasius as propagating the essence and energies distinction.[162]

159. See Torrance, *Trinitarian Faith*, 38–39, especially footnote 69 on p. 38. Torrance is highly critical of the way in which Maximus the Confessor, John of Damascus, and Gregory Palamas used the essence/energies distinction. Torrance argues that they were influenced by Pseudo-Dionysius' extreme apophaticism. See also *Theology in Reconciliation*, 252 for his critique of John of Damascus in a similar vein.

160. Torrance, *Trinitarian Faith*, 236–39.

161. See *Theological Dialogue*, 1:13–14. Cf. Dorothea Wendebourg's famous paper delivered in the 1980s at the Oxford Patristics Conference entitled "From the Cappadocian Fathers to Gregory Palamas: The Defeat of Trinitarian Theology," (published in *Studia Patristica* 17/1) whose critique is substantially similar. Wendebourg argues that the Cappadocian Fathers' emphasis on the distinction between essence and energies in God paved the way for Gregory Palamas to undo Trinitarian theology by conceiving of three tiers in God: his οὐσία, ὑπόστασεις, and ἐνέργεια and basically make God unknowable in himself. For Palamas, argues Wendebourg, God's activity in the world is only with his energies and thusly neither his ὑπόστασεις nor his οὐσία are touched at all by the world, ultimately putting up a wall between God's economy and ontology. Wendebourg argues that the Cappadocian Fathers' emphasis on the distinction between essence and energies in God paved the way for Gregory Palamas to essentially undo Trinitarian theology by conceiving of three tiers in God: οὐσία, ὑποσάστεις, and ἐνέργεια, thereby making God unknowable in himself.

162. See Florovsky, *Creation and Redemption*, 43–78. The argument typically runs that Athanasius' distinction between nature and will in God was a distinction between essence and energies.

In contrast, Torrance depicts Athanasius and Palamas as intrinsically op-posed to one another in basic theology on this point.[163]

Matthew Baker, an Eastern Orthodox scholar appreciative of Tor-rance, contends that Torrance's critique is really more of Lossky and other twentieth-century readings[164] of Gregory Palamas than of Palamas himself, suggesting Palamas might fair better if approached today.[165] The school of Romanides and Lossky indeed make a very strong distinction between God's essence and God's energies in their efforts at defending a strict apo-phaticism, following Pseudo-Dionysius. Vladimir Lossky, for example, con-tends "eastern theology always distinguishes between the gift and the Giver, between uncreated grace and the Person of the Holy Spirit who communi-cates it."[166] According to Lossky, Palamas' understanding is that in prayer the Christian is united to God's uncreated energies, but these energies are not a part of God as he is in himself.

According to recent readings[167] of Gregory Palamas, following the interpretation of John Meyendorff, for Palamas, God interacts with the world personally.[168] This reading, while still holding to the three-tiered view, holds that "the divine energies are given to us in a hypostatic, i.e., personal, form."[169] As Meyendorff states:

> The distinction between "essence" and "energy"—that focal point of Palamite theology—is nothing but a way of saying that

163. Torrance, *Theological Dialogue*, 1:11. In the Reformed-Orthodox Dialogue the Orthodox suggest that Torrance over-absolutizes Athanasius against the Cappadocians. See the Minutes in The Thomas F. Torrance Manuscript Collection. Special Collec-tions, Princeton Theological Seminary Library. Box 170. Perhaps Torrance's view was influenced by an untitled manuscript he preserved in his personal collection. See The Thomas F. Torrance Manuscript Collection. Special Collections, Princeton Theological Seminary Library. Box 198. The author argues that Palamas replaced the Athanasian emphasis on salvation via Christ's (vicarious) humanity with salvation via God's uncre-ated energies. Given this version of Palamism, of course Torrance would have problems.

164. Lossky, *The Mystical Theology of the Eastern Church*; Romanides, *Outline of Patristic Dogmatics*.

165. Baker, "The Place of St. Irenaeus," 42. This was also the critique of John Ziziou-las. See Zizioulas, *Communion and Otherness*, 139. He is highly critical of this reading as proffered by Wendebourg.

166. Lossky, *The Mystical Theology of the Eastern Church*, 213.

167. See e.g., Rossum, "Creation-Theology," 373–78.

168. Following his groundbreaking study: Meyendorff, *Introduction A l'étude de Grégoire Palamas*. See especially 195–256 and 279–310.

169. Zizioulas, *Communion and Otherness*, 139.

the transcendent God remains transcendent, as He also com-
municates Himself to humanity.[170]

If this were indeed the case, Torrance would surely have nothing with which
to disagree. One wonders what Torrance might have concluded himself had
he indwelt Palamas to the same extent as Athanasius and Cyril. There is no
textual evidence that he studied these later Fathers as closely as the earlier
ones.[171] Torrance does not often deal directly with Maximus or Palamas;
he simply argues that the Cappadocian distinction opened the door for the
Byzantine trajectory, which he sees in the Orthodox theology of his day.
Perhaps he would have less of a problem with the Byzantine theology of
this newer interpretation. Granted the prevailing viewpoint in Torrance's
time was that of Lossky and Romanides, the critique of Wendebourg and
Torrance was absolutely valid (i.e., of the prevailing interpretation of his
time). Thus, based on the current way in which the Byzantine trajectory
had manifested itself, Torrance, on the basis of his patristic reconstruction,
realizes the dualist elements and was appropriately apprehensive about the
Cappadocian-Byzantine dualist leanings.[172]

In light of recent scholarship, it seems likely that Torrance might
have found in Gregory Palamas a support for many of his key viewpoints.
According to the current readings, for Palamas, God's uncreated energies
are personal and to be viewed Christocentrically; without the sharp distinction often attributed to them.[173] Notably, in his defense of the essence/

170. See Meyendorff, "Introduction," 20.

171. He may have actually done so but his publications leave no indication of an
indwelling of Byzantine sources to the same extent he indwelt patristic sources from
fourth century. Rather, his interaction with John of Damascus, Maximus the Confessor,
and Gregory Palamas et al. usually consists of fairly general critiques. Torrance does
not refer to them more than a handful of times in either *Trinitarian Faith* or *Christian
Doctrine of God*. Rather, Torrance's interaction with them is primarily in his ecumenical
work (e.g., published texts such as *Trinitarian Perspectives* and *Theological Dialogue 1 &
2*. The Byzantine tradition and Gregory Palamas in particular do not receive the careful and detailed study that Torrance affords Athanasius, the Cappadocians, and, more
generally, the Nicene tradition.

172. In the Reformed-Orthodox Dialogue Torrance does suggest that he is mostly
apprehensive about Lossky's reading of Palamas (i.e., perhaps not necessarily apprehensive about Palamas himself). See Minutes from the Orthodox Reformed Consultation,
Orthodox Centre of the Ecumenical Patriarchate, Chambesy, Geneva, 6–11, March
1983 in The Thomas F. Torrance Manuscript Collection. Special Collections, Princeton
Theological Seminary Library. Box 170.

173. Palamas uses the example of geometry to show that the distinction of energies is purely linguistic and semantic. He says God's energies are "indivisibly divisible"
(ἀδιαιρέτως διαιρεῖται) and "united divisibly" (συνάπτεται διῃρημένως). See Gregory
Palamas, *The One Hundred and Fifty Chapters* in Sinkewicz, *Saint Gregory Palamas*.

energies distinction, Palamas was countering natural theology much like Torrance.[174] Palamas' insistence on knowledge of God and union with God via the divine energies is an insistence upon the divine initiative in salvation and revelation and it was an attempt to objectively root knowledge of God and Christocentrically root salvation. Throughout his writings he asserts God's full and personal presence in each of the energies[175] as well as the Christocentric[176] and enhypostatic nature of the energies.[177]

Perhaps if Palamas is accorded a place in future evangelical approaches to The Fathers following Torrance, much fruit can be harvested from a grace-centered and Christocentric reading of this Byzantine saint and the later Byzantine tradition. Meyendorff's reading of Palamas in addition to that of the new school of Palamism would certainly suggest this.[178]

See chapter 81. Palamas applies this to the essence/energies distinction as well and calls the division indivisible. See chapters 68–84. Thus, Torrance's issue with the division of essence from energies could be turned back on him: How can Torrance talk about God's being and God's acts separately? How can Torrance talk about Christ's person and Christ's work separately? This and the previous chapter have explored that Torrance does indeed do this, however he argues that the two are intrinsically connected. Likewise with Palamas' distinction: he discusses the two separately but this is simply a rhetorical tool. The two are ontologically connected but semantically distinguished.

174. Gregory Palamas, *Defense of those who practice hesychasm*, II.3.68. See Meyendorff, *Grégoire Palamas* for the critical edition of this text (future references are to this edition) and Palamas, *Gregory Palamas: The Triads*, for an English translation of a selection from Meyendorff's critical edition. See also Gregory Palamas, *The One Hundred and Fifty Chapters* in Sinkewicz, *Saint Gregory Palamas*, 26–29.

175. Palamas, *Defense of those who practice hesychasm*, III.2.7: "Ἀλλὰ καὶ ὡς ὅλον ἐν ἑκάστῃ ὄντα τῶν θεοπρεπῶν ἐνεργειῶν, ἀφ᾽ ἑκάστης ὀνομάζομεν αὐτόν, ἀφ᾽ οὗ διαδείκθται καὶ τὸ πασῶν τούτων ὑπερεξῃπῆσθαι." Palamas argues that the energies cannot be divided from one another; each is in each and the whole of the divine energies is in each. Palamas furthermore argues that the energies must be God; otherwise God is not simple but composite. See *The One Hundred and Fifty Chapters* in Sinkewicz, *Saint Gregory Palamas*, 109ff. Accordingly, Palamas' essence/energies could very well be interpreted as defending the very thing Torrance aims to preserve with the ὁμοούσιον, namely, the strong connection of the immanent and economic Trinity and the fact that God's being is fully present in God's acts.

176. E.g., Palamas, *Defense of those who practice hesychasm*, III.1.35.

177. E.g., Palamas speaks of the enhypostatic (ἐνυποστάτως) light, i.e., the light which is really substantiated (has a real existence). Palamas, *Defense of those who practice hesychasm*, II.3.8. See also III.1.9. Palamas is not talking about the hypostases of the Trinity here, however. See further Palamas, *Gregory Palamas: The Triads*, 131 n. 2. However, the implication is that each is substantiated in God's being.

178. Palamas himself discusses *theosis* effected by grace. See e.g., *Defense of those who practice hesychasm*, III.1.27.

CONCLUSION

This chapter has explored how Torrance creatively reconstructs the patristic tradition into a Reformed and evangelical version of the *Consensus Patrum*. By means of his connection of the Greek Fathers to the Reformed evangelical tradition found in Calvin and Barth, Torrance reconstructs the *consensus* into a golden thread running throughout theological history, the "evangelical stream." In Torrance's return to the Greek patristic tradition, he departs from the Augustinian tradition and is critical of the Cappadocian and Byzantine tradition, all for their supposed inherent dualism.

Herein Torrance appropriates The Fathers into his own context in a highly creative fashion. His connection of Athanasius to Calvin and Barth and, more generally, his connection of The Fathers to Reformed theology are all very creative. Torrance's most original connections are indeed between the Greek Fathers and the Reformed tradition, particularly Barth, whom Torrance sees as the true heir of the Greek Fathers. Torrance's vision of "streams," particularly his vision of the evangelical stream running through the church's history, is highly imaginative. It is to these aspects that modern theology is indebted to Torrance and this part of his thought that must be considered if contemporary scholarship is to gain a grasp on Torrance's unique contribution to patristic scholarship. He creates a plausible narrative of church history which offers a view of the evangelical tradition as inheriting the Greek patristic tradition.

Furthermore, Torrance's reconstruction of The Fathers into "streams" or "threads" is an exciting and creative reconstructive of the patristic era. This reconstruction shows Torrance's unique approach to The Fathers and highlights, in part, his genius. His reconstruction of The Fathers into these streams of thought, as argued above, offers a plausible and helpful template for Reformed evangelical theologians wishing to utilize the theology of the patristic era.

Torrance's emphasis on the first four councils, Nicaea, and the fourth century is, however, in many regards typically Protestant and Reformed. Flovosky critiques modern readings of The Fathers for containing an overemphasis on the first five centuries of patristic theology and therefore a failure to look at the theology of Maximus the Confessor.[179] Matthew Baker rightly points out that Torrance rarely cites any patristic figure after Cyril of Alexandria other than Severus of Antioch and John Philoponus.[180] Indeed, for Torrance, while theoretically open to more, practically classical ortho-

---

179. Florovsky, *Bible, Church, Tradition*, 111.
180. Baker, "The Place of St. Irenaeus," 25.

doxy ended with Cyril of Alexandria. For Florovsky (and others from the Eastern Orthodox tradition), Athanasius should be read alongside Maximus and the other Fathers.[181] Thus, for Florovsky it is hermeneutically possible to read Athanasius through the later Fathers; indeed, the *consensus* must be read in this way. Torrance's *Consensus Patrum* is, therefore, highly selective and very Protestant in contrast with Florovsky and the Eastern Orthodox whose entire reading causes them to draw different connections and conclusions than Torrance regarding the fourth century.[182] Chapter 1 discussed Georges Florovsky's assessment that Protestantism has generally assumed a "process of decay" regarding the tradition. However, chapter 1 also argued that Florovsky's critique is somewhat of a generalization and could not be applied toward the Reformed approach to which Torrance adheres. Though Torrance does assume the "golden age" notion of Calvin, emphasizing, at least implicitly, the first four centuries over the rest of church history. There are others who view church history similarly, albeit in a less developed form than Torrance.[183]

In their own reconstruction of patristic theology, John Meyendorff and Georges Florovsky[184] contend that patristics studies have been in a "Western captivity" by which they meant the Eastern/Greek Fathers were forced into foreign, Western, categories distorting their theology.[185] They propose a return to The Fathers and adopt the "patristic mind," articulating patristic theology in a patristic way. This chapter and the preceding chapter have argued that Torrance is largely successful in this regard. His attempt

181. Florovsky, *Bible, Church, Tradition*, 113–20.

182. Torrance does not cite Maximus or Palamas once in *Trinitarian Faith* nor discuss them in *Christian Doctrine of God*. He cites John of Damascus once in *Trinitarian Faith*. Rather, throughout these texts where he explores the classical tradition of theological history Torrance limits himself to primarily Athanasius, Epiphanius, Didymus, the Cappadocians, and Hilary. This is a self-imposed limitation and, no doubt, one has to limit oneself. As such, Torrance cannot be blamed; these two magisterial studies are solid contributions to patristic and theological scholarship. However, the palate he was working with does look selective in comparison with Florovsky and the Orthodox who are indeed open to a much broader tradition. As argued in chapter 1, the Orthodox are no less guilty of selectivity (in their case, a certain neopalamite lens through which they read The Fathers). The suggestion here is simply that theologians today assuming Torrance's Reformed evangelical version of the *consensus* need not be as selective a Torrance and thus should consider incorporating the Byzantine and Augustinian traditions as well. See the concluding chapter of this book for elaboration.

183. See for example Swete, *The Holy Spirit in the Ancient Church* and the magisterial work of Schaff.

184. Florovsky calls it a "neopatristic synthesis."

185. Meyendorff, *Byzantine Theology*, 128. See also Sutton and Bercken, *Orthodox Christianity*, 5–6.

at finding the "inner logic/connection" of the Greek Fathers is precisely an attempt at adopting and expressing the patristic mind, much like Florovsky calls for, and his reconstruction of The Fathers into streams of a *Consensus Patrum* is highly imaginative and fresh. As such Torrance offers a Reformed and evangelical version of Florovsky's neopatristic synthesis.

But, are the categories of themes and streams which Torrance organizes The Fathers into legitimate? This chapter has argued that Torrance's many distinctions can be somewhat overly-simplistic and the current scholarly view is that there is more overlap between the Cappadocian/Byzantine stream and the Athanasius-Cyril evangelical stream than Torrance argues.[186] This chapter discussed the development of Torrance's view of the Cappadocians and Byzantine theology and argued that though he was always focused upon Athanasius his attack on the Cappadocian/Byzantine stream notably surfaces only after his debate with John Zizioulas. Torrance's amalgamation of contemporary theological debate with patristic debate is, perhaps, his greatest strength because it is a way to successfully apply The Fathers today.[187] Torrance has a very dynamic way of using historical texts and he jumps from the fourth century to the sixteenth century to the twentieth century, often in one sentence.[188] He uses fifth-century heresies to critique much later theological problems.[189] This can be an extremely helpful application of The Fathers to contemporary problems and a successful attempt at a neopatristic synthesis; yet it can also be highly confusing.[190] For example, Torrance's discussion of the "Cappadocian distinction," particularly in regards to the procession of the Holy Spirit, is more about the 1980s than the 380s and his issue is more with John Zizioulas than the Cappadocians. Occasionally, Torrance's presentation of Basil and the Cappadocian distinction looks far too much like John Zizioulas, without reference to John Zizioulas himself.

Ultimately, Torrance's imaginative construction of the different streams, while indebted to earlier views in some cases and holding some

186. See also Morrison, Review of *The Trinitarian Faith*, 119.

187. Torrance states that theology must seek to "rethink and reformulate the essential dogmas of the Christian Church in the mode and idiom of our own day . . . " (*Theology in Reconciliation,* 12).

188. See e.g., Torrance, *Space, Time, and Incarnation* where he does this a lot.

189. For example "Nestorian type dualism" in Calvinist thought. See Torrance, *Theological Dialogue,* 1:5.

190. Newman did this with Athanasius many years earlier. Torrance is prone to the same temptation as Newman, namely, amalgamating contemporary debates with historical ones to the point that the historical lines are blurred substantially. See Daley, "The Church Fathers," 31 for a critique of Newman in this regard. See e.g., Torrance, "Karl Barth and the Latin Heresy," where Arianism and liberalism are compared.

unmentioned details in between the lines, is highly original and imaginative and ultimately a helpful (if occasionally simplistic) genealogy of church history.[191] If Torrance's project is approached with knowledge of what he is attempting to do the above issues become less problematic.

However, overall, Torrance's reconstruction of The Fathers into his Reformed evangelical version of the *consensus* has many gains. Both this and the preceding chapter have discussed Torrance's unique approach to the patristic tradition. As this chapter has argued, this primarily entails a departure from the Augustinian emphasis, which makes Torrance unique among western and Protestant theologians.[192] This chapter argued that Torrance presents the Greek Fathers as the "inheritance" of Protestants, evangelicals, and Reformed as much (if not more so) as they are the inheritance of Roman Catholics and Eastern Orthodox. Torrance paints the evangelical tradition as in line with classical Christianity, particularly the theology of the Greek Fathers. This provides an excellent guide for further evangelical appropriation and furthermore, a bridge for ecumenical dialogue. Torrance's approach is even more unique among Reformed theologians inasmuch as Torrance departs from the typical Reformed emphasis on Reformed confessions and figures and returns to the catholic themes discussed in the last chapter and the figures discussed in this chapter.[193]

Chapter 1 argued that, while not rejecting the Greek Fathers, the Protestant Reformers and the subsequent Protestant tradition emphasize Augustine and Augustinian theological themes. Typically Reformed and evangelical theology emphasizes these as well, furthermore emphasizing Reformed and evangelical creeds and confessions.[194] Torrance departs from this tradition and returns to the ecumenical Greek patristic tradition while reading it from his Reformed evangelical perspective. Accordingly, while evangelicals typically point to their rootedness in the early church evidenced

191. Torrance tends towards a very black and white view of theological history; good guys versus bad guys, heroes versus villains, evangelicals versus fundamentalists, Athanasius versus Gregory Palamas, and of course realism versus dualism. Torrance's distinctions can be very helpful and insightful but, sometimes, overly simplistic. See a critique in this vein by Morrison, Review of The Trinitarian Faith, 119.

192. There are, of course, others e.g., Colin Gunton who have also done this.

193. Torrance does not, however, reject Reformed confessions (though he does often critique the Westminster Catechism). He rather returns to the theology behind the catechisms and finds this in catholic themes and figures. See Torrance, "Introduction" in The School of Faith for a very appreciative introduction to Reformed confessions. Torrance's commitment to the Reformed evangelical tradition was explored in chapter 1.

194. A look at the subjects typically studied by almost any Reformed evangelical theologian would portray this as the case. See, e.g., McGrath, Iustitia Dei (on justification).

in Augustine, Torrance shows that the evangelical tradition is more deeply
rooted in the ancient tradition than this portraying that the evangelical tradition is in line with Irenaeus, Athanasius, Didymus, Epiphanius, Hilary,
Cyril and the many theological themes they emphasized.

Torrance's vision helpfully elaborates upon Calvin's reading of the
church fathers inasmuch as he clarified the "golden age" concept and explores the way in which the mindset of the golden age continues into contemporary times. The precedence for this in the Reformed and Protestant
tradition has been discussed and, as argued, Torrance's reading of the Reformed tradition (especially Barth) as the heir to Greek patristic tradition
is similar to the method applied by Calvin and the later Reformed in their
polemics against the Roman Catholics, namely, seeing the Protestant tradition as the true continuation of classical Christianity. One might question
whether Torrance, therefore, brings unfair presuppositions to The Fathers.
However, it is impossible to not bring presuppositions to a reading of The
Fathers and every tradition attempting to read The Fathers does so.[195] Torrance rightly sees overlap between Reformed and Greek patristic theology
and interprets them in light of one another from his Christological and
evangelical perspective. Thus, his reading is a good *Reformed evangelical*
reading of the Greek Fathers, which, as argued in both chapter 3 and this
chapter, brings a fresh perspective and sheds fresh light on The Fathers ex-
traditing them from traditional interpretations.

Torrance's appropriation of The Fathers is in line with the Reformation inasmuch as he, like the Reformers, sees the contemporary evangelical
church in line with the evangelical stream of patristic theology. Torrance
portrays that evangelicals today cannot only return to The Fathers because
they are not the "property" of Roman Catholics and Eastern Orthodox but
that, in fact, there was an evangelical stream in the early church to which
contemporary evangelicalism is more faithful than other traditions.[196] Furthermore, Torrance explores what a contemporary evangelical reading of
historical theology ought to look like (focus on Christology, the ὁμοούσιον,
and grace) and his ecumenical work depicts the wide-ranging significance

195. As argued in chapter 1, Newman read later the Greek Fathers through later Roman Catholic development, Roman Catholics read The Fathers through Aquinas, the
Eastern Orthodox read the Greek Fathers through Gregory Palamas and the essence
and energies distinction, and the liberal tradition reads the Greek Fathers through the
lens "kernel and chaff."

196. It should be noted that this approach is not entirely unique to Torrance. As
argued in chapter 1, Philip Schaff, for example, appropriated The Fathers similarly and
his translations and compilations of The Fathers as well as his work in historical theology has been very influential in Protestant evangelical circles. The approach of Swete
was also in this vein. See Swete, *The Holy Spirit in the Ancient Church*.

of such an approach.[197] Primarily, he shows that evangelicals can (and should) remain in their own tradition but work towards ecumenical rapprochement on the basis of the evangelical theology of the early church which continued through the medieval period and was preserved by the Reformers continuing in evangelical churches to this day. As such, Torrance's theological and evangelical appropriation of The Fathers provides a relevant guide for this reading of theological history.

Furthermore, Torrance's *consensus* is a proposal for a return not simply to some sort of general "Tradition"[198] but the classical and evangelical tradition of the Trinity and Christology.[199] This approach is helpful inasmuch as it provides a significantly more objective method of appropriation than an attempted retrieval of some sort of general and ideal[200] "Tradition," which, as argued in chapter 1 of this book, is the tendency of many evangelical retrievals of The Fathers.

Torrance's Christology/grace centered reading of theological history offers a viable template for further appropriation of the Greek Fathers and patristic themes by evangelicals. He has done the groundwork and evangelicals can move forward with his excellent work in the classical tradition[201] in hand, prepared for further exploration of the patristic tradition and, more broadly, theological history. A revisiting of some elements (such as Torrance's negative view of the Cappadocian Fathers and the Byzantine tradition) and an application of his method to themes in which he left room for further exploration (such as asceticism) can therefore take place.[202]

197. See the following chapter.

198. Cf. Thomas Oden, D. H. Williams, and others who propose a return simply to the "Tradition" tend to cast their nets extremely wide. For example, Oden's list of paleo-orthodox writers found at the end of one of his earlier books. Oden noted that this is a much bigger list than in his "Agenda for Theology" in 1979 when he listed Pannenberg, von Balthasar, and Congar. See Oden, *The Rebirth of Orthodoxy*, 165–66. The problem with a simple return to the general "Tradition" is indeed that there is no such thing and thus the list of people returning to it can be huge (as Oden's was). Torrance and others who return to the classical evangelical tradition of Trinity and Christology offer a more "objective" method which allows differentiation between different traditions in the history of the church. The problem with the approach of Oden is that the list of relevant authors becomes deceptively long on account of the fact that basically anyone returning to historical sources can be considered "paleo-orthodox" without differentiation.

199. As, for example. Bromiley points out. See Bromiley, "Promise of Patristic Studies" 135–140.

200. In the "Platonic" sense.

201. Explored most fully in *Trinitarian Faith*.

202. See the concluding chapter of this book for the beginnings of such an exploration.

Torrance is seriously under-utilized by theologians and patrologists alike, albeit with exceptions. Notably, Khaled Anatolios refers to Torrance in his book.[203] However, most references to Torrance by scholars are negative. Ernest is critical of Torrance's approach to The Fathers as a theologian.[204] Williams, one of the leading figures in current evangelical theologies of retrievals, refers to Torrance's doctoral thesis written on the Apostolic Fathers, noting Torrance's distinction of the Apostolic Fathers from Paul on the doctrine of grace.[205] Arguably, many probably do not know what to make of Torrance because he does not fit in the traditional categories. He is not a patrologist proper; so patristics scholars do not utilize him. He is a Reformed theologian but he does not talk about typical Reformed theological themes (and he is actually critical of many versions of them) nor does he only talk about typical Reformed theologians (and he is critical of many schools in Reformed thought), so Reformed theologians do not use him. Instead his books are full of explorations of Greek patristic figures and themes and so Reformed and evangelical theologians tend to avoid his patristic scholarship.[206] Regardless of the reason, he is typically overlooked or severely critiqued.

It is notable that most evangelical attempts at retrieving the Greek Fathers generally do not refer to Torrance either.[207] The reason for their turning east has been attributed to a number of reasons including the shift towards holism[208] and the turn from ahistorical to historical.[209] However, their retrievals are generally fairly broad. Thus, for them, Torrance is likely too binary in his retrieval as they wish to return to a more holistic and inclusive tradition. Torrance calls for a retrieval of the Greek Fathers over and against the Augustinian tradition and the Nicene tradition over and against the Byzantine tradition. However, these figures call for a holistic retrieval of the entire tradition of the church. For example, Oden's "Vincentian method of appropriation" calls for *ressourcement* of both eastern and western sources and Webber's "ancient future faith" does not discriminate between

203. Anatolios, *Athanasius,* 23–24. Here Anatolios cites Torrance, *Divine Meaning,* 179. See p. 214 for the endnote citation.

204. Ernest, *The Bible in Athanasius of Alexandria,* 13.

205. Williams, *Evangelicals and Tradition,* 131–39.

206. e.g., Bruce McCormack's criticism that to return to Greek patristic themes, bypassing Reformed confessions, is to no longer be Reformed. See McCormack, "The End of Reformed Theology?" 52–53.

207. With notable exceptions. See Oden, *The Rebirth of Orthodoxy,* 165–66. Oden sees Torrance as an importance figure in the movement.

208. Webber, *Ancient-Future Faith,* 21.

209. Webber, *Younger Evangelicals,* 71–82; Oden, *Requiem.*

Augustine and the Greek Fathers.[210] Herein these groups tend towards the numerical and very broad notion of the *consensus* to which a heavy reliance on Vincent of Lérins' statement lends itself and are, herein, closer to the medieval Roman Catholic approach than that of the Reformers.

Robert Webber's approach contains elements of this static, abstract, and numerical view of doctrine and the Rule of Faith as well.[211] These figures tend to not differentiate between an Irenaean approach and Tertullian type approach to the Rule of Faith. Ultimately, they define the *consensus* in a rather static and abstract way looking for some sort of truly numerical agreement amongst The Fathers in addition to reading their own tradition back into The Fathers. In contrast with these more static and abstract approaches, Torrance's many connections provide a much more dynamic template for Reformed and evangelical theologians. Torrance's *consensus* is faithful to The Fathers and his own tradition, while at the same time allowing the two mutually inform and reform one another. He provides an objective theological focus (Christology) and a viable template/lens through which evangelicals can read and appropriate The Fathers (the overarching evangelical stream running throughout theological history). Herein, Torrance successfully portrays evangelicals as the heir to the Greek Fathers (all the while shedding fresh light on The Fathers). Thus Torrance should be more utilized by patrologists, systematic theologians, and, especially, Reformed and evangelical theologians returning to the church fathers.

All of Torrance's connections do raise the question as to whether The Fathers would agree with what Torrance is doing with them. Simply put: is Torrance's ὁμοούσιον the same as Athanasius' ὁμοούσιον? Some say it is not. Foremost in the critiques along this vein is that Torrance's reading of The Fathers, primarily Athanasius and the ὁμοούσιον, sounds far too Barthian for the fourth century.[212] Colin Gunton argues that Torrance's reading of the ὁμοούσιον is too Western and sounds more Augustinian than Athanasian (as Torrance contends it is).[213]

---

210. Husbands and Greenman, *Ancient Faith for the Church's Future*, 230–45. See also Hall, *Learning Theology with the Church Fathers*, 53–81 and Olson and Hall, *The Trinity*, 31–49. They argue for a doctrine of the Trinity based on Gregory of Nyssa, Athanasius, Ambrose, and Augustine.

211. "An authoritative summary of what the church believed and taught." See Webber, *Ancient-Future Faith*, 183–85. See also Williams, *Evangelicals and Tradition*, 62–65 for a similar account. The problem may very well lie in the fact that both these theologians do not seem to differentiate between Irenaeus and Tertullian on this point.

212. Ernest, *The Bible in Athanasius of Alexandria*, 17. See also Molnar, *T. F. Torrance*, 325 for further accounts (and rebuttals) of critiques along these lines.

213. Gunton, *Father, Son, and Holy Spirit*, 44–52. Gunton wonders whether "the immense stress on the ὁμοούσιον does not run the risk of flattening out the particularities,

In Torrance's *Trinitarian Faith* he presents the "inner logic" of The Fathers. This method gives the impression that Torrance may think he understands The Fathers better than they understood themselves.[214] Many of Torrance's commentators are critical of him in this regard and proffer views that The Fathers are effectively mouthpieces for Torrance's theology and that his Athanasius is, rather than being an actual representation of the saint, some sort of construction of Torrance's pen.[215] Many contend that in an effort to adapt patristic theology to his own situation Torrance uses and molds patristic theology in such a way that The Fathers would not have recognized it. Some contend that Torrance misquotes or misrepresents The Fathers by making them espouse a theology that they never clearly articulated.[216]

Therefore, though in his use of the ὁμοούσιον Torrance sees himself as returning to patristic Christology and Triadology, the question remains as to whether in the Torrancian *Consensus Patrum* Torrance presents his readers primarily with The Fathers themselves or, in fact, more with Torrance and Barth. Holmes puts forward this critique of many contemporary "recoveries" of Trinitarian theology.[217] Holmes' contention is that modern Trinitarian theology, most of which claims to be returning to the patristic

---

so that the divine *being* tends to be stressed at the expense of the divine *persons*." He suggests that Torrance's reading of the Greek Fathers was perhaps more Western, Latin, and Augustinian than Greek patristic (50–51). Torrance does explicitly connect the ὁμοούσιον and Karl Barth's close identification of the being and acts of God. See *The Christian Doctrine of God*, 120 and 149 where Torrance refers to Athanasius *Contra Arianos* 2.2 and Barth, *Church Dogmatics* II.1, pp. 257ff.

214. See e.g., Torrance, *Incarnation*, 62. Robert Walker helpfully footnotes that this is Torrance's discussion of the "implications" of patristic theology. Problems arise, however, inasmuch as Torrance states the implications (in his view) of patristic theology in language that implies The Fathers were abundantly clear in their assertions, when in fact there are diverging opinions on many issues.

215. Rankin, "Carnal Union with Christ," 268; Morrison, Review of *The Trinitarian Faith*.

216. Copan, Review of *The Christian Doctrine of God*, 248.

217. See Holmes, *The Holy Trinity*. Though, Holmes is not critical of Torrance. In fact, he only refers to Torrance once in the book and this is on Calvin on the Trinity (169). Holmes is mainly critical of "social Trinitarian" accounts of The Fathers and argues that they filter their own viewpoints back into The Fathers. As such his critique is, in a sense, of those who are typically critical of Torrance (and of whom Torrance is typically critical) such as Colin Gunton who critiques Torrance for not insisting upon the particularity of the persons of the Trinity. See also Molnar, *T. F. Torrance*, 344–45 for a summary of this critique. Molnar rightly deals with this critique by pointing out that Torrance insists upon three persons dynamically substantiated in the being of God. Regarding Torrance on the doctrine of the Trinity, particularly in light of Holmes's book, see further Radcliff, "T. F. Torrance in Light," 21–38 and "T. F. Torrance and the Patristic Consensus."

(often Greek) doctrine of God, is in actual fact unfaithful to The Fathers.[218] Holmes suggests that contemporary attempts at the retrieval of classical patristic Trinitarian theology, though laudable in some regards, have been largely unsuccessful at retrieving The Fathers. According to Holmes, while ostensibly "patristic" they are not actually faithful to The Fathers.[219] Holmes concludes that many contemporary Trinitarian theologians, though desiring in many ways to return to The Fathers, construct something rather foreign to them. Holmes' stated thesis, in short, is that twentieth-century Trinitarian revival, while ostensibly patristic, in fact has more to do with the preconceptions and commitments of the twentieth-century figures leading the "revival" and less to do with classical (i.e., patristic, medieval, and Reformation) Trinitarian theology.[220]

It is probably fair to say that Athanasius' use of the ὁμοούσιον is not exactly the same as Torrance's[221] Thus, these critiques are certainly not unfounded; however, they are also not entirely fair. In a sense, Torrance would have contended that he understands what these Fathers meant and implied better than they did because of his own situation, hundreds of years later standing post-Reformation and post-Barth.[222] Historically, this may be unhelpful but theologically it is extremely insightful and constructive; furthermore, Torrance may actually be right.[223] The themes while perhaps not explicitly found in The Fathers in the form presented by Torrance, are indeed fair theological statements to make inasmuch as Torrance reads The Fathers

218. For example, Barth's new Trinitarian language, Rahner's identity between the ontological and economic Trinity, Zizioulas's stress on the personal, willful, nature of God as Trinity, and Moltmann, Pannenberg, and Jenson's amalgamation of God's economy and ontology. See Holmes, *The Holy Trinity*, 9ff.

219. Holmes argues that these attempts are commendable responses to the liberal theology of the eighteenth and nineteenth centuries and the insistence on God's unknowability and basic denial of Trinitarian theology. Thus, their starting point, the intimate connection between economy and ontology, is good. However, he contends that they take it too far for, as he concludes, for The Fathers it was important to emphasize God's simplicity and unknowability in his nature, thus all that can be said about God must be spoken in regard to his hypostases. Holmes argues that the emphasis for The Fathers is upon God mediating himself rather than the Son as mediator and upon inability to speak about the divine nature. See Holmes, *The Holy Trinity*, 198–200.

220. Ibid., 2.

221. As argued earlier in this chapter Torrance applies the ὁμοούσιον and other patristic terms much more broadly than The Fathers did themselves.

222. In this sense there is substantial overlap between Torrance and Newman. Torrance's *consensus* could very well be viewed as a Reformed version of Newman's "development of doctrine" discussed in chapter 1 of this book.

223. As such, a critique could very well be directed at Holmes regarding his potentially rigid and static approach to patristic theology.

from a dogmatic and Reformed evangelical perspective and unpacks the inner logic behind the classical theology of The Fathers. Torrance, by means of reading The Fathers in light of the his Reformed evangelical perspective and rooting them Christologically in the ὁμοούσιον, makes connections and asserts the implications of The Fathers' theology which allows deeper understanding of what they meant and their connections to his tradition. In this sense it is not far-fetched to say that Torrance understands the implications of The Fathers better from his point of view of the *Consensus Patrum*. For, The Fathers, says Torrance, are better understood in light of the Reformation, as explored earlier in this chapter. Ultimately, as argued in chapter 1, all theological interpreters of the patristic tradition have a lens through which they view The Fathers; the key must be to balance historical faithfulness (not putting words into the mouths of The Fathers) with confessional commitment (viewing The Fathers from within one's own tradition), which Torrance does successfully.[224] His reading of The Fathers is a creative Reformed evangelical rendering of the *consensus* which is neither statically Reformed nor statically patristic; it is rather dynamically Reformed *and* patristic.

In the final analysis then, Torrance is really only able to be critiqued in this regard historically: The Fathers did not explicitly hold to some of the ideas Torrance attributes to them; yet Torrance never claimed to be an historian. Rather, his is a constructive-theological endeavor.[225] Torrance never places his project in the field of history; it is rather constructive systematic theology, which ultimately makes it a tenable possibility.[226] Torrance uses historical sources and therefore he must be held at least somewhat accountable historically; his lack of clarity regarding what elements are his own interpretations and what is truly patristic can be sometimes be historically unhelpful.

Torrance's reconstruction of The Fathers around the ὁμοούσιον has much to offer and, indeed, provides a reading of the Athanasius and The

224. Overall, Holmes also balances historical faithfulness with theological acumen. See especially Holmes, *The Holy Trinity*, 56–143.

225. See further Radcliff, "T. F. Torrance and the Patristic Consensus" and Radcliff, "T. F. Torrance in the Light."

226. While Torrance says theology is necessarily "historical" by this he means "historically informed." However, Torrance simply was a not a historian; he was a theologian. See Torrance, "Introduction" in *The School of Faith*, lxvii–lxviii. Interestingly Ernest critiques Torrance for approaching The Fathers as a systematic theologian rather than as a historian. See Ernest, *The Bible in Athanasius of Alexandria*, 13. John Behr, on the other hand, takes issue with patrology becoming a study of the history of late antiquity. See Behr, *The Mystery of Christ*, 18. Would Ernest have systematic theologians ignore The Fathers? Should they leave the Bible to the biblical scholars as well? This would certainly be problematic. The key, no doubt, is to balance history and theology.

Fathers with which scholars at the forefront of current patristic scholarship (such as Behr and Anatolios) often agree, at least in substance, emphasis, and trajectory, if not explicitly.[227] Torrance's emphasis on the ὁμοούσιον may be influenced by Barthian commitment to God's self-giving in revelation and reconciliation, but this allows Torrance fresh insight into Athanasius and the other Fathers. Torrance sees in Athanasius and the other Fathers on the ὁμοούσιον commitment to Barthian views and Torrance uses this to draw out what had not been before.[228] Torrance's emphasis on the ὁμοούσιον and the inner meaning behind it (that revelation and reconciliation come from the side of God) provides fresh insight into The Fathers by paring away patristic theology that did not focus on this commitment and highlighting the classical theology that did focus upon it.

Torrance's reading of The Fathers on the doctrine of the Trinity, particularly on the *filioque* debate is a fresh insight and his ὁμοούσιον reconstruction allows him this new reading. Torrance's connection of God's being and acts and emphasis on God's immediate presence in Christ sheds further insight in the *filioque* debate. Torrance offers a potential answer to the ongoing debate between "social Trinitarians" and those emphasizing the unity of God.[229] The following chapter of this book will discuss Torrance's immense work in this regard and how he brought about significant rapprochement between Reformed and Orthodox churches on the doctrine of the Trinity.[230] Here Torrance provides insight into the question of the procession of

---

227. Primarily the Christocentric emphasis. See e.g., Behr, *Mystery of Christ*, 19.

228. Despite strong overlap between Barth and Athanasius and Arianism and nineteenth-century liberal theology, they are surely different. Torrance's greatest strength may have also been his greatest weakness. He made The Fathers highly relevant to his contemporary time by viewing the ways that Athanasius' attack on Arianism overlapped with, for example, his own contemporary battle with liberal theology. However, this is somewhat over simplified simply because Arianism, though similar, was not the same as 19th century liberal theology. See e.g., Torrance, "Karl Barth and the Latin Heresy," 461–82 and Torrance's depiction of Athanasius and Barth both fighting the same perennial battle against dualism. See the concluding chapter of this book for elaboration upon this critique. Daley similarly critiques Newman on this. See Daley, "The Church Fathers," 31.

229. Basically, those who emphasize the unity of God's persons and his economy and ontology (e.g., Barth and Rahner) and those who emphasize the distinctiveness of the three persons of the Trinity (e.g., Moltmann and Zizioulas). See Noble, *Holy Trinity*, 201–3 for a summary of the debate. On p. 203 Noble helpfully summarizes: "In the current climate, opinion appears to be polarized between those who focus on the *unity* of the Trinity and those who focus on the *distinct Persons* of the Trinity; that is, those who focus on the *One* and those who focus on the *Three*."

230. See Torrance, *Theological Dialogue I* and Torrance, *Theological Dialogue II* particularly the *Agreed Statement*.

the Holy Spirit. It is highly unfortunate that scholars writing on the subject today do not often discuss Torrance's significance.[231]

Gunton's critique that Torrance's Triadology, while ostensibly Greek, is in actual fact Augustinian has merit, and, no doubt, Torrance agrees, at least in part. As Torrance states:

> Augustine was said not to know much Greek but there is no doubt that his *De Trinitate*, surely one of the greatest works on theology ever written, is steeped in the teaching of the Greek fathers, which he got to know partly through Hilary who did have a good knowledge of Greek and was well versed in Athanasian and Cappadocian theology.[232]

The long-held "de Régnon thesis"[233] which sharply distinguishes between Latin (Augustinian) and Greek (Cappadocian) doctrines of the Trinity is currently falling out of fashion with patristics scholars[234] and current scholarship is moving forward seeing Augustine and Latin Triadology in line with Greek (both Athanasian and Cappadocian) Triadology.[235] Torrance, though still falling into some now outdated categories perhaps based, in part, on the de Régnon thesis is at the same time a pioneer (and stands along the current reading) in his time inasmuch as he sees Augustine in line with Greek Trinitarian thought.[236] As such Torrance's scholarship in this area has much to offer the current Trinitarian conversation and he is seriously under-utilized by patristics scholars and theologians alike on this topic. Torrance's doctrine

231. See e.g., Siecienski, *The Filioque*. Siecienski wrote a chapter on contemporary discussion without any mention to Torrance. Cf. Noble, *Holy Trinity*, who utilizes Torrance substantially.

232. Torrance, *Trinitarian Faith*, 22.

233. The distinction between Greek/Eastern (Cappadocian) doctrine of the Trinity focusing on the threeness of the persons in God and of Latin/Western (Augustinian) doctrine of the Trinity emphasizing rather the oneness of the being of God. See Régnon, *Études de théologie positive*. Whether de Régnon actually held to the paradigm that took his name has been called into question. See Hennessy, "An Answer to de Régnon's Accusers," 179–97.

234. Therein, Gunton's categories (and critiques of Torrance) are somewhat out of date.

235. Ayres, *Nicaea and Its Legacy,* particularly pp. 188–221 and 365–83; Ayres, *Augustine and the Trinity*; Barnes, "Rereading Augustine's Theology of the Trinity." Even the Orthodox, though still somewhat critical of Augustine on the Trinity, are beginning to see more similarities than they once did. See Papanikolaou and Demacopoulos, *Orthodox Readings of Augustine* for a collection of essays from a conference exploring this subject.

236. Noble makes a similar connection, pointing to Augustine as not necessarily absolutely contrary to the Greek Fathers. See Noble, *Holy Trinity*, 215–17.

of the Trinity is a resource for the current *via media* for the current Trinitarian debate with his dynamic conception of the Trinity and three hypostases inhering in the one ousia and it offers a compromise between historically contradicting traditions that can be of ecumenical import.[237] Voicing this sentiment precisely, Noble states: "Torrance's Trinitarian theology holds out the best hope of combining the concerns for divine Unity with the concerns of the social Trinitarians."[238] Torrance's conception of three hypostases inhering in one divine ousia emphasizes the distinctiveness of each hypostasis of the Trinity while not compromising a strong assertion of divine unity. His reading of the Greek Fathers along these lines offers a reading of the patristic tradition along the line of Holmes and the current trajectory, seeing the patristic tradition as fairly integrated and consensual.[239]

Owing to his portrayal of the Greek Fathers as the inheritance of the Reformed and evangelical tradition, Torrance is able approach other similarly minded traditions in ecumenical dialogue on the basis of a common heritage in the Greek patristic tradition. The next chapter of this book will discuss the outcome of Torrance's retrieval of the Greek Fathers and his uniqueness and ecumenical relevance, particularly the way in which the Torrancian *Consensus Patrum* consisting of catholic themes and figures undergirds his ecumenical work, particularly with the Eastern Orthodox, enabling him to remain evangelical whilst also ecumenical.[240] So, next, this book will explore the "fruits" of the Torrancian *Consensus Patrum*, the Reformed-Orthodox Dialogue and Torrance's wide-ranging ecumenical work conducted in large part on the basis of shared commitments to the Greek Fathers.

---

237. See chapter 5. See also Noble, *Holy Trinity,* 201–3 for a summary.

238. See ibid., 215 n. 41.

239. Though, as discussed earlier, Torrance does see certain divergences such as the "Cappadocian distinction."

240. Torrance believed his book *Trinitarian Faith* was directly relevant to the Reformed-Orthodox Dialogue. See correspondence with His All-Holiness Demetrius I dated February 1988. The Thomas F. Torrance Manuscript Collection. Special Collections, Princeton Theological Seminary Library. Box 172.

CHAPTER 5

The Ecumenical Relevance of T. F. Torrance's *Consensus Patrum*

It is my plea to the Orthodox that they should resist the temptation to take their main stand today, somewhat one sidedly, on the Cappadocian development from Athanasius, but reconsider the centrality of the Athanasius-Cyril axis on which there can be deep agreement throughout the Eastern Orthodox Churches between the so-called 'Chalcedonian' and 'Monophysite' Churches, as well as between East and West. And it is my plea to the Roman Catholics that a rapprochement be made with Greek patristic understanding of the Trinity and the vicarious humanity of Christ, which is in fact the theology lying behind their own great liturgical renewal, and especially with the non-dualistic theology of Athanasius and Cyril . . . My plea to Protestants is that they learn to look behind the pluralist society and the fragmented pattern of the Reformation Churches to the 'wholeness' that belongs to the apostolic foundation of the Church in Christ . . . "

Thomas F. Torrance, *Theology in Reconciliation*, 9–10.

INTRODUCTION

Torrance's reconstruction of patristic theology in light of the evangelical perspective of the Reformation into a Torrancian *Consensus Patrum* is of great ecclesiastical and ecumenical importance. Chapters 3 and 4 of this book argued that the Torrancian Reformed evangelical version of the *Consensus Patrum* is centered upon the catholic themes (chapter 3) and figures (chapter 4), the central theme being the Nicene doctrine of ὁμοούσιον and the central figure being Athanasius of Alexandria. Torrance returns to Greek patristic themes and figures emphasizing them instead of Reformed confessions and creeds (as is typical for Reformed and evangelicals) and Augustine and Augustinian themes (as is typical for the Western tradition in general). Currently, as argued in chapter 2 of this book, the evangelical church is in the midst of a resurgence of interest in the theology of the early church. This chapter will argue that Torrance's Christocentric, evangelically informed, and ecumenically open reconstruction of The Fathers into the *Consensus Patrum* offers a highly relevant guide for contemporary ecumenical dialogue and retrieval of the classical, especially Greek, Fathers. This is seen especially in light of the other Protestant returns to the theology of the classical Greek Fathers discussed in chapter 2 who are less objective (e.g., the emerging movement), more rigidly Protestant/Western (e.g., those who read Augustinian theological themes back into the Greek Fathers), or driven by objectivity to some static confession (e.g., those who convert to Roman Catholicism or Eastern Orthodoxy).

As has been proffered throughout this book, Torrance reads and appropriates the church fathers, especially the classical Greek Fathers, in a unique and imaginative way inasmuch as his reading is Christ-centered on the Nicene doctrine of ὁμοούσιον and in light of the evangelical theology arising out of the Protestant Reformation. As explored in chapter 3, in his use of The Fathers Torrance imaginatively reconstructs patristic themes and figures around this core aspect to Nicene theology as he sees it and, as such, the Torrancian *Consensus Patrum* is objectively focused on God as revealed in Jesus Christ and informed by the evangelical tenets surrounding this revelation. As seen in chapter 4 in this book, because of Torrance's centering of his reading of The Fathers on the Nicene doctrine of ὁμοούσιον Torrance's patristic spotlight shines upon the "Athanasius-Cyril axis" and also the surrounding theological thread including such supporters as Irenaeus of Lyons, Gregory Nazianzen, Epiphanius of Salamis, Didymus the Blind and later John Calvin and Karl Barth. As argued in chapter 1, Torrance's project is by no means untraditional as his appropriation and reconstruction of the classical Greek Fathers is traditionally Protestant in many ways and has its precedent in John Calvin and, later, Philip Schaff. However, by means of his focus on the ὁμοούσιον and the Athanasius-Cyril thread of theology, Torrance draws out elements of patristic theology not traditionally garnered from The Fathers and indeed brings a fresh reading and interpretation of the patristic era to the table of historical and systematic theology.

This chapter will argue that the fruit of Torrance's re-reading and imaginative reconstruction of The Fathers is his immense and unique ecumenical work. By means of his returning to catholic themes and figures with Christological objectivity and commitment to evangelical tenets Torrance is able to engage other similarly focused Christian traditions in fruitful theological dialogue bringing about connections not previously existent and additionally further informing his own Reformed tradition as well as those with whom he was in contact, showing how a Reformed evangelical theologian can return to the Greek Fathers while remaining within their own tradition.

THE ECCLESIASTICAL AND ECUMENICAL FRUITS OF TORRANCE'S RETRIEVAL

As seen in chapters 3 and 4 of this book, Torrance's use of The Fathers is Reformed. Throughout his discussion of Greek patristic themes and figures Torrance remains faithful to traditional central tenets of Reformed theology, particularly God's providential effectiveness (or the "divine initiative") in salvation as well as the Word centeredness of theological activity and he approached ecumenical dialogue as a Reformed churchman. However, Torrance does not remain statically faithful to Reformed creeds and confessions nor any other external dogmatic construction but objectively re-centers everything upon Christ and the Gospel by means of a stress upon the Nicene-Athanasian ὁμοούσιον. As such, in his ecumenical work Torrance remains faithfully Reformed, Protestant, and evangelical while looking at patristic themes and figures with an aim towards true dialogue and reform on both sides of the conversation. Torrance's biggest role in ecumenical relations was in the Reformed-Orthodox Dialogue though he spent time in other realms of the ecumenical conversation as well.

This chapter will examine the fruit of Torrance's return to and retrieval of the Greek Fathers, his ecumenical work, specifically the role played by his imaginative reconstruction of The Fathers around the ὁμοούσιον. It will explore how Torrance is unique inasmuch as he remains decidedly Reformed, Protestant, and evangelical but allows the Greek Fathers to inform his tradition; this is done by means of Torrance's Christocentric/evangelical approach and his unique ecclesiological perspective. It will examine the way in which Torrance's objective and Christ-centered reconstruction of The Fathers around the ὁμοούσιον sets him apart from other Protestant returns to the Greek Fathers who are less objective in their approach to the patristic era. This chapter will argue that Torrance's unique ὁμοούσιον centered retrieval of the Greek Fathers, though open to particular critiques, is an example to be followed by other Protestants and evangelicals who wish to retrieve The Fathers for their own theological setting for reform and ecumenical dialogue.

This book has been exploring the way in which Torrance appropriates the classical Fathers and reconstructs them into a Reformed evangelical version of the *Consensus Patrum*. Torrance, unlike the evangelicals discussed in chapter 2 who convert after "discovering" The Fathers, remains within his own broadly evangelical tradition, and unlike evangelicals discussed in chapter 2 who tendentiously appropriate The Fathers based on their own subjective reasons, has an objective guiding principle, namely, God in Christ and the Gospel of salvation fully by grace (the ὁμοούσιον); indeed a Christocentric approach to classical Christianity. Torrance produces and paves the way for what could be called an "evangelical patristic theology."[1] Accordingly, the rest of this chapter shall explore the fruit of Torrance's return to the Greek Fathers, Torrance's Reformed evangelical *consensus* arguing this is best illustrated in his vast ecumenical work and, herein, his reform of his own Reformed tradition.

Chapters 3 and 4 of this book examined and assessed Torrance's creative reconstruction of The Fathers. This chapter will further explore how Torrance reconstructs The Fathers around the Christological/evangelical perspective of the Reformation (the ὁμοούσιον) in ecumenical dialogue. Torrance's reconstruction allows him fresh insight into The Fathers, and his own tradition. The outcome of this is Torrance's insight into and reformation of his own tradition and other traditions by means of his ecumenicity, as will be explored below. This is based on Torrance's (a) Christ-grace-Trinity (ὁμοούσιον) centered objective reading of classical patristic theology and (b) the catholic themes and figures of the shared tradition which act as points of contact for ecumenical conversation, which allows Torrance to, in many ways, reform the theology of his own tradition as well as others and thus is of great ecumenical significance.

---

1. This same method has been applied to Calvinism by the "Evangelical Calvinists." See Habets and Grow, *Evangelical Calvinism*. While remaining committed to "evangelicalism," namely, the Gospel of grace and the centrality of Christ, the Evangelical Calvinists read and, in some cases, reform Calvin. See the concluding chapter of this book for a proposal as to what an "evangelical patristic theology" might look like.

TORRANCE'S ECUMENICITY

In Torrance's thorough introduction to his collection of Reformed catechisms, *The School of Faith*,[2] he contends, "it belongs to the nature of theology to be *catholic*," which he sees as involving both historicity and ecumenicity.[3] Torrance believes that theology is inherently "dialogical" meaning that it is conversational, a conversation between God and his people.[4] Thus, for Torrance, theology is necessarily historical and ecumenical; historical "because it is historical dialogue with God" and ecumenical because "the exposition of theology as hearing of the Word and understanding of the Truth cannot be private to one particular Church."[5] Therefore, Torrance understands theology to be, by its very nature, catholic, historical, and ecumenical. Indeed, to be otherwise would point to "theology" not being, in fact, real theology. What he means by this shines clear in Torrance's own contribution to the ecumenical dialogue. Essentially, as will be shown, it means looking at theology's object, God revealed in Christ, alongside other denominations, which, practically, means doing theology through the theology surrounding the Nicene doctrine of ὁμοούσιον focused on the doctrine of the Trinity by means of the help of one its most faithful exponents, Athanasius. As will be seen, this entails the potential critique and reform of Torrance's own Reformed tradition as well as potential critique and reform of the other partners in the dialogue; albeit, always reforming by means of alignment with Christ.

In many ways Torrance was born into the ecumenical context. He was born to missionary parents in China. His father was Presbyterian and his mother was Anglican and so an ecumenical mentality was likely to have been a part of his daily family life from his genesis.[6] Additionally, Torrance sees himself within the Scottish evangelical tradition of theology, which he sees in line with classical patristic Christianity through John Calvin.[7]

2. Torrance, "Introduction" in *The School of Faith*, xi–cxxvi. According to Robert Walker and Tom Noble, two former students of Torrance's, Professor Torrance used to recommend this introduction to his students as preparatory reading for his dogmatics lectures. See Torrance, *Atonement*, lxxxiv.

3. Torrance, "Introduction" in *The School of Faith*, lxv.

4. Ibid., lxv–lxvii.

5. Ibid., lxvii–lxviii.

6. *Itinerarium Mentis In Deum: T. F. Torrance—My Theological Development.* The Thomas F. Torrance Manuscript Collection. Special Collections, Princeton Theological Seminary Library, Series II, Box 10.

7. Torrance, *Preaching Christ Today*, 18–19; Torrance, *Theology in Reconciliation*, 83–84; Torrance, *The Mystery of the Lord's Supper*, 32. Torrance sees Robert Bruce, a minister at St Giles' in Edinburgh in the 16th century, as steeped in classical Christian

McGrath's observation has already been noted how, more generally, British evangelicals tend to see themselves in continuation with historical Christianity (at least more so than North American evangelicals tend to).[8]

Torrance's ecumenical work proper has been broad and present throughout the majority of his career as both a churchman and theologian. For example, early in his career (in the 1950s and 1960s), Torrance published the two-volume work, *Conflict and Agreement*, concerning ecumenical dialogue with Anglicans, Presbyterians, and Roman Catholics on subjects such as theology, ministry, and sacraments.[9] During his year as Moderator of the General Assembly of the Church of Scotland, Torrance was ordained "Honorary Protopresbyter" of the Orthodox Archdiocese of Alexandria. During the 1980s and 1990s Torrance led the Reformed side of the Reformed-Orthodox Dialogue, and subsequently published two volumes accounting this discussion.[10] While all of these were done on the basis of Torrance's appropriation of classical Christian theology, the Reformed-Orthodox Dialogue portrays this the most clearly as his connection and discussion with the Eastern Orthodox was primarily on the basis of the classical Greek Fathers.

Torrance primarily turns to the Orthodox (and not the Roman Catholics) for a plethora of reasons. First and foremost, as shall be explored below, Torrance sees himself within the Western Christian tradition. Ecumenical dialogue for Torrance does not so much entail dialogue with Roman Catholics[11] because he sees his own Reformed evangelical tradition as a part of the same Western tradition of the Catholics.[12] Torrance understands his

theology. See also Torrance, *Scottish Theology*. Among others, Torrance saw Robert Boyd as following in the Greek patristic tradition. See further his correspondence with George Dragas on this subject. The Thomas F. Torrance Manuscript Collection. Special Collections, Princeton Theological Seminary Library. Box 104. Torrance also sees John Forbes of Corse as indebted to the Greek patristic tradition. See Box 178.

8. See McGrath, "Trinitarian Theology," 52.

9. Torrance, *Conflict and Agreement 1*; Torrance, *Conflict and Agreement 2*.

10. Torrance, *Theological Dialogue I*; Torrance, *Theological Dialogue II*. See the recent issue (volume 4, 2013) of *Participatio: The Journal of the Thomas F. Torrance Theological Fellowship* for further discussion of Torrance and Eastern Orthodoxy. This excellent issue contains articles written in large part by Orthodox theologians (but also some evangelical theologians) on the patristic bases of Reformed-Orthodox relations through the lens of Torrance himself. See also the forthcoming volume edited by Matthew Baker and Todd Speidell: *T. F. Torrance and Eastern Orthodoxy* (forthcoming 2015).

11. Though, he does include an article on Rahner and Vatican II in a collection of essays in ecumenical perspective *Trinitarian Perspectives* (77–102) and he writes about Catholics in his *Forward* to *Theology in Reconciliation*.

12. See e.g., Torrance, *Theological Dialogue*, 1:3.

tradition to have arisen out of and to still be a part of the same Western Christian tradition of which Roman Catholics are also a part.[13] Therefore, a dialogue with Roman Catholics would have not been significantly different in form[14] from a dialogue between the Reformed and Anglicans.[15] However, Torrance approaches the Orthodox on account of the great gulf that had developed between his own Reformed tradition and the Orthodox tradition. More practically, Torrance approaches the Orthodox on account of a shared love of The Fathers in general and the Greek Fathers in particular. Whereas disagreements do arise between the Reformed and Orthodox on the place of the later Byzantine tradition,[16] Torrance (rightly, as it turns out) sees that the Reformed and the Orthodox share in their love of the classical Greek tradition of Athanasius and Cyril of Alexandria and their emphasis on Christology and the Trinity. The last chapter discussed Torrance's departure from Augustine and chapter 1 discussed the fact that Catholics emphasize Augustine (often through Aquinas). Torrance wants to avoid this typically Western emphasis of which his own Reformed tradition is no less guilty and sees this possibility in dialogue with the Orthodox.

According to Colin Gunton, Torrance's reading of the church fathers has provided a "reopening of a major historical conversation."[17] Though there had been informal dialogue between the Reformed and Orthodox churches since the mid-twentieth century, the Reformed-Orthodox Dialogue formally occurred in 1981, 1983, 1988, and 1990. The impetus for the dialogue came from "deep theological rapport" between Torrance (on the Reformed side) and Methodios (on the Orthodox side) over the understanding of classical Alexandrian theology as represented above all by Athanasius and Cyril.[18]

Their shared goal was to explore the common roots between the two churches on the basis of Apostolic faith and order as explicated in classical Christianity. Accordingly, the doctrines of Triadology and Christology conditioned their conversation throughout. According to the Minutes, in his introductory greeting to the Orthodox patriarchate during their official proposal for dialogue, James McCord, president of the World Alliance of Reformed Churches at the time, "stressed how the Reformed feel themselves

---

13. Once again, the overlap between Torrance and Schaff on this point is substantial. Schaff, *History of the Church*, 4.

14. But there would be differences in substance.

15. Which Torrance does engage. See *Conflict and Agreement I* and *II*.

16. See below.

17. Colin Gunton, *Father, Son, and Holy Spirit*, 51.

18. Torrance, *Theological Dialogue*, 1:x.

historically very close to the Orthodox in a common concern for the truth of the Apostolic Faith and for the unity of the Church in that same faith"[19] and Torrance notes how he developed the view, while Moderator, that Orthodox/Reformed dialogue should usefully begin on the doctrine of the Trinity.[20]

TORRANCE'S ECUMENICAL USE OF CATHOLIC THEMES AND FIGURES

In his ecumenical work Torrance, in the language of Methodios of Aksum, a leader on the Eastern Orthodox side of the Reformed-Orthodox Dialogue, returns to truly catholic themes and figures.[21] The themes and figures which Torrance returns to were explored in full in chapters 2 (themes) and 3 (figures) and, as argued there, are absolutely centered upon the Nicene ὁμοούσιον and the Athanasius-Cyril axis of classical theology. Below, the catholic themes and figures to which Torrance returned will be explored in the ecumenical context wherein Torrance uses them, portraying Torrance's ecumenical significance as well as his influence towards reform within his own tradition.

Reformed Catholicity

In the first instance, the basic reason why Torrance sees himself able to enter into ecumenical dialogue is because of the fundamental catholicity of the Reformed tradition. Torrance sees the Reformed church as a movement of reform within the greater universal catholic church tethered to the foundation of the Apostolic Faith.[22] He states: "The Reformed Church is the

19. See the Minutes in The Thomas F. Torrance Manuscript Collection. Special Collections, Princeton Theological Seminary Library. Box 170.

20. See the Minutes in The Thomas F. Torrance Manuscript Collection. Special Collections, Princeton Theological Seminary Library. Box 170. Chapters 3 and 4 explored the centrality of the doctrine for Torrance.

21. Methodios' actual words in a letter dated May 19, 1988: "I admire your patristic expressions and your use of catholic terms like *perichoresis*." See The Thomas F. Torrance Manuscript Collection. Special Collections, Princeton Theological Seminary Library. Box 172.

22. Torrance states: "The Reformation was not a movement to refound the Church, or to found a new Church; for the whole reforming movement would undoubtedly have continued within the Roman Church had it not been for the bigoted and arrogant recalcitrance of its hierarchy, which insisted in binding the movement of the Word and Spirit by the traditions of men and making it of none effect, and when that failed, in throwing

Church reformed according to the Word of God so as to restore to it the face of the ancient Catholic and Apostolic Church."[23] At the very outset of his first *Memorandum* which he presents at the opening of the first session of the dialogue, Torrance articulates that the Reformed church "does not set out to be a new or another Church but to be a movement of reform within the One Holy Catholic and Apostolic Church of Jesus Christ . . . "[24] Torrance understands himself as a part of the Western tradition inheriting the great tradition of the Greek Fathers. For him it is not and should not be unusual for Reformed to look to their rootedness in the Greek patristic tradition. As such, Torrance's ecclesiology enables him to remain in the Reformed church while also correcting his own tradition from within (precisely what he does in the Reformed-Orthodox Dialogue). Torrance explains that the Reformed churches have always been guided by "classical Greek theology," the "great Alexandrian and Cappadocian theologians," the Augustinian doctrine of grace, and the Triadology of the classical Greek Fathers.[25]

Notably, Torrance elaborates that the Reformed are in line with classical Greek Christianity in more than just basic theology. He contends that the Reformed conception of the "real presence" of Christ in the Eucharist as well as ministry deriving from "Christ himself the Lord and Head of the Church" rather than from the membership of the church is more in line with Greek patristic thought and practice than Latin theology, patristic or medieval.[26] According to the Official Minutes of the dialogue, in the ensuing discussion, some of the Orthodox delegates noted with great interest the analogy between Orthodox autocephalous[27] churches and Reformed autonomous churches[28] which Torrance discusses in his paper.[29]

---

it out altogether, just as the early Christians were thrown out of the synagogues and followed with maledictions and anathemas." See Torrance, *Conflict and Agreement*, 1:77.

23. Ibid., 1:76.

24. Torrance, *Theological Dialogue*, 1:3.

25. Ibid., 1:4. He sees Calvin particularly indebted to Gregory Nazianzen, in terms of theology. See Torrance, *Trinitarian Perspectives*, 21–40.

26. Torrance, *Theological Dialogue*, 1:4–5.

27. From the Greek αὐτοκεφαλὶα, self (αὐτο) κεπαλὶα (heading). It is a type of Orthodox Church typically not under an Archbishop (e.g., the Cypriot Orthodox Church is an ancient autocephalous church and the Orthodox Church in America is a much newer, receiving its autocephalous status from Moscow in the twentieth century).

28. The Thomas F. Torrance Manuscript Collection. Special Collections, Princeton Theological Seminary Library. Box 170.

29. Torrance, *Theological Dialogue*, 1:10.

Torrance sees the Reformed tradition rooted to the foundation of the Apostolic Faith, albeit with different forms of piety and worship.[30] Thus, there are differences between the Reformed and Orthodox; differences in worship practices, differences in prayer practices, and differences in church order among other things. However, Torrance sees a shared commitment to the substance of theology. First, Torrance contends that the Reformed tradition adheres to the Apostolic Faith[31] and practice.[32] He holds that the way forward in ecumenicity is a focus on the truly catholic Apostolic Deposit of Faith as well as the Apostolic *kerygma*,[33] indeed the ὁμοούσιον and the epistemological and soteriological implications contained therein.

Combined with this commitment to ecumenical theology, Torrance contends that the Reformed tradition, no less than the Orthodox tradition, developed within its own context and "cultural and historical milieu."[34] For Torrance both the Orthodox and Reformed should embrace their own pietistic developments while seeking to return to the theological core that they share with one another. Thus, the Reformed tradition, while being distinctive in many ways was and is rooted, according to Torrance, in Apostolicity and catholicity.[35] On this basis the two traditions could hope for rapprochement and theological agreement.

30. For Torrance these differences in pietistic practice are not necessarily problematic. His view is not unlike the Lutheran view propagated in the *Formula of Concord* regarding *adiaphora* or "secondary things." See Torrance, *Conflict and Agreement*, 1:82 for Torrance's discussion of the difference between the Lutheran, Anglican, and Reformed approaches to *adiaphora*. Torrance sees the Reformed approach as best, approaching *adiaphora* as secondary and always able to be shaped and reformed by "Christological correction."

31. Torrance, *Theological Dialogue*, 1:6. He says: "While the Reformed Churches in the sixteenth and seventeenth centuries produced catechetical and confessional formulations for the guidance of their life, teaching and proclamation of the Gospel, these were and are held only as 'secondary standards' subordinate to the Apostolic Faith as mediated through the New Testament, and to the Catholic doctrine as defined by the Apostles' and Nicene-Constantinopolitan Creed."

32. Ibid., 1:8–10.

33. Ibid., 1:91. Torrance says: "The *kerygma* refers not merely to proclamation about Christ but to the Reality proclaimed, Jesus Christ who is personal, actively and savingly at work through the *kerygma*." As argued, this equals the ὁμοούσιον for Torrance. See also Torrance's discussion on p. 1:91–107.

34. Ibid., 1:5, 10.

35. According to the Official Minutes, the Orthodox delegates wondered how the Reformed could hold to any doctrine (i.e., from whence came their authority?). The Reformed response pointed to the Reformed emphasis on synodical/conciliar consensus as opposed to mere individualism. See the Minutes in The Thomas F. Torrance Manuscript Collection. Special Collections, Princeton Theological Seminary Library. Box 170.

Torrance proposes that the Reformed and Orthodox explore truly catholic themes and figures in order to work towards rapprochement. Accordingly it is to the themes and figures discussed in the previous two chapters to which Torrance urges the dialogue to return.

The ὁμοούσιον and the Athanasius-Cyril, Irenaeus, Epiphanius, Didymus stream contra the Cappadocian-Byzantine trajectory

Throughout Torrance's ecumenical work, particularly the Reformed-Orthodox Dialogue, Torrance urges for a return to the Athanasius-Cyril stream of classical Greek theology and their strong emphasis on the Nicene ὁμοούσιον contra the Cappadocian-Byzantine trajectory as the means of ecumenical rapprochement.[36] Methodologically, Torrance believes that the best approach towards theological and ecumenical dialogue is on the basis of the Trinity, Christology, and Pneumatology; and, on that basis the Eucharist, the church, and the ministry.[37] Indeed, this is the approach he proposes in the Reformed-Orthodox Dialogue. Torrance contends that the best method for discussion and the best approach for agreement is on the basis of Athanasian-Cyrilline theology[38] and the common roots of Alexandrian and Cappadocian theology, as well as the Conciliar Statements which they informed so heavily.[39] Torrance reminisced that in the discussions following the papers presented, everyone "kept returning to the need for a dynamic understanding of the living Triune God in the inseparability of his Being and Act," or, the ὁμοούσιον.[40] By means of this realist focus, Torrance thought the Reformed and Orthodox traditions would be able to return to their common fount and "cut behind" the cosmological and epistemological dualism which problematically informed later developments in the Byzantine East and Augustinian West.[41] Such an approach, Torrance thinks, would bring about agreement between Chalcedonians and non-Chalcedonians, Orthodox and Reformed, and Roman Catholics and Evangelicals.[42] Torrance

36. Torrance, *Theological Dialogue*, 2:5.

37. Ibid., 1:10.

38. According to the Official Minutes, in the ensuing discussion, Emilianos from the Orthodox side states: "Is not Torrance in danger of over-absolutizing Athanasius in relation to the Cappadocians?" See The Thomas F. Torrance Manuscript Collection. Special Collections, Princeton Theological Seminary Library. Box 170.

39. Torrance, *Theological Dialogue*, 1:11.

40. Ibid., 1:xxiii.

41. Ibid., 1:11.

42. Ibid., 1:10–11.

proposes that all traditions in ecumenical dialogue need to admit, however, that there are elements which they need to "unknow" in their tradition; extra-Apostolic/patristic theological developments, generally cosmologically and epistemologically dualist.[43] It is to Athanasian theological realism that Torrance urges everyone to return.

Torrance proposes a return to the Athanasian-Cyrilline axis of theology.[44] Torrance sees the Cappadocian development as a move away from the Athanasian focus.[45] However, Torrance sees in Didymus the Blind[46] and Epiphanius of Salamis[47] a return to the Athanasian-Cyrilline emphasis. The later Byzantine developments are considered dualist in orientation.[48]

As discussed, the objective focus on the ecumenical discussion between the Reformed and Orthodox is the doctrine of the Trinity. Throughout Torrance's ecumenical work his approach to the Trinity was essentially as outlined in chapters 3 and 4 of this book, namely, through the Nicene-Constantinopolitan doctrine of ὁμοούσιον. Indeed, this doctrine is not only a theological but also an ecumenical lynchpin for Torrance. He contends that the Nicene ὁμοούσιον is a "king-pin" of the Nicene-Constantinopolitan Creed which expresses the core evangelical belief that in Jesus humans are confronted with the very self-giving and self-revealing of God as he is in himself.[49]

43. Ibid., 1:5. Torrance lists some of these in his second Memorandum: Nestorian dualism in Calvin's doctrine of God and soteriology, the Cappadocian dualistic distinction between God's essence and energies, the Dionysian Neoplatonic distinction between generic and particular substance, dualism in the Byzantine liturgy and the Orthodox understanding of the liturgy in Nicholas Cabasilas, and the dualism of Leonine and Augustinian theology (1:13–18). And, further on he states: "In the general development of the Evangelical Churches . . . there has been a failure to appreciate adequately the living embodiment of faith and truth in the corporate life and structure of the Church . . . tensions have developed between Scripture and Confession, or biblicism and confessionalism, in which we find a Tertullian type of approach adopted both toward the Scripture and toward creedal formulations of Christian doctrine. This is very evident in the way in which the *Canons of the Synod of Dordt* or the *Westminster Confession of Faith* have had the effect of reducing the church's Confession of Faith to systems of doctrinal propositions which are invested with prescriptive authority." Torrance proposes that these "dualist and legalist" ways of thinking are to continue to be undone by focus on the *kerygma*.

44. Torrance, *Theological Dialogue*, 2:3–13.

45. Ibid., 2:13–21.

46. Ibid., 2:21–24.

47. Ibid., 2:24–32.

48. Ibid., 2:35–37.

49. Torrance, *The Incarnation*, xi–xv. Torrance articulates further that in this doctrine theology passes from the economic to the ontological Trinity (xx). The Orthodox agree that this is a lynch-pin. See, e.g., 1–15.

Additionally, though the discussion worked with the Cappadocian and Alexandrian Trinitarian formula "mia ousia, treis hypostaseis,"[50] Torrance still urges his fellow churchmen and theologians to return to a more Athanasian way of approaching the Triadological phrase, namely, through the ὁμοούσιον, and the insistence on the "perfect equality of the Father, Son and Holy Spirit, in each of whom the Godhead is complete."[51] He often asserts this, as in his dogmatic works (as discussed more fully in chapters two and three) against the Cappadocian and Byzantine bifurcation of God's οὐσια and ὑπόστασεις and God's οὐσια and ἐνέργια. For Torrance the ὁμοούσιον was used by The Fathers and should be used as an "exegetical and clarificatory expression."[52]

In the ensuing discussion the Official Minutes bring to light a number of points brought forward by both sides in regards to methodology for classical patristic appropriation.[53] The Orthodox side mentions the importance of the "line of continuity" for the *Consensus Patrum*. Chrysostomos states: "There is a magisterial element in the weight of tradition." Torrance responds:

> We must be aware of the Apostolic nature of the church, and the obedience of the church to the truth of the Apostles. That is why The Fathers were not infrequently criticized and corrected by the Councils. *We have to note the magisterial authority of the Councils vis-à-vis The Fathers.*[54]

Accordingly, as a method, both the Reformed and Orthodox agreed to move forward with the intention of basing their ecumenical discussion on the doctrine of the Trinity per Torrance's suggestion.[55] The subject of authority is subsequently discussed by other figures throughout the dialogue[56] and throughout the dialogue the focus is upon the Trinity as understood

---

50. Torrance, *Theological Dialogue*, 1:79 referring to Athanasius, Gregory Nazianzen, Cyril of Alexandria, and John of Damascus.

51. Ibid., 1:87.

52. Ibid., 1:98.

53. See The Thomas F. Torrance Manuscript Collection. Special Collections, Princeton Theological Seminary Library. Box 170.

54. The Thomas F. Torrance Manuscript Collection. Special Collections, Princeton Theological Seminary Library. Box 170. Italics not in original.

55. The Minutes state that Torrance "suggested the group continue to move forward on an objective basis, that is, a focus on the doctrine of the Trinity, the Canon of Truth, most helpfully done working on the basis of original texts, a shared exegesis of certain patristic writings." See The Thomas F. Torrance Manuscript Collection. Special Collections, Princeton Theological Seminary Library. Box 170.

56. Torrance, *Theological Dialogue*, 1:50–75.

by the classical Fathers and the way in which this informs other theological doctrines as well as church, ministry, and the sacraments.

Throughout the dialogue questions often arose concerning whether God interacts with the world primarily by means of his uncreated energies (the Orthodox view) or in Christ (the Reformed view).[57] Torrance argues that perhaps the essence/energies distinction was taken too seriously because of Vladmir Lossky's reading. Torrance considers stressing the theology of Palamas is unhelpful because of Palamas' Neo-Platonic dualism, a sort of "eastern Augustinianism."[58]

Trinity

Torrance's conversation on the doctrine of the Trinity in the dialogue between Reformed and Orthodox is consistent with his view as discussed in chapters 3 and 4 of this book. Torrance's strong hesitation about the Cappadocian practice of speaking of God the Father as αἰτία, πηγὴ, and ἀρχή is on the basis of its move away from the more Athanasian principle that one can say of the Son everything said of the Father, except "Father."[59] He sees this as a formalizing of the more dynamic use of terms by Athanasius.[60]

57. See e.g., the Official Minutes: Following the presentation of Emilianos' paper on "God's Immutability and Communicability" Chrysostomos brings forward 4 focal points: (1) The relationship of God to mankind through his energy [ἐνέργια], (2) how does God relate himself to space and time? (3) how does God in his grace come to mankind through the church?, and (4) how do we understand the relationship of a personal God to the person of man?" Following this Torrance states his view that "the paper did not do adequate justice to the central thrust in the thought of Athanasius at the critical point of the relationship between *ousia* [οὐσία] and *energia* [ἐνέργια]. Athanasius did not separate them as in the Cappadocians and later Byzantines. [Georges] Florovsky has shown how the Cappadocians did make the radical separation with their more inflexible Aristotelian outlook but Athanasius rather stressed the co-essentiality of the Father, Son, and Holy Spirit." Chrysostomos felt that The Fathers must be viewed as a synthetic whole and thus Athanasius, whom Torrance was referring to, should be read alongside, for example, Maximus the Confessor. See The Thomas F. Torrance Manuscript Collection. Special Collections, Princeton Theological Seminary Library. Box 170.

58. The Thomas F. Torrance Manuscript Collection. Special Collections, Princeton Theological Seminary Library. Box 170. Torrance's issue with the essence/energies distinction is that it ultimately makes God unknowable as he is in himself. Torrance sees this basic dualism asserted in Gregory of Nyssa, John of Damascus, Thomas Aquinas, Peter Lombard, Gregory Palamas, et al.

59. Torrance, *Theological Dialogue*, 1:15.

60. Ibid., 1:15.

As discussed in chapters 3 and 4, Torrance feels that, following Athanasius, the doctrine of the Trinity is central[61] and that the only proper place to begin theological reflection on the doctrine of the Trinity was through the Son.[62] Accordingly, the first two major meetings focused on authority[63] and Triadology[64] and the final meetings focused on the Son and the Spirit[65] and concluded with the Trinity as well.[66] Herein Torrance, following Athanasius, insists on the Christological conditioning of Trinitarian discussion.[67] Torrance contended that Cyril of Alexandria unpacked this basic Athanasian commitment further:

> It is highly significant that Cyril of Alexandria turned back to the teaching of Athanasius, rejecting like him all idea of a hierarchy in God, while accepting the Cappadocian formula, *mia ousia, treis hypostaseis,* he eliminated the ambiguity that had arisen, by rejecting the notion of causal relations within the Trinity as quite unbiblical . . . Here we have the full orthodox doctrine of the *Holy Trinity in one Godhead, One God in three Persons,* in which the Persons are understood as wholly coinhering in one another, as completely coequal and coeternal as well as consubstantial, with one authority, glory, power, will, activity and goodness, and who as such are *one arche,* as Athanasius had claimed.[68]

For Torrance, the Cappadocians and later Byzantines departed from this insistence and basic commitment. The job of the Reformed-Orthodox Dialogue, as he saw it, was to return to this common evangelical foundation and move forward from there.

The outcome of the dialogue was the "Agreed Statement on the Holy Trinity"[69] which was written Torrance and his former student George Dragas wherein "they insisted that they agree on the content of the doctrine."[70]

61. Ibid., 1:81f.

62. Ibid., 1:84–85.

63. Ibid., 1:21–75.

64. Ibid., 1:79–158.

65. Ibid., 1:39–106.

66. Ibid., 2:109–232.

67. Ibid., 1:85.

68. Ibid., 1:89 citing Cyril of Alexandria, *Thesaurus* and Athanasius of Alexandria, *Ad Antiochenos.* Torrance also sees Gregory Nazianzen following in this stream of Trinitarian thought.

69. Ibid., 1:219–26; Torrance, *Trinitarian Perspectives,* 115–22.

70. Torrance, *Theological Dialogue,* 2:xxi.

After studying patristic texts such as Athanasius, *Ad Serapionem*, Basil, *On the Holy Spirit*, Gregory Nazianzen's *Theological Orations*, Calvin's *Institutes* and Karl Barth's *Church Dogmatics*,[71] and a number of papers presented at the dialogues, they drafted and agreed upon the *Agreed Statement on the Holy Trinity*, which emphasized the centrality of the doctrine of the Trinity, the monarchy of the Father, the dynamic nature of unity and Trinity and, as such, *perichoresis*. In many ways this was a compromise of Torrance's earlier stauncher position resisting any assertion of the sole monarchy of the Father. However, at the core, it is faithful to his position throughout his life inasmuch as it strays from emphasizing the hypostasis of the Father as monarchy.

In regards to pneumatology, Torrance sees Athanasius' Triadology and his conception of the procession of the Spirit from the οὐσία of the Father as cutting behind the divisions between East and West on the matter.[72] According to Torrance's estimate, the Reformed tradition had historically accepted the *filioque* but as a way of saying that the Spirit proceeds from the Father through the Son and leads us through the Son to the Father.[73]

Ministry

According to Torrance, any legitimate doctrine of ministry must flow from Triadology. Accordingly he applies his "consubstantial Trinitarian focus" discussed above to the ministry of the church in a variety of ways. Indeed, he contends that a hierarchical Triadology and subordinationist Christology lies behind authoritarian eccclesiologies and that the more Athanasian Triadology he is proposing would bring about a significantly different view of ecclesiastical authority and ministry.[74]

Accordingly, Torrance contends that the Reformed tradition always understood ministry as "from above and not from below"[75] rooted in the one Priesthood of Christ.[76] Thus, the ministry is never focused, according to Torrance, on the human side of things. Indeed, the focus is always upon Christ who is the one "effecting" the ministry.[77]

71. Ibid., 1:xxvii.

72. Ibid., 1:xi.

73. Ibid., 1:7.

74. Ibid., 1:xxv. Basically, less hierarchichal and more Presbyterian.

75. Ibid., 1:5.

76. Ibid., 1:8.

77. See Torrance, *Conflict and Agreement*, 13–57. Notably, Torrance also applies this to the question of women in ministry, concluding that as Christ the effector of ministry

Torrance applies this Trinitarian conception of ministry and church authority to a reconstruction of the notion of bishops; a reconstruction which Torrance sees as a return to the classical patristic ecclesiastical structure.[78] In his words:

> It became distinctive of the Reformed Church that the *episcope* was held to be lodged not individually in the persons but corporately in the body of Presbyters i.e. in the Presbytery as a whole . . . the "Bishop" was understood as the presiding Presbyter . . . the Reformed Church sought to take its pattern of reform from the pattern of the Early Church before the bishop became separated from the presbytery over which he presided . . .[79]

Torrance works this notion out in full elsewhere[80] and essentially concludes that the ecclesiastical organization most faithful to the classical patristic era is what he terms the "corporate episcopate" and is essentially a combination of Presbyterian and episcopal church structure.[81] Torrance understands this to be both in line with classic Reformed thinking (e.g., Calvin) but also to have been the way of the patristic church, as discussed above.

Torrance sees in this structure a way towards more organizational union with other denominations set up in an episcopal structure. Notably, in dialogue between the Church of Scotland and the Church of England/ the Scottish Episcopal Church, Torrance proposes a way forward directly on the basis of his notion of "corporate episcopate."[82] Torrance suggests that the Church of Scotland have one presbyter-bishop over each presbytery and that they would also serve at an individual parish, with one "Archbishop-Moderator" over all the presbyteries. For the episcopal structure of the Anglican Church, Torrance suggests that bishops have a less hierarchical role and that lay leaders become elders. Here, Torrance calls for a scheme of

---

and the minister represents or "images" Christ, the sex of the minister makes no difference. See Torrance, *Gospel, Church, and Ministry*, 216–17.

78 Cf. Zizoulas, *Eucharist, Bishop, Church*.

79 Torrance, *Theological Dialogue*, 1:9.

80 Torrance, *Royal Priesthood*.

81 Ibid., 88–108.

82 The Thomas F. Torrance Manuscript Collection. Special Collections, Princeton Theological Seminary Library. Box 89. See also Torrance, *Conflict and Agreement 1*, 83–98 for further elaboration upon this point. Torrance sees precedent for the corporate episcopate in Scotland in Erksine and Knox and, more generally, in the Reformed tradition. Torrance refers to Calvin's *Letter to the King of Poland* as precedent for a version of apostolic succession in Reformed churches (86). See also Torrance, *Scottish Theology*, 33. Here he discusses John Knox's rooting of succession in Christ rather than a simple linear succession.

"mutual adaptation between Presbytery and Episcopacy," an "act of God in bringing together in all their fullness and historical continuity two streams of Spiritual life and growth in the Church which is the one body of Christ."[83]

Torrance had high hopes for this proposed structure as a way forward in ecumenicity. He states:

> In the light of this it would appear proper to work for a mutual adaptation of our churches and a re-ordering of their ministries in such a way as to assimilate into unity the three main aspects of the ministry that appear in churches of the Congregational, Presbyterian, and Episcopal types. In such an adaption there would take place an integration of the Episcopate with the Presbytery and an integration of this Episcopal Presbytery with the corporate priesthood of the whole body.[84]

To Torrance's disappointment, the Church of Scotland would not come on board with this proposal and this method for ecumenical rapprochement was no longer Torrance's primary way; he took the more theological route discussed above.

---

83. Torrance lists a number of doctrinal principles which he thinks are central for this merger: "1) Jesus Christ is the Head of the Church, and presides of it in all things.

2) Through baptismal incorporation into Christ all members of the Body are given to share in their appropriate way in His Royal Priesthood. They are joined together by the One Spirit in such a way that they are ordered by the Head according to a diversity of function and in a mutual subordination of love.

3) Within the Body and within its royal priesthood there is a special modification of the corporate priesthood bound with the ordering of the Eucharist. This is the ministry of the Word and Sacrament instituted and given by the ascended Lord to the Church and placed within the Body and it is continuously renewed in every age. It is essentially a subministration which by its very place and nature must not seek to dominate or lord it over the body, i.e., to usurp the place of the Head. As placed within the Body this ministry is essentially corporate, and must be given corporate expression serving the corporate priesthood, and must manifest a unity in the Body corresponding to its one Head.

4) Within and over the ministry of the Word and Sacrament, or the special priesthood of the Church, there is the 'episcopate,' not as a higher ministry, but as a special gift for the oversight of the ministry, and as the sign both of the corporate nature of the priesthood and the corporate continuity of the Church." See The Thomas F. Torrance Manuscript Collection. Special Collections, Princeton Theological Seminary Library. Box 89.

84. The Thomas F. Torrance Manuscript Collection. Special Collections, Princeton Theological Seminary Library. Box 89.

Sacraments

Torrance's view of the Sacraments is rooted in the patristic notion of the vicarious humanity of Christ. He conceives of this doctrine as truly Reformed
(through Calvin) and also patristic (primarily Athanasius and Cyril).[85] Torrance holds a very high view of the sacraments and liturgy placing him very
much in line with those discussed in chapter 1 who are attracted to the early
church and often convert to Orthodoxy or Catholicism on the basis of their
rich sacramental and liturgical life.

Regarding baptism, Torrance sees the New Testament and patristic
conception of baptism to have been rooted, not in the act itself, but in the
reality it points to, namely Christ's vicarious baptism and act of saving.[86]
Similarly, Torrance holds a very high view of the Lord's Supper that he sees
as patristic. In his introduction to his translation of Robert Bruce's sermons
on the sacraments[87] Torrance discusses how he sees Bruce following The
Fathers in his doctrine of the sacraments and particularly the Eucharist.[88]
Throughout his sermons, which from his appreciative introduction Torrance clearly agrees with, Bruce puts forward a "spiritual union" in the Lord's
Supper whereby Christ is really present and believers are made to truly feed
upon the actual body and blood of Christ. As stated, Torrance sees this as a
return to the early church and more faithful to The Fathers than the Roman
Catholic notion of transubstantiation.[89]

CONCLUSION

Currently the evangelical church is on the brink of a "neopatristic"[90] revival
on the basis of their *ressourcement* of classical Christian theology. As argued
in chapters 1 and 2 of this book, although the Reformers were rooted in The

85. See Torrance, *Theological Dialogue*, 1:11 and also the section in chapter 2 on the
vicarious humanity.

86. Torrance, *Conflict and Agreement*, 125–32. Torrance arrives at this notion on
the basis of both his theology of the vicarious humanity and by his comparison of the
Greek word *baptisma* to *kerygma*. He contends that, like *kerygma*, *baptisma* points to
the reality beyond itself. James Barr is highly critical of this and other similar steps
Torrance took with both Hebrew and Greek words. See Barr, *Semantics of Biblical Language*, 140f for Barr's critique of Torrance's interpretation of *baptisma*.

87. Torrance, *The Mystery of the Lord's Supper*, 13–36.

88. Ibid., 32.

89. This would further explain Torrance's turn to the Orthodox in ecumenical
dialogue (rather than Roman Catholics).

90. To use Florovsky's phrase.

Fathers and resolutely saw themselves as a continuation of the evangelical tradition in the early church over against the Roman Catholics who had departed, subsequent Protestantism turned their back on the tradition of the classical Fathers for a variety of reasons. However, owing to the shift from a modern to postmodern paradigm and, even more so, the work of figures such as Torrance, evangelicalism is currently returning to the classical tradition of The Fathers in full force.

The evangelical, Christological, and Trinitarian method of patristic appropriation while remaining in one's own tradition begun by Torrance has been followed by a number of scholars. Some of these theologians see themselves following in the footsteps of Torrance whereas others should simply be considered to be in the same evangelical stream of Torrance. The full outcome of the recent (and very much ongoing) evangelical re-appropriation of the classical Christian Fathers discussed in chapter 2 remains to be seen as it is those who are currently writing and publishing whom "carry the torch" now. Torrance has played a role in igniting this return and ought to continue to provide an example and serve as a guide for evangelicals wishing to return to the classical Greek Fathers.

Chapter 2 argued that upon discovery, evangelicals typically convert to another denomination (erroneously confusing faith and order by holding to a static view of confessions and theology) or (at varying levels) tendentiously appropriate a general Great Tradition (subjectively selecting ideas to appropriate). The subsequent chapters have explored Torrance's approach. His Christocentric, Trinitarian, and evangelical appropriation allows him objective appropriation and reconstruction of the patristic tradition as well as reformation of his own tradition. This chapter argued, furthermore, that Torrance's approach is commendable considering his objectivity, faithfulness to The Fathers, evangelical commitment, and inherent ecumenical openness.

Torrance's return to the Greek Fathers is both objective and ecumenical. Placed next to other Protestant evangelical retrievals, Torrance's return to the Greek Fathers over and against Augustine is unique for his Reformed and Protestant tradition. The most unique element of Torrance is that he remains decisively Reformed while objectively appropriating the Greek Fathers. As such, he is an excellent example for Reformed and evangelical theologians wishing to appropriate the Greek Fathers. Torrance provides a viable template for appropriation. He portrays the Greek Fathers as the inheritance of the Reformed and evangelical tradition and he helpfully explores how this is so.

However, Bruce McCormack critiques Torrance's bypassing of Reformed confessions in his return to patristic theological themes.[91] McCor-

---

91. McCormack, "The End of Reformed Theology?" 46–64. Griffith is similarly

mack voices concern over the current trend in confessional Protestantism. As he sees it, Protestants who care about theological orthodoxy return to ancient Christianity instead of the confessions of the Reformed church.[92] As argued in chapter 1, this trend indeed exists. These Protestants are either subjective/self-norming (thus essentially liberal), converting to Roman Catholicism/Eastern Orthodoxy, or (as with many evangelicals) returning to Greek patristic theological themes and viewing them from an evangelical and Protestant (but sometimes too tendentiously Western) standpoint. McCormack contends that if present trends continue the only churches left in the west in the next century will be Roman Catholic, Eastern Orthodox, and conservative evangelical. He states: "Protestantism as we know it will have ceased to exist. The end of Reformed theology may well coincide with the end of Reformed churches."[93]

McCormack attributes part of the problem to Reformed Protestant theologians who, while claiming to remain Reformed and Protestant, return to the Nicene Creed and the theology of the early church. McCormack contends that those attempting to return to the Nicene Creed and patristic theology can no longer be called "Reformed" because "Reformed" means interpreting the creed and the early church through the Reformed confessions.[94] Indeed, McCormack considers this return to be basically liberal. As he sees it, liberals and orthodox; converge here on the doctrine of "union with Christ" and ultimately it is not really objective but subjective and self-norming-indeed, a union of the soul with Christ.[95] McCormack proposes that Reformed theologians (if they are really Reformed) must submit to the Reformed confessions and he urges for a return to sources, namely, the

---

critical. He argues that Torrance's departure from a forensic notion of justification "marks a decisive break with Calvin and the Reformed tradition" (Griffith, "High Priest in Heaven," 238). Griffith is, more generally, critical of Torrance for combining Christ's accomplished work with the application of this work to Christians, arguing that the two must be separated (ibid., 221).

92. McCormack, "The End of Reformed Theology?" 10.

93. Ibid., 53.

94. Ibid., 52.

95. McCormack argues that the emphasis on Nicaea/patristic theology outside the Reformed confessions tends to emphasize themes such as union with Christ. He contends this emphasis is not really objective but subjective and self-norming. See McCormack, "The End of Reformed Theology?" 52–53. In his Croall Lectures at the University of Edinburgh in 2011 he similarly compared the theology of Athanasius and Schleiermacher. As discussed in chapter 1 of this book, this critique assumes a Harnackian reading of Athanasius. McCormack's critique is part of a much bigger dissatisfaction with Protestant theology departing from typical Protestant emphases such as Penal Substitution, which McCormack considers to be central to traditional Protestantism.

Reformed confessions.[96] His conclusion is that, unless patristic theology is read through the Reformed confessions one is not really Reformed.[97]

McCormack's critique of Torrance's approach assumes a seriously static view of what it means to be Reformed, much like the static approach to tradition taken up by those who confuse faith and order and consider it necessary to Roman Catholicism or Eastern Orthodoxy after discovering The Fathers. This static approach is akin to the approach that Torrance sees in the Western church; the "Tertullian type of approach" towards both Scripture and confession.[98] According to Torrance the Reformed and evangelical churches often tend, rather unfortunately, towards this "Tertullian approach" and this "had the effect of reducing the church's Confession of the Faith to systems of doctrinal presuppositions which are invested with prescriptive authority."[99] Torrance sees this as "dualist" and "legalist" and believes that a more proper approach would be with a dynamic conception of the object of the Confession of Faith, or as he puts it, "we must learn to distinguish the Substance of the Faith from explicit doctrinal formulations. Thus here again we have a return to the perspective of Nicene theology."[100]

No doubt Torrance prefers a more dynamic notion of dogma/theology and theological language; the more "evangelical" and indeed "scientific" approach discussed in chapter 3 of this book. Indeed, Torrance argues that the Protestant churches often tend towards a legalist approach to the confessions.[101] His critique of the Reformed churches in this regard is strong.[102]

Ultimately Torrance's separation of faith and order as well as the object of truth and expressions of truth is helpful in this regard. As he sees it, the

96. McCormack, "The End of Reformed Theology?" 64.

97. He strongly critiques Torrance (inter alia) in a footnote. McCormack questioned whether the enterprise of theologians such as Torrance who make themes such as "union with Christ" and even go so far as to label it *"theosis"* could be rightly called "Reformed." He takes takes issue with (1) the fact that these emphases are not in the Reformed confessions and (2) that theologians such as Torrance return to these emphases while bypassing the Reformed confessions. See McCormack, "The End of Reformed Theology?" 51 n. 51.

98. See Torrance, *Theological Dialogue*, 1:107.

99. Ibid.

100. Ibid.

101. See ibid., 91–107 particularly 103–7. He urges for evangelicals to depart from the Tertullian type legalist approach where expression of the truth becomes abstract and detached from the truth itself to which it points and to return to the Bible and the confessions with a more Irenaean and personal approach wherein the focus is not on the Deposit of Faith or the *kerygma* itself but to the person/work of Jesus Christ to whom/which it points, namely, the Nicene doctrine of ὁμοούσιον.

102. See Torrance, "Introduction" in *The School of Faith*, xvii–xi.

Reformed tradition always views confessional formulations as subordinate to the core of the faith.[103] Those pioneering the "evangelical Calvinist" movement are following a similar mindset with much fruit.[104] Here, Torrance's reading is relevant in today's theological climate. This chapter explored where Torrance's approach uniquely fits not only among evangelicals returning to The Fathers but also evangelicals appropriating The Fathers in similar ways to Torrance. The argument was proffered that Torrance's approach is highly relevant. Therefore, a critical adoption of it is much in order. The following chapter will offer an overall assessment of Torrance's project and explore his uniqueness more fully. This concluding chapter will also offer a proposed way forward, namely, critical adoption of Torrance's lens and method.

---

103. Torrance, *Theological Dialogue*, 1:6–10.

104. Habets and Grow, *Evangelical Calvinism*. Thus their situating themselves more with the Scots Confession than with Westminster, in a very Torrancian fashion (5). They view theology as a "centered set" rather than a "bounded set" to use mathematical language.

CONCLUSION

An Assessment and Proposed Adoption of Torrance

Few contemporary theologians in [Torrance's] tradition have so thoroughly and consistently appropriated the spiritual wealth of Greek patristic theology and particularly the theology of the Alexandrian Church as it was given expression and formulation by the great Fathers, Athanasius and Cyril.

George Dion. Dragas, "The Significance for the Church of Professor Torrance's Election As Moderator of the General Assembly of the Church of Scotland," 216.

INTRODUCTION

This book has explored the substance, merit, place, and relevance of the patristic scholarship of Thomas F. Torrance. The study has shown that Torrance imaginatively reconstructs the Greek Fathers in light of the evangelical tenets of the Reformation, and accordingly, reconstructs elements of Reformed theology in light of Greek patristic theology into a Reformed evangelical version of the *Consensus Patrum*.[1] Torrance combines the

1. Torrance states: "When Greek Patristic Theology is studied and interpreted in the strong Biblical perspective restored through the Reformation of the Church in the West that its permanent place in the foundations of Evangelical Theology may be appreciated in a new way . . . [and] when Reformed Theology is reassessed and interpreted

Christological emphasis the classical Greek Fathers and the evangelical/ soteriological emphasis of Reformed Christianity and reconstructs The Fathers around this basis.[2] For Torrance, this essentially means a reconstruction of The Fathers around Athanasius and the Nicene doctrine of ὁμοούσιον τῷ Πατρί, which, as he sees it, encapsulates these dual core emphases, captured by the patristic era and the Nicene era.[3] Consequently, Torrance sees an "evangelical stream" of theology running from Irenaeus through Athanasius, Cyril, Didymus, Epiphanius, Calvin, and culminating in the theology of Karl Barth. This evangelical stream is the Torrancian *Consensus Patrum*. In many ways, Torrance sees his vocation involving a preservation of this "stream" and he uses it to "evangelize" contemporary theology that had fallen into epistemological, cosmological, and soteriological dualism in both the Eastern and Western churches.

Torrance's project offers an evangelical and theologically driven reading of classic Christianity. This has much to offer not only to Reformed evangelical Protestantism's generally functional (as opposed to ontological/ personal) Christology but also to, more generally, the current patrological climate where the church fathers are often studied in the context of a history of late-antiquity rather than theology.[4] Ecumenically, Torrance's project opens the door for dialogue with both the Roman Catholic and Eastern Orthodox churches because, on the one hand, it assists evangelicals in seeing themselves in line with patristic Christianity and, on the other hand, offers a basis for rapprochement with other churches.[5]

The overall argument in this book has been that Torrance imaginatively reconstructs the Greek Fathers in light of the evangelical tenets of the Reformation and, more particularly, around Athanasius and his doctrine of the ὁμοούσιον. This study has been focused upon Torrance's reading and use of the church fathers and thus has emphasized the patristic side of Torrance's historical reconstruction though, no doubt, much could be explored

---

in light of its ancient roots in the evangelical theology of the early centuries that its essential catholicity and its unifying force are to be understood" (*Trinitarian Perspectives*, 21–22).

2. Torrance, *Reality and Evangelical Theology*, 14–15; Torrance, *Preaching Christ Today*, 20; Torrance, *Theology in Reconciliation*, 235–37, 285; Torrance, *Theology in Reconstruction*, 267.

3. Or, the "epistemological and evangelical significance of the ὁμοούσιον." See e.g., Torrance, *The Trinitarian Faith*, 133–59.

4. A critique proffered recently by the Eastern Orthodox patrologist John Behr. See Behr, *The Mystery of Christ*, 18.

5. Perhaps, in the words of Colin Gunton, because it provides a "reopening of a major historical conversation." See Gunton, *Father, Son, and Holy Spirit*, 51.

in regards to Torrance's reconstruction of the Reformed tradition in light of classic patristic theology.

Chapter 1 of this book explored the historical precedent of Torrance's project by means of a study of the *Consensus Patrum* in historical Protestantism, Roman Catholicism, and Eastern Orthodoxy, whilst chapter 2 placed Torrance's reading of The Fathers in the context of recent evangelical retrievals of The Fathers. Chapters 3 and 4 explored the Torrancian *Consensus Patrum* itself, arguing that it consists of catholic themes (chapter 3) and figures (chapter 4), centered upon Athanasius and the ὁμοούσιον. In chapter 5 this book unpacked the ecumenical significance of Torrance's project arguing that Torrance's *consensus* enables him to remain in his own Reformed evangelical tradition while retrieving the Greek Fathers in an ecumenical fashion. This concluding chapter will offer an appreciative yet critical assessment of the Torrancian *Consensus Patrum* and a proposed way forward, toward an "evangelical patristic theology," critically adopting the Torrancian *Consensus Patrum*.

A CRITICAL APPRECIATION

Throughout each chapter of this book, appreciative criticism has been offered on Torrance's reading of the church fathers in the form of critical exposition, comment, comparison, and analysis. The Torrancian *Consensus Patrum* has much merit inasmuch as it is largely faithful to the catholic themes and figures of classical patristic (especially Greek patristic) Christianity while remaining substantially evangelical and Reformed. In addition to this objectivity, the Torrancian *consensus* is inherently ecumenical and has paved a path for others to follow.

As Bromiley helpfully points out, the way forward for evangelical studies of classical Christianity has to do with the fact that classical patristic views do not necessarily lead to medieval Roman Catholic views.[6] Indeed, nor do they lead to contemporary Roman Catholic or Eastern Orthodox views. Rather, classical patristic Christianity, in fact, can lead just as much to contemporary evangelicalism. Thus, instead of being only Roman Catholic or Eastern Orthodox resources, The Fathers are equally (if not more so) evangelical resources. The church fathers have, as Bromiley notes, provided excellent guides for discussion of the Trinity, Christology, atonement, (and more), and are excellent resources for evangelicals.[7] Ultimately, then, to use the words of Williams, evangelicals learn from Torrance that:

6. Bromiley, "Promise of Patristic Studies," 130–35.

7. Ibid., 135–40.

To be 'deep in history' for evangelical Protestantism need not be and should not be oxymoronic. One should not leave evangelicalism or a believer's church setting to be nourished by the substantial resources available in ancient (or patristic) Christianity. The great model for this undertaking was and is Philip Schaff, whose scholarly work of the last century in producing translations of primary texts of church history, the early church especially, is a sufficient demonstration that any oxymoron between Protestantism and the whole of the church's history is artificially self-imposed.[8]

Indeed, Schaff, the younger evangelicals, and especially, as this book has argued, Torrance are great examples to be followed; and, hopefully more will continue to work on the ground which they have so wonderfully tilled. This book has explored how Torrance provides a viable model for Reformed evangelicals.

Ultimately, Torrance not only offers fresh insight into patristic and Reformed theology, offering challenges to traditional readings of both, but also provides a genealogy of church history and a lens through which evangelicals and Reformed can confidently see the patristic tradition as their inheritance and read the Greek Fathers. Torrance has paved the way for his method to be critically taken up and applied in further theological studies of the church fathers. Indeed, patrology, systematic theology, and evangelicals/ Reformed wishing to retrieve The Fathers have much for which to thank Torrance and much that they can learn from him both substantially and methodologically.

Chapters 1 and 2 both explored how the typical Western and Protestant tradition, often uncritically, focuses upon Augustine and Augustinian theology. Torrance, rather, returns to Athanasius and was somewhat critical of Augustine and the Latin tradition. Chapter 4 discussed Torrance's uniqueness as a Reformed Protestant returning to Athanasius and the other Greek Fathers rather than Augustine and the Augustinian tradition. The Torrancian *Consensus Patrum*'s truly catholic breadth can be seen particularly in light of those discussed in chapter 1 (a) who return to the Greek Fathers and convert to Roman Catholicism or Eastern Orthodoxy, (b) who return to the Greek Fathers and tendentiously appropriate them, and (c) the current trend within evangelical circles, especially in North America, towards a return to the Greek Fathers.

This book argued that the evangelical return to classical Christianity (the third group discussed in chapter 2), while most like Torrance and

---

8. Williams, *Evangelicals and Tradition*, 12.

commendable in many regards, tends towards amalgamation of the many strands of patristic tradition into one great "Tradition" and can tend towards unfairly Western reading of The Fathers by continuing to focus on Augustinian and Western theological themes. Torrance stands unique among them inasmuch as he, while remaining staunchly evangelical and Reformed, returns to truly catholic themes and figures. Therefore, this group could learn much from Torrance as his appropriation of the themes from patristic theology, while remaining committed to his own Reformed and evangelical tradition, can serve as an example for others wishing to retrieve The Fathers objectively into their own tradition in the future. Torrance's genealogy of theological history provides a helpful template to be used critically by evangelicals and Reformed theologians wishing to appropriate The Fathers into their own tradition.

Torrance's approach potentially sheds light upon why many others are "heading east." Many theologians (academic, clerical, and lay) are dissatisfied with typical Western/Augustinian emphases on the *ordu salutis,* double predestination, and the forensic elements of the atonement.[9] Torrance's departure from this and his emphasis on Greek patristic themes and figures (e.g., Athanasius, Cyril, union with Christ, and the personal/Christocentric nature of the atonement) can be viewed as a part of this greater movement. Additionally, Torrance's separation of faith and order as well as the substance of the faith from the expression of the faith provides a helpful parameter for ecumenical dialogue allowing evangelical theologians to remain evangelical but not remain statically evangelical. Ultimately, Torrance's approach, namely, remaining substantially Reformed and evangelical while appropriating the Greek Fathers provides an example and guide for further appropriation.

Torrance's project of patristic reconstruction is successful, generally faithful to the theological ideas and commitments of The Fathers, and highly imaginative and constructive. Indeed, as his former student George Dragas put it:

> Few contemporary theologians in [Torrance's] tradition have so thoroughly and consistently appropriated the spiritual wealth of Greek patristic theology and particularly the theology of the Alexandrian Church as it was given expression and formulation by the great Fathers, Athanasius and Cyril.[10]

9. Notably, those in the evangelical Calvinist movement. See Habets and Grow, *Evangelical Calvinism.*

10. Dragas, "The Significance for the Church," 216.

Torrance returns to The Fathers and attempts to not only grasp what they mean but also seeks to creatively apply them in his own context. This book has argued that Torrance is largely successful in his attempt and reconstructs both his own Reformed evangelical tradition and many standard readings of The Fathers in light of one another into a Reformed evangelical rendering of the *Consensus Patrum*. As such, Torrance's Reformed evangelical *consensus* offers a helpful Reformed and evangelical approach to the church fathers.

Torrance has "cleared the ground" for others to continue his work. He successfully presents the Greek Fathers as the "inheritance" of Protestants, evangelicals, and Reformed as much as they are the inheritance of Roman Catholics and Eastern Orthodox. He also paints the evangelical tradition as in line with classical Christianity, particularly the theology of the Greek Fathers. This provides an excellent guide for further evangelical appropriation and a bridge for ecumenical dialogue. Torrance's approach offers a legitimate method to be adopted by Reformed and evangelical theologians and his reading offers a helpful lens through which to view The Fathers.

Whereas the more holistic approaches of Webber, Oden, and Williams discussed in chapter 2 have much to offer, they do offer some hermeneutical problems. Primarily, their approach, while in theory looking to all of the evangelical tradition, in practice tends to focus on particular eras and figures without offering a reason why.[11] Other than Oden, there is no prescribed method of appropriation and even Oden's project offers no method for choosing particular streams over others; and there most certainly were different streams that can all be considered classical Christianity. There are nuances among The Fathers and one need only to read The Fathers to see that disagreement existed among them. There is no seamless "Tradition."[12] Torrance provides a viable reading of these differences, while at the same time preserving certain nuance and making distinctions.

Typically, scholars in the these Protestant movements of retrieval acknowledge but do not substantially use Torrance, perhaps owing to lack of

11. Williams voices a similar critique of Oden's appropriation (Williams, *Retrieving the Tradition*, 34).

12. Though the current trajectory of Ayres, Holmes, et al., in large part, disagrees. Holmes asserts a seamless garment, a "one voice," of the classical and truly ecumenical Christian tradition on the doctrine of the Trinity spanning East and West, Greek and Latin (Holmes, *The Holy Trinity*, 144–46). There are others who agree with Torrance that there is distinction in the patristic era. See Behr, "Calling upon God as Father," 153–65 for an account that is more nuanced than traditional East-West distinctions but that argues for important differences. The way forward may be somewhere in the middle of the spectrum between Torrance's strong distinctions and the newer readings' "one voice."

knowledge of his patristic appropriation[13] or perhaps owing to his overly binary depiction/emphasis on Greek patristic themes such as *theosis*.[14] Torrance approaches the Greek Fathers on their own terms and allows what he finds to reform his own tradition; the outcome is Torrance, a Reformed theologian, talking about, for example, *theosis*, the vicarious humanity of Christ, and bishops. This stands out amongst the many current evangelical retrievals which look for Protestant themes in the Greek Fathers.

Thus, while the entirety of these figures offer a helpful corrective to Torrance's sometimes simplistic and binary reading of the patristic era, their more holistic and synthetic approach is equally as problematic. The Fathers are indeed not a seamless garment and a hermeneutic for appropriation is much needed. Furthermore, the Greek Fathers simply did not work with the same themes as the Western Fathers.[15] Accordingly, Torrance's objective focus on Greek patristic themes such as the ὁμοούσιον and the epistemological and soteriological/evangelical implications contained within it remains a helpful guide for evangelical appropriations of classical Christianity who want to remain evangelical on the one hand and faithful to The Fathers on the other hand. It is important to approach The Fathers on their own terms. Torrance does this and extracts what he learns applying it to his own tradition. The temptation is to tendentiously look for certain themes in The Fathers and Torrance is an example of how to successfully approach The Fathers from a certain perspective while also being fair to The Fathers themselves.

There are theologians more in line with Torrance's objective focus, evangelical commitments, and faithfulness to The Fathers such as Colin Gunton and his return to the "classical tradition" as he called it and his strong focus on the doctrine of the Trinity.[16] Bromiley also proposes a more

13. With notable exceptions: See Oden, *The Rebirth of Orthodoxy*, 165–66 who was clearly influenced by Torrance. Notably, Williams' only reference to Torrance is a critique of misreading the early Greek Fathers on justification. Williams is critical of Protestant theologians returning only to Augustine for proof of a Protestant doctrine of justification and sees the early Greek Fathers asserting substantially the same position as the Reformers. Accordingly, he is critical of Torrance for accusing the Greek Fathers of not holding to an Augustinian notion of justification. See Williams, *Evangelicals and Tradition*, 130–39.

14. Typically Protestants in this movement tend towards very broad ecumenism and look to a general "Great Tradition" (whilst at the same time focusing on a few select figures).

15. See McGrath, *Iustitia Dei*.

16. Gunton, *Promise of Trinitarian Theology*. Though Gunton's conclusions are different than Torrance and more in line with Torrance's "Cappadocian distinction," in methodology Gunton is more in line with Torrance than the more holistic approaches discussed above.

objectively focused appropriation.[17] Additionally, Donald Fairbairn offers a Christologically-centered and grace based approach much akin to Torrance.[18] Finally, Andrew Purves' publications and teaching focus upon a similar approach to classical patristic theology.[19]

Ultimately, Torrance can and should continue to act as a helpful guide. By showing that The Fathers are precursors to the evangelical tradition and that evangelicalism is a continuation of the evangelical stream in the early church he provides impetus for evangelical appropriation of The Fathers. Furthermore, the example of Torrance's ecumenical work should act as a guide for how to approach The Fathers as an evangelical while remaining in one's own tradition. It is notable that although, as discussed in chapter 4 of this book, Torrance's work on The Fathers has generally not been utilized by patristics scholars or Reformed evangelical theologians, there has been a very positive reception of it by Eastern Orthodox theologians, particularly patrologists. For example, Orthodox theologians such as George Dragas,[20] Matthew Baker,[21] John Behr (to a certain extent),[22] and even Georges Florovsky[23] are all fairly positive in their reception of Torrance.[24] The appreciation generally has to do with Torrance's appreciation of The Fathers, the Greek Fathers in particular.

17. Bromiley, "Promise of Patristic Studies," 145–51.

18. Fairbairn, *Grace and Christology*; Fairbairn, "Patristic Soteriology," 289–310.

19. Purves' teaching currently entails Reformed theology and he teaches very much from a patristic perspective much akin to Torrance. His publications focus on his former role as Professor of Pastoral Theology and place pastoral theology in a Christological and Trinitarian context by means of The Fathers and also Torrance himself. See Purves, *Reconstructing Pastoral Theology*.

20. Dragas, "The Significance for the Church."

21. Baker, "The Place of St. Irenaeus."

22. Behr, Review of *Divine Meaning*.

23 See Baker, "The Eternal 'Spirit of the Son'" for an argument for substantial similarity between Florovsky and Torrance in both Triadology and, more generally, basic theology. In his classes, George Dragas, who studied under both Torrance and Florovsky has commented that the two were close and both voiced deep appreciation for the other to him.

24. See also the many essays written by, in large part, Orthodox theologians contained in the recent issue of *Participatio: The Journal of the Thomas F. Torrance Theological Fellowship* (vol. 4, 2013) on Torrance and Orthodoxy as well as the forthcoming volume edited by Matthew Baker and Todd Speidell: *T. F. Torrance and Eastern Orthodoxy* to be published by Wipf & Stock. Such appreciation from Orthodox theologians augurs well for the continuation of ecumenical dialogue between the Reformed and Orthodox traditions on the basis of Torrance (and more deeply his rootedness in Greek patristic theology and theologians).

Torrance's *Consensus Patrum* is therefore highly relevant not only ecumenically but also for the current generation of evangelicals. Theologians in the "evangelical Calvinism" movement are currently using the method with figures from the Reformation.[25] Practically, Torrance's method can be applied very directly by exploring what the evangelical stream of the *Consensus Patrum* looked like in specific instances and in contemporary evangelical application.[26]

A CRITICAL ADOPTION

Accordingly, the rest of this conclusion will offer a proposed "way forward" from this study; a projected application of the fruits of this study and of Torrance's method. This will entail (1) pointing to which elements of the Torrancian *Consensus Patrum* should be adopted, (2) pointing to which elements of the Torrancian *Consensus Patrum* should be left behind, and (3) proposing a way forward, towards an "evangelical patristic theology." This will be done by means of by an exploration of Torrance's article "Karl Barth and the Latin Heresy"[27] as an illustrative point of departure.

This book has offered much appreciation of the Torrancian *Consensus Patrum* throughout each chapter. Torrance is both objectively focused upon God in Christ and theologically constructive. Torrance consistently begins his reading of the *consensus* from a starting point in Christ and, therein, God himself. Herein, Torrance sees himself following Athanasius.[28] His project remains focused upon Christology and, therein, Triadology and he continually reconstructs patristic theological themes in light of the Reformation doctrine of grace while at the same time attempting to do The Fathers justice by using their own themes and terms. Torrance contends that the affirmations in the fourth century at Nicaea and in the sixteenth century during the Protestant Reformation are complementary; the former emphasizing God's presence with humankind in Christ and the latter emphasizing the connection of the identity of the gift of grace and the Giver of grace.[29] For Torrance, both of these movements in the church preserved essential aspects to the great emphasis on the Greek patristic theme of the ὁμοούσιον,

25. Habets and Grow, *Evangelical Calvinism*. It is basically a reconstruction of Calvin's theology around the central tenets of the Gospel. Evangelical Calvinism is "constructive theology" (ibid., 7–8).

26. Such as asceticism. See Radcliff, "A Reformed Asceticism."

27. Torrance, "Karl Barth and the Latin Heresy," 461–82.

28. Ibid., 461.

29. Ibid., 462.

namely, that in Christ God has completely given himself to humankind in revelation and reconciliation.[30] Torrance's connection of Nicene theology and Reformation theology is extremely insightful and offers a convincing picture of the way in which The Fathers are the inheritance of evangelical Protestants while at the same time remaining inherently ecumenical and faithful to The Fathers. Furthermore, Torrance's reading of Nicene theology through the lens of the evangelical theology of the Reformation allows for fresh insight into the theology of The Fathers and a reconstruction of his own theological tradition in a plethora of areas, but most notably in Christology and, generally, all other areas flow out of Christology for Torrance.

The Torrancian *Consensus Patrum*'s focus upon Christology contributes to Reformed Protestant Christology. Chapter 3 of this book argued that the kernel of the Torrancian *consensus* is Athanasius' doctrine of the ὁμοούσιον, by which Torrance means "God Himself is the actual content of His revelation and God Himself is really in Jesus Christ reconciling the world to Himself."[31] For, Torrance, this insistence was key for the Nicene Fathers, especially Athanasius, and serves as the cornerstone of the *consensus* and, accordingly, acts as the cornerstone of dogmatic theology in general. Torrance's emphasis upon the Nicene and Athanasian ὁμοούσιον, offering much methodologically, offers, more pointedly, a contribution to Reformed Protestant Christology.

Reformed Protestant Christology has, historically, been tempted towards a "functional" emphasis, rather than on the person of Jesus Christ, more so upon the work of Christ.[32] In "Karl Barth and the Latin Heresy," Torrance traces varying versions of this "Latin Heresy" in western Christianity from Leo the Great through Anselm into contemporary western theology.[33] In Reformed Protestant theology, such as in the *Westminster Confession of Faith*, the ontological aspect of Christology is not denied, but the emphasis tends towards the functional side (Christ's work), sometimes at the expense of who Christ is (Christ's person).

Serving as an important contribution to this perspective, Torrance's Athanasius-ὁμοούσιον emphasis offers an important re-situating of Reformed Protestantism on Christology. Working off the ground tilled by Karl

---

30. Ibid., 464

31. Torrance, *The Christian Doctrine of God*, 7.

32. This is what Torrance calls the "Latin Heresy." See Torrance, "Karl Barth and the Latin Heresy."

33. Torrance, "Karl Barth and the Latin Heresy," 477–78. Here, he surely also has in mind the Reformed scholastic tradition, particularly the Westminster Tradition of which he was so critical in, e.g., his Introduction to *School of Faith*.

Barth on this,[34] and by tracing it back further to Athanasius, Nicaea, and the Greek Fathers Torrance widens the perspective and shows the broader context for this Christological emphasis. Torrance argues throughout "Karl Barth and the Latin Heresy" that the person and work of Christ cannot be separated and throughout his other works, as chapter 3 of this book argued, the ontological/personal aspect of Christology—the ὁμοούσιον—is absolutely central.

In addition to the purely Christological aspect discussed above, Torrance's approach offers challenges on a variety of levels, as argued in chapter 3 of this book. The ontological emphasis in Torrance's Christology challenges traditional Reformed Protestant emphases on the Penal Substitutionary theory of the atonement and incorporates it into a much broader atonement theory involving *theosis* and union with Christ. The ontological and personal emphasis in Torrance's Christology, combined with his view of the vicarious humanity of Christ, illuminates more fully the importance of the entire life of Christ, viewing the atonement in light of the incarnation, rather than the incarnation in light of the atonement.

Furthermore, Torrance's *consensus* offers much in regards to a holistic approach in contrast to a more dualistic approach. In his article "Karl Barth and the Latin Heresy," Torrance discusses his viewpoint that Karl Barth, following in the classical tradition of the church, was attacking Augustinian, Cartesian, and Newtonian dualism which had been running rampant in the church.[35] Torrance sees this dualism problematically undergirding Western theology in their doctrines of revelation[36] and reconciliation.[37] Torrance sees the dualism prevalent throughout the Western church, evident in such theologians as Leo the Great, Anselm, Peter Lombard, Aquinas, and, more generally, Roman Catholic and Reformed theology. Torrance sees "obvious connections" between Karl Barth and Athanasius[38] and sees a broad tradition in the church following in this stream.[39]

Certain elements of the Torrancian *Consensus Patrum* can be left behind as theologians of the next generation attempt to build on the fertile soil laid by Torrance. Torrance brings The Fathers into his own context and, very successfully, applies them to his own situation. While there is much

34. Torrance acknowledges this and speaks very highly of Barth's role in re-directing the emphasis in Reformed and evangelical thought in "Karl Barth and the Latin Heresy" and elsewhere.

35. Torrance, "Karl Barth and the Latin Heresy," 463.

36. Ibid., 463–73.

37. Ibid., 473–79.

38. Ibid., 464.

39. Ibid., 476.

to be commended in this, Torrance sometimes amalgamates modern and patristic theology and, even more so, Torrancian/Barthian and patristic theology in ways that can be unfair to The Fathers. Sometimes, instead of "obvious connections," between Athanasius and Barth (as Torrance puts it), Athanasius begins to look nearly identical to Barth.[40]

So, the method for figuring out what to "shave off" Torrance might look something like: what elements are more a part of Torrance's specific context than otherwise? These elements can then be revisited with fresh eyes and, perhaps, left behind with Torrance.

The first element is Torrance's attack on dualism. As discussed, Torrance sees his vocation as involving attacking the dualism embedded in Western theology.[41] The Fathers often become Torrance's tools in the fulfillment of this endeavor. Torrance sees elements of this problem present in patristic theology (such as in the debate between Athanasius and Arius). However at times Torrance's rendering of Athanasius' battle with Arianism looks suspiciously like his own attack on dualism in modern theology. Torrance sees himself combatting cosmological and epistemological dualism throughout his many texts. Accordingly, one of the aspects to Torrance's approach to The Fathers is that he is searching for elements of this in theological history. In turn, Torrance attacks many figures for elements of dualism in their thought: Augustine, Gregory Palamas, and Aquinas are all accused of this at some point and because of this Torrance does not really accord them much space in his texts. Torrance's broad critiques (such as "the Latin heresy") can herein tend towards over-simplicity at times. It is surely an over simplification to say that the entire west was dualist in epistemology and soteriology from Augustine until Barth.[42] Thus, perhaps more nuance

---

40. See e.g., Torrance, *Theology in Reconciliation*, 240f and Torrance's discussion of Athanasius' scientific theology. The point here is not that Torrance's connections are unfounded (chapter 4 argued that his connections are highly creative and helpful); rather, the point is simply that sometimes Torrance's "obvious connections" (as creative and helpful as they are) are not explicitly stated by Torrance and this gives the impression that Athanasius' theology is Barthian theology written in patristic Greek and Arius is propagating basically the same heresy as Schleiermacher, etc. Torrance often jumps between Barth and The Fathers sounding as if they are saying basically the same thing. See e.g., *Trinitarian Faith*, 93 and *Christian Doctrine of God* wherein Barth is referred to fairly often. See also *Space, Time, and Incarnation*.

41. See e.g., Torrance, *Karl Barth: Biblical and Evangelical Theologian*, 213–40.

42. Torrance accuses Augustine of dualism based on neoplatonic commitments. See e.g., Torrance's comments in Minutes from the Orthodox Reformed Consultation, Orthodox Centre of the Ecumenical Patriarchate, Chambesy, Geneva, 6–11, March 1983 in The Thomas F. Torrance Manuscript Collection. Special Collections, Princeton Theological Seminary Library, Box 170. Current Augustine scholarship now tends to avoid viewing Augustine in light of neoplatonism. See e.g., Ayres, *Augustine and the*

is needed here; one could reasonably say that Torrance has dealt with the problem of dualism so prevalent in his own time. Torrance rightly saw certain interpretations of these figures as dualist and attacked that; however, today scholars can nuance their approach to these figures more than Torrance did in his day, perhaps even leaving Torrance's critique of dualism behind with Torrance.

Chapter 4 discussed Torrance's attack on the "Cappadocian distinction" and the "Byzantine trajectory" of Gregory Palamas. The argument was put forward that this attack was, more deeply, aimed at John Zizioulas and, therefore, Torrance's distinction between Nicene theology and the Cappadocian distinction is really more about the 1980s than the 380s. Embedded within this debate is Torrance's more negative reception of the Augustinian West and the Byzantine East. However, the attacks are, once again, aimed more at theologians of his own context. His battle with Augustinian soteriological dualism is perhaps more deeply with the Federal/Scholastic/Westminster theology that he came across in his own context and his critique of the Cappadocians and Gregory Palamas is more of John Zizioulas and, even more so, the neopalamite theology of e.g., Lossky. On the one hand, these are largely successfully applications of The Fathers in his own time and in his own tradition. On the other hand, however, for theologians not in deep debate with the theology of the neopalamites, Zizioulas, and Federal theology, these elements of the Torrancian *Consensus Patrum* can be revisited and perhaps left with Torrance. Torrance successfully dealt with these problems and it is up to theologians today to move forward without elements of the Torrancian *Consensus Patrum* which were more contextual.[43]

In his reading of the patristic tradition Torrance hardly discusses other patristic scholars or secondary texts and is not always entirely transparent about his filters for reading The Fathers. Indeed, the list of his secondary sources is very limited.[44] As Behr notes, any look at the footnotes of Torrance's texts leaves the reader in wonderment at the number of primary source citations and at the same time the lack of secondary citations.[45]

Trinity.

43. See Farrow, "T. F. Torrance," 25–31 for a similar approach. In his article Farrow generally argues for the positive qualities of Torrance's theology and his return to The Fathers whilst also suggesting the unhelpfulness of Torrance's "Latin Heresy."

44. If his personal library catalogue is any indicator, he was working primarily with Protestant secondary sources (such as Dorner and Bethune-Baker), especially liberal (such as Harnack and Zahn). See his catalogue in The Thomas F. Torrance Manuscript Collection. Special Collections, Princeton Theological Seminary Library. Box 209.

45. Behr, Review of *Divine Meaning*, 107.

Furthermore, Torrance clearly has a number of ideas he considers core. Chapter 3 explored Torrance's view of Christ's assumption of fallen humanity arguing it may have come, in part, from H. R. Mackintosh's reading of Gregory Nazianzen. Chapter 3 also explored Torrance's discussion of the Greek versus the Latin views of the atonement and notes that his view has elements similar to John McLeod Campbell along with the Greek Fathers. Additionally, Torrance's vision assumes some notion of the Newmanian notion of "Development of Doctrine" discussed in chapter 1, which is very possible via Orr.[46]

Chapter 4 explored Torrance's commitment to Barthian theology. Additionally, chapters 3 and 4 explored Torrance's fondness for Augustinian Triadology which he considers to be basically Greek patristic. Finally, Torrance's reading of Athanasius on the doctrine of the Holy Spirit sometimes sounds very much like Swete and Shapland.[47] Torrance could have been clearer about his filters and what ideas were really from Athanasius, Barth, etc., and what was, in fact, Torrance. Indeed, it sometimes seems that Torrance thinks they were all saying basically the same thing and the line between what each figure actually said and Torrance's own conclusions is not always evident.

WHAT IS THE WAY FORWARD? AN "EVANGELICAL PATRISTIC THEOLOGY"

When the items relevant only to Torrance's context are removed, and the perennially beneficial elements of the Torrancian *Consensus Patrum* kept, an "evangelical patristic theology" emerges. The rest of this chapter will attempt to offer a basic outline of a way forward, an "evangelical patristic theology."

First, as explored in chapter 1, every interpreter of the *Consensus Patrum* has a lens. Therefore, Protestant evangelicals should not be ashamed

46. Torrance's reading of the patristic era looks very much like that of James Orr at times. See Orr, *The Progress of Dogma*. Notably, the Torrance archives at Princeton Seminary contain notes taken by Torrance on this text highlighting such ideas as situating Athanasius in the episcopal side of the Alexandrian school as well as Irenaeus as in line with Athanasius as a biblical theologian. Torrance also included Orr's text on the reading list for his Dogmatics course at New College. See The Thomas F. Torrance Manuscript Collection. Special Collections, Princeton Theological Seminary Library. Box 16 and 51 respectively. None of this is conclusive evidence for Orr's influence upon Torrance, but the similarities between the two and Torrance's utilization of Orr, are interesting nonetheless.

47. See Shapland's "Introduction" and see also Swete, *The Holy Spirit in the Ancient Church*, 212–21.

to have an "evangelical lens" through which they approach the *consensus*. Torrance has successfully reminded evangelicals and Reformed that The Fathers are their inheritance as much, if not more, than Roman Catholic and Eastern Orthodox. Furthermore, he has shown that patristic themes and figures can (and should) be approached through the lens of the evangelical commitments of the Reformers in the sixteenth century. Indeed, this is the proper approach for an evangelical.

Second, Torrance has offered a very helpful way to objectively approach the *Consensus Patrum*, namely, through the Athanasian ὁμοούσιον, Christology, and Triadology. Chapter 2 explored ways in which contemporary appropriation of The Fathers can tend towards tendentiousness without an objective principle. Torrance has offered an example of how to remain objective; by focusing on the central doctrine of Christ and, therein, the Trinity.

Thirdly, through the above two commitments, Torrance sheds fresh light on many truly catholic patristic themes and figures. While remaining evangelically committed, Torrance approaches The Fathers essentially on their own terms. This generally sets him apart from those in the paleo-orthodox movement which often approaches The Fathers with the desire of finding Western and Protestant themes and remains too statically committed to their confessions in a "Tertullian fashion." Torrance's themes and figures were discussed in chapters 3 and 4 respectively. Examples of the fresh light shed by Torrance are his reading of the vicarious humanity of Christ in Athanasius and Irenaeus, his reading of the science of theology in the Alexandrian tradition, his reformation of the *filioque* debate, and his manifold insights into ministry and ecclesiology in light of the early church and Christology.

Torrance has paved the way and it is up to theologians today to pick up where he left off and work towards constructing an "evangelical patristic theology." An evangelical patristic theology need not adopt the elements purely relevant to Torrance's context discussed above. Then, an evangelical patristic theology can revisit some of the more contextual elements of the Torrancian *consensus* and, following Torrance's example, approach truly catholic patristic themes and figures on their own terms, while remaining committed to the evangelical tenets of the Reformation.

An evangelical patristic theology is more capacious and less binary than Torrance, whilst at the same time learning from Torrance that The Fathers are not a seamless tradition but rather full of differing, but complementary, "streams." This can be done through an application of Torrance's grace/Christ-centered reading towards further readings of patristic themes and figures. Such scholarship as that of Lewis Ayres in re-reading the Nicene era can be utilized.[48] With Ayres, an evangelical patristic theology revisits Nicaea and the doctrine of the Trinity, perhaps seeing less of a distinction between Athanasius and the Cappadocians.[49] Also relevant is Ayres re-reading of Augustine.[50] The Western tradition may have much fruit which has not been picked on account of Torrance's widespread attack on dualism in the Latin and Byzantine traditions. Patristics scholars are now viewing the patristic era in a much more nuanced fashion than during Torrance's era. Along with Ayres, Rist,[51] Barnes,[52] and Hart,[53] to name a few, an evangelical patristic theology sees Augustine as, at least somewhat, in line theologically with the Greek Fathers (their emphasis is typically on the doctrine of the Trinity). Their argument is that Augustine was not as strong a proponent on such things as the *filioque* as later interpreters would have it. Perhaps he is in line with the Greek Fathers on more than this; there is much room indeed for further exploration.[54]

Furthermore, an evangelical patristic theology might explore a re-reading of Gregory Palamas, along the lines of the re-reading offered earlier in this book. The *hesychastic* tradition of Palamas is an area that has been

48. Ayres, *Nicaea and Its Legacy*. See pp. 188–221 for Ayres on Basil and pp. 365–83 for Ayres on Augustine. Though, as aforementioned, the trajectory of Holmes, Ayres, Barnes, et al. tends towards seeing the patristic tradition speaking with "one voice." This is probably an oversimplification on the opposite extreme of Torrance. Torrance helpfully shows that there are differences among figures in the patristic era, the newer readings show that these differences are not as clear-cut as Torrance contends; however, the *via media* is likely the best route forward: The Fathers were in basic agreement but with different emphases and nuances.

49. An evangelical patristic theology is also open to discussion of figures left out by Torrance such as Marcellus of Ancyra. See Parvis' groundbreaking work on Marcellus: *Marcellus of Ancyra and the Lost Years of the Arian Controversy, 325–345*. Parvis sees Marcellus as substantially more central than often thought by the rest of twentieth-century scholarship.

50. Ayres, *Augustine and the Trinity*.

51. Rist, *Augustine*. Rist argues that Augustine should be viewed less as a neo-Platonist and more as a Christian theologian.

52. Barnes, "Rereading Augustine's," 145–76.

53. Hart, "The Hidden and the Manifest," 191–226.

54. Current scholarship on Aquinas is also working more along these lines. See Kerr, *After Aquinas*, 56–65 for Kerr's appraisal of Aquinas on his so-called "natural theology." While not equating Barth and Aquinas, Kerr offers a reading that sees Barth and Aquinas more in line than traditionally thought. Karen Kilby offers a related reading of Aquinas on the doctrine of the Trinity. She sees Aquinas as emphasizing the distinctiveness of each person of the Trinity more than traditionally thought. See Kilby, "Aquinas," 414–27. Torrance considers Aquinas dualist in his theology cutting of the doctrine of the One God from the doctrine of the Triune God. See Torrance, *Theology in Reconciliation*, 285.

central to Byzantine theology for centuries and does not receive any attention from Torrance on account of his attack. Torrance's attack on both the Latin and Byzantine tradition is based on his battle against dualism. Evangelical patristic theology exists in a different era from Torrance and, accordingly, it can approach both traditions with the basic commitments of the Torrancian *Consensus Patrum* but can mine the depths of both traditions in ways not done by Torrance. Further studies of Palamas, the latter Byzantine tradition, and, indeed, non-Byzantine theological traditions from a less binary perspective than Torrance would likely bear much fruit.[55]

Moreover, an evangelical patristic theology can approach many themes not explored by Torrance on account of his avoidance of Latin and Byzantine theology because of their dualism. First, an evangelical patristic theology might explore a grace-based study of asceticism. Asceticism is often viewed as a "work" to do. However, if viewed in light of the Reformation the Byzantine ascetic tradition may have much to offer evangelicals. Second, the great ascetic tradition offers the vocation of monasticism. This has much to offer the evangelical churches today in many regards.

Some of Torrance's other themes may be picked up and explored further. For example, Torrance's reconstruction of the patristic notion of the bishropic regarding "Presbyterian bishops" may have more fruit on, for example, North American soil where fewer wars have been fought over church-related issues. Figures such as Habets pick up elements of Torrance and explore them further.[56] However, many elements of Torrance's remain to be applied throughout in the current conversations wherein they are relevant, for example, Torrance's doctrine of the Trinity, particularly his potential role as a *via media* between current debates in Trinitarian theology.[57]

Further studies may also explore other classical patristic themes or even different figures appropriating The Fathers into their evangelical

---

55. Iain Torrance (T. F.'s son) has written a magisterial text on Severus of Antioch (born c. 465 C.E.). Rather than as a "Monophysite," Torrance presents Severus as in line with the classic patristic on Christology and, as such, paves the way for ecumenical rapprochement between Oriental Orthodox and other non-Chalcedonians with adherents to Chalcedon seeing the two sides as less polarized than once thought. As such, Iain Torrance carries his father's work into post-Chalcedonian patristic theology. See Torrance, *Christology After Chalcedon*. His book is based on his PhD thesis and provides a substantial theological introduction to Severus' theology (pp. 37–74) and an introduction (75–139) and translation (143–236) of a selection of Severus' letters. It should be noted that T. F. Torrance was very appreciative of his son's work and referenced it in *The Christian Doctrine of God* (on page 160)

56. E.g., Habets, *Theosis in the Theology.*

57. Noble suggests the same in his book *Holy Trinity: Holy People.*

traditions.[58] For example, Philip Schaff's genealogy of church history may offer more elements by which an evangelical patristic theology can move forward.

CONCLUSION

In conclusion, T. F. Torrance has much to offer in regards to his reading and reconstruction of the *Consensus Patrum*. The best way to move forward is to appropriate Torrance's *Consensus Patrum*, revisit and possibly even leave behind the purely contextual elements, and continue the work which Torrance began, namely, a re-reading of the classical Christian tradition in light of the Reformation and continuing to tap into the bounteous well of the *Consensus Patrum* seeing what can be learned from the theology and lives of the classical, truly ecumenical, church fathers.

58. *Participatio: The Journal of the Thomas F. Torrance Theological Fellowship* is currently projecting an issue on Torrance and the church fathers which shall hopefully do this precisely.

Patristic Sources Cited in
Trinitarian Faith

Chapter 1: Faith and Godliness (121 footnotes)

Hilary of Poitiers
Contra Constantium Augustum Liber (1)
De Trinitate (31)
De Synodis (2)

Athanasius
Epistola ad Monachos (1)
De Synodis (9)
Ad Antiochenos (2)
Ad Afros (8)
Ad Adelphium (1)
Ad Serapionem (6)
De Decretis (5)
Contra Arianos (6)
Ad Epictetum (1)
Contra Gentes (1)
De Incarnatione (3)
Epistola Encyclica (3)
Expositio Fidei (1)
Apologia Contra Arianos (4)
Historia Arianorum ad Monachos (1)

Ad Episcopos Aegepti (4)
Vita Antonii (1)
Epistola 55 (3)
Epistola 56 (3)
Epistola 2 (3)
Epistola 39 (1)
Epistola 51 (1)
Epistola 59 (1)
Epistola 61 (1)
Epistola 62 (1)
Epistola 11 (1)

Basil
Epistola 125 (1)
Epistola 127 (1)
Epistola 140 (1)
Epistola 159 (1)
Epistola 204 (1)
Epistola 251 (1)

Theodoret
Historia Ecclesiastica (5)

Gregory Nazianzen

Epistola ad Cledonium, 102 (2)
Oratione 21 (2)
Oratione 19 (1)

Socrates
Historia Ecclesiastica (2)

Eusebius
Vita Constantinii (1)

Irenaeus
Demonstration of Apostolic
Preaching (3)
Adversus Haereses (64)

Clement of Alexandria
Stromateis (6)

Cyril of Jerusalem
Catecheses (1)

Augustine
De Trinitate (1)
In Joannem Evangelium (3)
De Libero Arbitrio (1)
De Diversis Quaestionibus (1)
In Psalmos (1)

Epistlola 120 (1)
De Spiritu et Littera (2)
The Liturgy of St James (1)

Tertullian
De Virginibus Velandis (1)

Origen
De Oratione (4)
De Principis (44)
Commentaria in Evangilium
Joannem (18)
Contra Celsum (47)
In Canticum canticorum (1)
In Mattheum (3)
In Deuteronomium (1)
In Jeremiam (2)
In Lucam (1)
Epistola ad Gregorium (1)
Epistle ad Afros (1)
Dialogue with Herakleides (1)

Prosper of Aquitaine
De gratie Dei et libero volunta-
tis arbitrio (1)

Chapter 2 : Access to the Father (73 footnotes)

Athanasius
De Synodis (10)
De Sententia Dionysii (1)
Ad Episcopos (6)
Ad Afros (2)
Ad Antionchenos (1)
Ad Monachos (3)
Ad Jovianum (3)
Ad Epictetum (2)
Contra Apollinarem (5)
Contra Arianos (28)
De Decretis (8)
Epistola Encyclica (2)

Contra Gentes (4)
Ad Serapionem (8)
Expositio Fidei (2)
In illud "Omnia mihi tradita"(1)
In Illud Omnia (4)
De Incarnatione (1)

Athenagoras
Legatio pro Christianis (1)

Origen
Contra Celsum (3)

Eusebius
Opera (1)

Gregory Nazianzen
  Oratione 30 (1)
  Oratione 28 (2)
  Oratione 29 (1)
  Oratione 31 (4)
  Oratione 6 (1)
  Oratione 25 (1)
  Oratione 38 (2)
  Oratione 1 (1)
  Oratione 18 (1)
  Oratione 21 (1)
  Oratione 34 (1)
  Oratione 38 (1)
  Oratione 39 (1)

Hilary of Potiers
  De Trinitate (42)
  De Synodis (4)

Basil
  Contra Eunomium (1)
  Homilia (1)

Hexaemaron (1)
Epistola 189 (1)
Epistola 210 (1)
Epistola 265 (1)
De Spiritu Sancto (6)

John of Damascus
  De Fide Orthodoxa. (1)

Gregory Nyssa
  Oratio Catechetica (3)
  De Spiritu Sancto adversus Macedonium (1)
  Contra Eunomium (3)
  Epistola 2 (1)

Irenaeus
  Adversus Haereses (1)

Cyril of Jerusalem
  Catecheses (1)

Cyril of Alexandra
  De Trinitate (1)

Chapter 3: The Almighty Creator (137 footnotes)

Athanasius
  Contra Arianos (87)
  De Decretis (16)
  De Synodis (9)
  Ad Antiochenos (5)
  Ad Afros (3)
  Ad Serapionem (3)
  Contra Gentes (14)
  De Incarnatione (10)
  In Illud Omnia (3)
  Expositio Fidei (6)
  Ad Episcopos (1)
  Epistola 11 (1)
  In Psalmos (1)
  Contra Apollinarem (1)

Hilary of Poitiers

De Trinitate (25)
Com. In Psalmos (1)
De Synodis (1)

Gregory of Nyssa
  De Trinitate (1)
  Antirrheticus contra Apollinarem (1)
  Non sint tres Dei (1)
  Oratio Catechetica (2)
  De Hominis Opificio (3)
  De anima et resurrectione (3)
  Contra Eunomium (8)

Evagrius/Basil
  Epistola 8 (1)

Athenagoras

Legatio pro Christianis (12)

De Resurectione mortuorum (5)

Origen
Contra Celsum (2)
De Principis (8)
In Joannem (2)

Theodoret
Historia Ecclesiastica (2)

Overture of the Council of Antioch to the Council of Nicaea (1)

Photius
Bibliotheca (1)

Epiphanius
Haereses (1)

Basil
Hexaemaron (25)
De Spiritu Sancto (3)
Contra Eunomium (1)
Epistola 6 (1)

Gregory Nazianzen
Oratione 39 (2)
Oratione 29 (2)
Oratione 28 (1)
Oratione 38 (4)

Oratione 45 (3)

Gregory Thaumaturgos
In Origenem (1)

Irenaeus
Adversus Haereses (41)
Demonstration of Apostolic Preaching (3)

Clement of Rome
1 Clement (1)
2 Clement (1)

Tatian
Oratio (1)
Oratio 7 (1)

Aristides
Apologeticum (2)

Theophilus
Ad Autolycum (12)

Justin Martyr
Dialogus cum Tryphone Judaeo (1)

Shepherd of Hermas (3)

Tertullian
De praescriptione Haereses (1)

Apostolic Constitutions (3)

Chapter 4: God of God, Light of Light (117 footnotes)

Justin Martyr
Dialogus cum Tryphone Judaeo (1)

Irenaeus
Adversus Haereses (19)
Demonstration of Apostolic Preaching (1)

Hippolytus

Refutatio Omnium Haeresium (4)

Clement of Alexandria
Stromatis (1)

Origen
De Principis (11)
Contra Celsum (1)

Minucius Felix

Octavius (1)

Tertullian
De Praescritione Haereses (2)
Adversus Praxean (1)
De Virginibus Velandis (1)
De anima (1)
De spectaculis (1)
De carne Christi (1)
De Resurrectione (1)

Eusebius
Historia Ecclesiastica (4)

Theodoret
Haereses (1)
Epistola 82 (1)

Hilary of Poitiers
De Trinitate (5)
De Synodis (8)

Jerome
Epistola 112 (1)

Ignatius
Philadelphians (1)
Magnesians (2)
Ephesians (2)
Trallians (1)
Smyrnans (1)

Alexander of Alexandria
Epistola 1 (1)

Theodoret
Historia Ecclesiastica (4)
Haereses (1)
Epistola 103 (1)

Eustathius
De an. Adv. Ar. (1) (Migne labels this "Fragmenta")

Socrates
Historia Ecclesiastica (2)

Gelasius

Historia Ecclesiastica (1)

Epiphanius
Ancaoratus (4)
Haereses (9)

Cyril of Jerusalem
Catecheses (2)

Athanasius
Contra Arianos (110)
De Incarnatione (4)
Contra Gentes (1)
Ad Maximum (1)
De Synodis (39)
Ad Epictetum (2)
De Decretis (40)
De Sententia Dionysii (2)
Ad Serapionem (24)
Ad Jovinium (1)
Ad Afros (13)
Ad Episcopos Aegyptii (1)
Festal Epistle 2 (1)
Festal Epistle 39 (1)
Festal Epistle 4 (1)
Festal Epistle 5 (1)
Festal Epistle 10 (1)
Ad Adelphium (4)
Ad Antiochenos (6)
In Illud Omnia (5)
Expositio Fidei (4)
Ad Episcopos (13)
De Sententia Dionysii (2)
Contra Apollinarem (6)
De Incarnatione et contra Arionos (1)
Sermo major de fide, fragmentum (1)

Ambrose
De Fide

Basil
Epistola 52 (5)

Epistola 125 (1)
Epistola 214 (1)
Epistola 236 (1)
Epistola 28 (1)
Epistola 9 (1)
Contra Eunomium (3)

Gregory/Basil
Epistola 38 (2)

Evagrius/Basil
Epistola 8 (2)

Gregory Nazianzen
Epistola 101 (1)
Oratione 45 (1)
Oratione 30 (3)
Oratione 29 (3)
Oratione 31(2)
Oratione 20 (1)
Oratione 42 (1)

Gregory of Nyssa
Contra Eunomium (7)
Oratio Catechetica (1)

Chapter 5: The Incarnate Saviour (153 footnotes)

Theodoret
Historia Ecclesiastica (1)

Alexander of Alexandria
De Anima et Corpore Deque
Passion Domini (4)

Athanasius
De Decretis (7)
Con Arianos (103)
Ad Afros (2)
Ad Adelphium (8)
Epistola 10 (1)
In Psalmos (2)
De Vita Antonii (2)
Contra Apollinarem (16)
Festal Epistle 10 (1)
Epistola 2 (1)
Epistola 14 (1)
Ad Maximum (3)
De Synodis (2)
De Incarnatione (19)
Ad Serapionem (7)
Ad Epictetum (16)
Ad Antichenos (8)
De Synodis (1)

Liturgy of St James (1)

Liturgy of St Mark (1)

Clement of Alexandria
Paedagogus (2)
Protrepticus (1)
Stromateis (7)
In Joannem (1)
Quis dives salvetur (3)

Origen
Dialektos (1)
In Matt. (2)
In Rom. (2)
In Num. (1)
In Lev. (3)
De Principis (2)
In Joannem (2)

Adamantius
De Recta Fide (1)

Epiphanius
Haereses (2)

Didymus
De Trinitate (3)
De Spiritu Sancto (1)

Irenaeus
Adversus Haereses (64)
Demonstration of Apostolic
Preaching (2)

Ad Diognetum (2)

Eusebius of Caesarea
Demonstratio Evangelica (6)

Theodoret
Dialogus (4)
Historia Ecclestiastica (1)

Augustine
Mediator inquantum Homo (1)
Confessiones (2)
Sermone 293 (1)
In Joannem Evangelium (2)
In Psalmos (1)
De Trinitate (3)
De Civitate Dei (1)
Enchiridion (1)

Apostolic Constitutions (1)

Gregory of Nyssa
Contra Eunomium (3)
Adversus Apollinarem (2)
Epistola Adversus Apollinarem
(1)
De Perfecta Christiani (1)
De Occursu Domini (1)
Oratia Catechetica (14)
Antirrheticus contra Apollina-
rem (1)
Oratia Catechetica (5)

Gregory Nazianzen
Oratione 1 (4)
Oratione 3 (1)
Oratione 30 (9)
Epistola 101 (2)
Oratione 2 (1)
Oratione 45 (3)

Oratione 28 (1)
Oratione 39 (1)
Oratione 4 (1)
Oratione 38 (2)
Carminum Theologica (4)
Oratione 22 (1)

Hilary of Poitiers
De Trinitate (14)

Cyril of Alexandria
In Joannem (3)
Dialogus cum Nestorium (1)
De Recta Fide (3)
Apologeticus Contra Theode-
tum (1)
Adversus Anthropomorphitas
(1)
Thesauruas de Sancta et Con-
substantiali Trinitate (2)
Epistola 17 ad Nestorium (1)
Adversus Nestorium (5)
Quod unus sit Christus (2)
De Incanatione Domini (1)
Epistola I (Ad Monachos Ae-
gytii) (1)

Evagrius/Basil
Epistola 8 (1)

Basil
Epistola 261 (3)
Epistola 236 (1)
In Psalmos (3)

Marius Victorinus
Adversus Arium (1)

Ambrose
Epistola 261 (1)

John Chrysostom
In Epistolam ad Romanos (1)
In Epistolam ad Hebraeos (1)

Cyril of Jerusalem

Catecheses (1)

Chapter 6: The Eternal Spirit (281 footnotes)

Athanasius
  Ad Serapionem (99)
  Contra Arianos (50)
  De Decretis (9)
  De Synodis (12)
  Ad Afros (1)
  Ad Antiochenos (5)
  Ad Adelphos (1)
  Ad Maximum (1)
  De Sententia Dionysii (2)
  Epistola 1 (1)
  Ad Jovinium (4)
  Contra Apollinarem (3)
  Ad Afros (2)
  In illud omnia (3)
  De Incarnatione et contra Aria-
    nos (1)
  Expositio Fidei (1)
  Ad Episcopos (2)

Epiphanius
  Haereses (142)
  Ancaoraturs (57)
  Ref Aet (from Haereses) (13)
  Expostitio Fidei Catholoicae et
    Apostolicae Ecclesiae (6)
  Expositio Fide (2)

Basil
  Epistola 236 (7)
  Entir. (1) (Athens edition)
  Epistola 125 (3)
  Homilia 111 (6)
  Contra Sabellianos (4)
  Contra Eunomium (19)
  De Spiritu Sancto (47)
  Epistola 38 (3)

Epistola 159 (2)
Epistola 226 (1)
Ep. Ad Epiph. (1) (Athens
  edition)
De Fide (1)
Hexaemeron (3)
Epistola 231 (1)
Epistola 159 (1)
Epistola 189 (1)
Epistola 69 (1)
Epistola 125 (3)
In Pas. (1) (Athens edition)
Epistola 21 (1)
Hom. Con. Syc. (1) – p. 237
  (Athens edition 54, pp.
  234–237)
Epistola 8 (1)
Epistola 31 (1)
Epistola 39 (1)
Epistola 210 (1)
Epistola 214 (3)
Epistola 336 (1)
Epistola 258 (2)
Epistola 52 (2)
Epistola 243 (1)
Epistola 234 (2)
Epistola 235 (2)
Epistola 236 (1)
Epistola 152 (1)
Epistola 188 (1)
Epistola 251 (2)
Oratione 35 (1)
Epistola 90 (1)
De Obs Se (1) (Athens edition)
Lit (1) (Athens edition)

Gregory of Nyssa
Oratia Catechetica (6)
Ref. Eun. (1)
Contra Eunomium (18)
De Spiritu Sancto (10)
Epistola 24 (1)
De Trinitate (4)
Non Treis Dii (7)
Ex Communibus Notionibus (5)
Adversus Macedium (from Jaeger) (2)
De Fide (1)

Dionysius of Alexandria (1)

Cyril of Alexandria
Thesauruas de Sancta et Consubstantiali Trinitate (4)
Dialogi de Trinitate (1)
In Joannem (1)

Didymus
De Trinitate (83)
De Spiritu Sancto (23)
Contra Eunomium (17)
Contra Manichaeos (1)
Expositio in Psalmos (5)

Hilary
De Trinitate (24)
De Synodis (2)

John of Damascus
De Fide Orthodoxa (1)

Evagrius/Basil
Epistola 8 (2)

Apostolic Constitutions (3)

Didache (1)

Ignatius
Magnesians (1)

Polycarp Martyrdom (1)

Irenaeus
Adversus Haereses (6)
Demonstation of Apostolic Preaching (1)

Adamantius
Dialogus de rectra in deum fide (1)

Origen
De Principis (8)
In Joannem (3)
De Oratione (2)

Hippolytus
Apostolic Tradition (2)

Justin Martyr
1 Apologia (1)

Cyril of Jerusalem
Catecheses (65)
Procatecheses (1)
Epistola ad Constantiam (1)

Eusebius
De Ecclesiastica Theologia (3)

Gregory/Basil
Epistola 38 (9)
Epistola 189 (1)

Ps. Basil
Contra Eunomium (2)

Gregory Nazianzen
Oratione 41 (6)
Oratione 37 (2)
Oratione 24 (1)
Oratione 28 (2)
Oratione 29 (7)
Oratione 30 (8)
Oratione 31 (34)
Oratione 34 (3)
Oratione 36 (1)
Oratione 58 (1)

Oratione 43 (2)

Oratione 38 (2)

Oratione 21 (1)

Oratione 45 (2)

Oratione 40 (6)

Oratione 39 (7)

Oratione 30 (1)

Oratione 43 (3)

Oratione 25 (1)

Oratione 26 (1)

Oratione 32 (1)

Oratione 20 (1)

Oratione 14 (1)

Oratione 41 (1)

Oratione 18 (3)

Oratione 20 (1)

Epistola 101 (1)

Oratione 29 (5)

Oratione 2 (2)

Oratione 34 (3)

Oratione 33 (1)

Oratione 32 (1)

Oratione 15 (1)

Oratione 1 (1)

Oratione 42 (4)

Oratione 38 (1)

Oratione 20 (2)

Oratione 21 (2)

Ps. Gregory Nazianzen

Epistola 243 (1)

Theodoret

Historia Ecclesiastica (2)

Ps. Macarius

Homilia 17 (1)

Novation

De Trinitate (2)

Theophilus

Ad Autolycum (1)

Tertullian

Adversus Praxean (3)

Apologeticum (1)

Athenagoras

Supplicatio (1)

Legatio pro Christianis (2)

Ps. Athanasius

Quastiones aliae (1)

De Trinitate (1)

Amphilochius

Contra Haereses (1) (Athens edition)

Epistola Synodica (3)

Fragmenta (4)

John of Damascus

De Fide Orthodoxa (2)

Theodoret

Dialogus (1)

Historia Ecclestiastica (4)

Serapion

Euch. (3) (Athens edition, 43, P. 76)

Sozomen

Historia Ecclesiastica (1)

Augustine

De Trinitate (2)

Ps Dionysius

De Divinis Nominibus (2)

De Mystica Theologia (1)

Liturgy of St Mark (1)

Tertullian

De praescriptione haereses (1)

Chapter 7: The One Church (151 footnotes)

Cyprian
Epistola 70 (1)
Epistola 72 (1)
Epistola 74 (1)
Epistola 76 (1)
Episcopatus unus est (1)
On the Unity of the Church (4)
Cuius a singulis in solidum pars tenetur (1)

Origen
In Joannem (8)
De Principis (5)
Contra Celsum (1)
In Canticum Canticorum (1)

Augustine
De Trinitate (2)
In Joannem Evangelium (2)
In Psalmos (8)

Hilary
De Trinitate (8)
In Psalmos (8)

Theodoret
Historia Ecclesiastica (4)
Dialogus (1)

Gregory Nazianzen
Oratione 21 (1)
Oratione 2 (1)
Oratione 32 (1)

Cyril of Jeruselem
Catecheses (23)

Didymus
De Trinitate (4)
De Spiritu Sancti (1)
In ac (1) (Athens edition)

Eusebius
Historia Ecclesiastica (1)

Tertullian
De Baptisma (4)
De Pudicitia (1)
De Oratione (2)
Apologeticum (1)
De praescriptione haereses (1)
Adversus Praxean (2)
De Virginibus Velandis (3)
De anima liber (1)
De Spectaculis (1)
De Carne Christi (1)
De resurrectione carnis liber (1)

Athanasius
Ad Afros (1)
De Decretis (2)
Contra Arianos (43)
De Synodis (3)
Ad Adelphium (1)
Ad Serapionem (8)
In Psalmos (2)
De Sententia Dionysii (1)
De incarnatione et contra arianos (1)
Apologia contra arianos (1)
De incarnatione (2)

Clement of Alexandria
Paedagogus (1)
Stromateis (4)

Theophilus
Ad Autolycum (1)

Vincent of Lerins
Commonitorium (1)

Epistola Apostolorum (1)

Epiphanius
Haereses (15)

Ancaoratus (9)
Expositio Fidei (6)

Irenaeus
Adversus Haereses (74)
Demonstration of Apostolic
   Preaching (14)

Clement
1 Epistle (1)
2 Epistle (1)

Shepherd of Hermas (3)

Didache (1)

Hippolytus
Demonstratio de Christo et an-
   tichristo (1)
Commentarium in Danielem
   (4)
Apostolic tradition (1)

Gregory of Nyssa
In illud tunc ipse (1)
Oratio Catechetica (1)
Contra Eunomium (1)
De Hominis Opificio (1)
En at res (1) (Jaeger)

Socrates
Historia Ecclesiastica (2)

Anonymous
De Rebaptisme (1)

Apostolic Constitutions (1)

Novation
De Trinitate (1)

Basil
Epistola 113 (1)
Epistola 146 (1)
Epistola 203 (1)
Epistola 243(1)
Epistola 266 (1)
Epistola 69 (1)
Epistola 125 (1)
Epistola 263 (1)
Epistola 265 (1)
Epistola 125 (1)
Hexaemeron (1)
De Spiritu Sancti (5)

Justin Martyr
Dialogus cum Tryphone Ju-
   daeo (4)
1 Apology (1)
De Resurectione (1)

Ignatius
Ephesians (1)
Magnesians (2)
Trallians (2)
Smyrnans (6)
Ephesians (1)
Philadephians (1)

Basil
Epistola 236 (1)

Chapter 8: The Triunity of God (173 footnotes)

Encyclical Letter of Constantinople (1)

Basil
Epistola 111 (1)
Epistola 236 (4)

Epistola 131 (1)
Homilia 241 (1)
Homilia 231 (1)
Epistola 234 (1)
Epistola 235 (1)
Contra Eunomium (7)

Epistola 214 (2)
Epistola 210 (2)
Epistola 52 (2)
De Spirtu Sancto (19)
De Fide (2)
Epistola 8 (1)
Epistola 69 (1)
Epistola 125 (3)
Epistola 128 (1)
Epistola 140 (1)
Epistola 159 (1)
Epistola 204 (1)
Epistola 92 (1)
Epistola 52 (1)
Epistola 258 (1)

Ps. adver
Contra Sabellianos (1)

Theodoret
Historia Ecclesiastica (5)

Gregory of Nyssa
De Spiritu Sancto (1)
Contra Eunomium (1)
Adversus Macedonium (1)
Non tres dii (2)
Ex Communibus Notionibus (2)

Gregory/Basil
Epistola 38 (9)

Evagrius/Basil
Epistola 8 (2)

Athanasius
Contra Arianos (40)
Ad Afros (5)
De Synodis (8)
Contra Gentes (3)
De Incarnatione (1)
De Decretis (2)
In Illud Omnia (3)

Contra Apollinarem (2)
Ad Antiochenos (4)
Expositio Fidei (2)
De Decretis (4)
De Incarnatione et Contra Arianos (1)
Ad Serapionem (49)
De Fuga (1)
De Sententia Dionysii (3)

Cyril of Alexandria
Dialogi de Trinitate (3)
Thesauruas de Sancta et Consubstantiali Trinitate (5)
In Joannem (3)
Contra Nestorium (2)
De Sacrosanta Trinitate (1)
De Adoratione (1)

John of Damascus
De Fide Orthodoxa (1)

Ps. Dionysius
De Divinis Nominibus (2)
De Mystica Theologia (1)

Gregory Nazianzen
Oratione 6 (1)
Oratione 1 (2)
Oratione 2 (1)
Oratione 20 (1)
Oratione 4 (1)
Epistola 58 (1)
Oratione 43 (1)
Oratione 31 (14)
Oratione 23 (3)
Oratione 42 (3)
Oratione 12 (1)
Oratione 29 (4)
Oratione 40 (8)
Oratione 42 (2)
Oratione 2 (1)
Oratione 25 (2)

Oratione 26 (1)

Oratione 36 (1)

Oratione 29 (4)

Epistola 58 (1)

Oratione 38 (1)

Oratione 19 (1)

Oratione 30 (4)

Oratione 32 (1)

Oratione 33 (1)

Oratione 34 (4)

Oratione 42 (4)

Oratione 20 (1)

Oratione 45 (3)

Oratione 38 (1)

Oratione 6 (1)

Oratione 25 (1)

Oratione 43 (1)

Oratione 31 (3)

Oratione 39 (5)

Oratione 21 (1)

Hilary

De Trinitate (4)

Didymus

De Spiritu Sancto (13)

De Trinitate (27)

Contra Eunomium (6)

Epiphanius

Ancaoratus (25)

Haereses (78)

Expositio Fidei (5)

Ref. Aet. (from Haereses) (8)

Hippolytus

Apostolic Tradition (1)

Bibliography

Abraham, William J. *The Logic of Renewal*. Grand Rapids: Eerdmans, 2003.

Anatolios, Khaled. *Athanasius: The Coherence of His Thought*. New York: Routledge, 2004.

———. *Retrieving Nicaea: The Development and Meaning of Trinitarian Doctrine*. Grand Rapids: Baker Academic, 2011.

ΑΠΟΣΤΟΛΙΚΗΣ ΔΙΑΚΟΝΙΑΣ ΤΗΣ ΕΚΚΛΗΣΙΑΣ ΤΗΣ ΕΛΛΑΔΟΣ. ΒΙΒΛΙΟΘΗΚΗ ΕΛΛΗΩΝ ΠΑΤΕΡΩΝ ΚΑΙ ΕΚΚΛΗΣΙΚΩΝ ΕΥΓΓΡΑΦΕΩΝ. ΑΘΝΑΙ: 1955FF.

Arnold, Duane. *The Early Episcopal Career of Athanasius of Alexandria*. Notre Dame: University of Notre Dame Press, 1991.

Athanasius, Saint, Patriarch of Alexandria. *Works on the Spirit PPS43*. Edited by John Behr. Translated by Mark DelCogliano, Andrew Radde-Gallwitz, and Lewis Ayres. Crestwood, NY: St. Vladimir's Seminary Press, 2011.

Ayres, Lewis. *Augustine and the Trinity*. Cambridge: Cambridge University Press, 2010.

———. *Nicaea and Its Legacy*. Oxford: Oxford University Press, 2004.

Backus, Irena. *Historical Method and Confessional Identity in the Era of the Reformation (1378–1615)*. Leiden: Brill, 2003.

———. *The Reception of the Church Fathers in the West: From the Carolingians to the Maurists*. Leiden: Brill, 2001.

Baker, Matthew and Todd Speidell, eds. *T. F. Torrance and Eastern Orthodoxy*. Eugene, OR: Wipf & Stock (forthcoming 2015).

———. "The Eternal 'Spirit of the Son': Barth, Florovsky and Torrance on the Filioque." *International Journal of Systematic Theology* 12/4 (October 2010) 382–403.

———. "The Place of St. Irenaeus of Lyons in Historical and Dogmatic Theology According to Thomas F. Torrance." *Participatio: The Journal of the Thomas F. Torrance Theological Fellowship* 2 (2010) 5–43.

Barnes, Michel René. "Rereading Augustine's Theology of the Trinity." In *The Trinity: An Interdisciplinary Symposium on the Trinity*, edited by Stephen T. Davis, Daniel Kendall, and Gerald O'Collins, 145–78. New York: Oxford University Press, 1999.

Barr, James. *Semantics of Biblical Language*. Oxford: Oxford University Press, 1961.

Barth, Karl. *Church Dogmatics*. Edited by T. F. Torrance. Edinburgh: T. & T. Clark, 1957ff.

———. *The Epistle to the Romans*. Translated by Edwyn Clement Hoskyns. London: Oxford University Press, 1933.

———. *Evangelical Theology*. Translated by Grover Foley. Edinburgh: T. & T. Clark, 1979.

———. *Humanity of God*. Translated by Thomas Wieser and John Newton Thomas. Louisville: Westminster/John Knox, 1999.

———. *Der Römerbrief*. Munich: Kaiser, 1922.

Bathrellos, Demetrios. "The Sinlessness of Jesus: A Theological Exploration in the Light of Trinitarian Theology." In *Trinitarian Soundings in Systematic Theology*, edited by Paul Metzger, 113–36. London: T. & T. Clark, 2005.

Bebbington, David. *Evangelicalism in Modern Britain*. Oxford: Routledge, 1989.

Behr, John. "Calling upon God as Father: Augustine and the Legacy of Nicaea." In *Orthodox Readings of Augustine*, edited by Aristotle Papanikolaou and George E. Demacopoulos, 153–65. Crestwood, NY: St. Vladimir's Seminary Press, 2008.

———. "Introduction." In *Saint Athanasius the Great: On the Incarnation: (Greek/ English) PPS44a*, translated and edited by John Behr, 19–49. Crestwood, NY: St. Vladimir's Seminary Press, 2012.

———. *The Mystery of Christ: Life in Death*. Crestwood, NY: St. Vladimir's Seminary Press, 2006.

———. *The Nicene Faith: Part I*. Crestwood, NY: St. Vladimir's Seminary Press, 2004.

———. *The Nicene Faith: Part II*. Crestwood, NY: St. Vladimir's Seminary Press, 2004.

———. Review of *Divine Meaning: Studies in Patristic Hermeneutics*, by T. F. Torrance. *St. Vladimir's Theological Quarterly* 42/1 (January 1, 1998) 104–8.

———. *The Way to Nicaea*. Crestwood, NY: St. Vladimir's Seminary Press, 2001.

Berkhof, Louis. *Systematic Theology*. Rev. ed. Grand Rapids: Eerdmans, 1996.

Biemer, Gunter. *Newman on Tradition*. Berlin: Herder and Herder, 1967.

Billings, J. Todd. *Union with Christ: Reframing Theology and Ministry for the Church*. Grand Rapids: Baker Academic, 2012.

Bougerol, Jacques-Guy. "The Church Fathers and the *Sentences* of Peter Lombard." In *The Reception of the Church Fathers in the West: From the Carolingians to the Maurists*, edited by Irena Backus, 113–64. Leiden: Brill, 2001.

Breen, Tom. "More Americans Join Orthodox Christian Churches." *USA Today*, January 11, 2007. http://usatoday30.usatoday.com/news/religion/2007-01-11 orthodox_x.htm.

Bromiley, Geoffrey W. "Promise of Patristic Studies." In *Toward a Theology for the Future*, edited by David F. Wells, and Clark H. Pinnock, 125–56. Carol Stream, IL: Creation, 1971.

Byasee, Jason. "Emerging From What, Going Where? Emerging Churches and Ancient Christianity." In *Ancient Faith for the Church's Future*, edited by Mark Husbands and Jeffrey P. Greenman, 249–63. Downers Grove, IL: InterVarsity, 2008.

Calvin, John. *Institutes of the Christian Religion*. Translated by John Thomas McNeill and Ford Lewis Battles. Philadelphia: Westminster, 1960.

Campbell, J. McLeod. *The Nature of the Atonement*. Rev. ed. Grand Rapids: Eerdmans, 1996.

Canlis, Julie. *Calvin's Ladder: A Spiritual Theology of Ascent and Ascension*. Grand Rapids: Eerdmans, 2010.

Carroll, Colleen. *The New Faithful: Why Young Adults Are Embracing Christian Orthodoxy*. Chicago: Loyola, 2002.

Carson, D. A. *Becoming Conversant with the Emerging Church: Understanding a Movement and Its Implications*. Grand Rapids: Zondervan, 2005.

Chadwick, Henry. *Tradition and Exploration: Collected Papers on Theology and the Church*. Norwich: Canterbury, 1994.

Claiborne, Shane. *Irresistible Revolution: Living as an Ordinary Radical.* Grand Rapids: Zondervan, 2006.

Clapp, Rodney. *Border Crossings: Christian Trespasses on Popular Culture and Public Affairs.* Grand Rapids: Brazos, 2000.

Colliander, Tito. *Way of the Ascetics: The Ancient Tradition of Discipline and Inner Growth.* Crestwood, NY: St. Vladimir's Seminary Press, 1985.

Colyer, Elmer. *How to Read T. F. Torrance: Understanding His Trinitarian and Scientific Theology.* Downers Grove, IL: InterVarsity, 2001.

Copan, Paul. Review of *The Christian Doctrine of God: One Being Three Persons,* by T. F. Torrance. *Trinity Journal* 18/2 (Fall 1997) 245–49.

Cunningham, Mary Kathleen. "Karl Barth." In *Christian Theologies of Scripture: A Comparative Introduction,* edited by Justin Holcomb, 183–201. New York: New York University Press, 2006.

Cutsinger, James S. *Reclaiming the Great Tradition: Evangelicals, Catholics and Orthodox in Dialogue.* Downers Grove, IL: InterVarsity, 1997.

Daley, Brian E. "The Church Fathers." In *The Cambridge Companion to John Henry Newman,* edited by Ian Ker and Terrence Merrigan, 29–46. Cambridge: Cambridge University Press, 2009.

D'Costa, Gavin. "The Impossibility of a Pluralist View of Religions." *Religious Studies* 32/2 (1996) 223–32.

Davis, Leo D. *The First Seven Ecumenical Councils, 325–787: Their History and Theology.* Wilmington, DE: Michael Glazier, 1992.

Davis, Stephen T., Daniel Kendall, and Gerald O'Collins, eds. *The Trinity: An Interdisciplinary Symposium on the Trinity.* Oxford: Oxford University Press, 1999.

Dawson, Gerrit. *An Introduction to Torrance Theology: Discovering the Incarnate Saviour.* New York: T. & T. Clark, 2007.

Denny, James. *The Christian Doctrine of Reconciliation.* London: Hodder and Stoughton, 1917.

Dragas, George. "The Eternal Son." In *The Incarnation: Ecumenical Studies in the Nicene-Constantinopolitan Creed,* edited by Thomas F. Torrance, 16–57. Edinburgh: Handsel, 1981.

———. "Interview Regarding T. F. Torrance." *Participatio: The Journal of the Thomas F. Torrance Theological Fellowship* 4 (2013) 30–46.

———. *Saint Athanasius of Alexandria: Original Research and New Perspectives.* Rollinsford, NH: Orthodox Research Institute, 2005.

———. "The Significance for the Church of Professor Torrance's Election As Moderator of the General Assembly of the Church of Scotland." *ΕΚΚΛΗΣΙΑΣΤΙΚΟΣ ΦΑΡΟΣ* 58/3–4 (1976) 214–31.

———. "St. Athanasius Contra Apollinarem." PhD thesis, University of Durham, 1985.

Eerdman, Chris. "Digging Up the Past: Karl Barth (the Reformed Giant) as Friend to the Emerging Church." In *An Emergent Manifesto of Hope,* edited by Doug Pagitt and Tony Jones, 242. Grand Rapids: Baker, 2007.

Elders, Leo J. "Thomas Aquinas and the Fathers of the Church." In *The Reception of the Church Fathers in the West: From the Carolingians to the Maurists,* edited by Irena Backus, 337–66. Leiden: Brill, 2001.

Ernest, James. *The Bible in Athanasius of Alexandria.* Boston: Brill Academic, 2004.

Fairbairn, Donald. *Grace and Christology in the Early Church.* Oxford: Oxford University Press, 2003.

————. "Patristic Soteriology: Three Trajectories." *Journal of the Evangelical Theological Society* 50/2 (June 1, 2007) 289–310.

Farrow, Douglas. "T. F. Torrance and the Latin Heresy." *First Things* (December 2013) 25–31.

Fergusson, David F. "The Ascension: Its Significance in the Theology of T. F. Torrance." *Participatio: The Journal of the Thomas F. Torrance Theological Fellowship* 3 (2012) 92–107.

————. *Bultmann*. Outstanding Christian Thinkers. London: Chapman, 1992.

Florovsky, Georges. *Aspects of Church History*. Collected Works of Georges Florovsky 4. Belmont, MA: Nordland, 1975.

————. *Bible, Church, Tradition: An Eastern Orthodox View*. Collected Works of Georges Florovsky 1. Belmont, MA: Nordland, 1972.

————. *Creation and Redemption*. Belmont, MA: Nordland, 1976.

Flynn, Gabriel, and P. D. Murray. *Ressourcement: A Movement for Renewal in Twentieth-Century Catholic Theology*. Oxford: Oxford University Press, 2012.

Foster, Richard J. *Celebration of Discipline: The Path to Spiritual Growth*. New York: HarperCollins, 1998.

Gillquist, Peter E. *Becoming Orthodox: A Journey to the Ancient Christian Faith*. Ben Lomond, CA: Conciliar, 1992.

———— , ed. *Coming Home*. Ben Lomond, CA: Conciliar, 2006.

Gregg, Robert, and Dennis Groh. *Early Arianism: A View of Salvation*. London: SCM, 1981.

Griffith, Howard. "High Priest in Heaven: The Intercession of the Exalted Christ in Reformed Theology, Analysis and Critique." Ph.D. diss., Westminster Theological Seminary, 2004.

Grillmeier, Alois. *Christ in Christian Tradition*. Atlanta: John Knox, 1975.

Gudziak, Borys. "Towards an Analysis of the Neo-Patristic Synthesis of Georges Florovsky." *Logos* 41 (2001) 197–238.

Gunton, Colin. *Father, Son, and Holy Spirit: Essays Toward a Fully Trinitarian Theology*. London: T. & T. Clark, 2003.

————. *Promise of Trinitarian Theology*. London: T. & T. Clark , 2003.

Gwatkin, Henry Melville. *Studies of Arianism: Chiefly Referring to the Character and Chronology of the Reaction Which Followed the Council of Nicaea*. Cambridge: D. Bell, 1882.

Habets, Myk. "Reformed *Theosis*? A Response to Gannon Murphy." *Theology Today* 65 (2009) 489–98.

————. *Theosis in the Theology of Thomas Torrance*. Farnham, UK: Ashgate, 2009.

Habets, Myk, and Bobby Grow, eds. *Evangelical Calvinism: Essays Resourcing the Continuing Reformation of the Church*. Eugene, OR: Wipf & Stock, 2012.

Hall, Christopher A. *Learning Theology with the Church Fathers*. Downers Grove, IL: InterVarsity Academic, 2002.

————. *Reading Scripture with the Church Fathers*. Downers Grove, IL: InterVarsity Academic, 1998.

Hanson, R. P. C. *The Search for the Christian Doctrine of God: The Arian Controversy, 318–381*. London: T. & T. Clark, 1988.

Harnack, Adolf von. *History of Dogma*. London: Williams & Norgate, 1894.

————. *What Is Christianity?* New York: Putnam's, 1901.

Harnack, Adolf von, and Theodor Mommsen. *Die Griechischen Christlichen Schriftsteller Der Ersten Drei Jahrhunderte.* Berlin: Deutsche Akademie, 1891.

Harper, Michael. *The True Light: An Evangelical's Journey to Orthodoxy.* London: Hodder & Stoughton, 1997.

Hart, David Bentley. "'The Hidden and Manifest: Metaphysics After Nicaea." In *Orthodox Readings of Augustine*, edited by Aristotle Papanikolaou and George E. Demacopoulos, 191–226. Crestwood, NY: St. Vladimirs Seminary Press, 2008.

Hart, Trevor. *Christ in Our Place.* Milton Keynes, UK: Paternoster, 1989.

Hennessy, Kristin. "An Answer to de Régnon's Accusers: Why We Should Not Speak of 'His' Paradigm." *Harvard Theological Review* 100 (2007) 179–97.

Holcomb, Justin. *Theologies of Scripture: A Comparative Introduction.* New York: New York University Press, 2006.

Holmes, Stephen R. *The Holy Trinity: Understanding God's Life.* Milton Keynes, UK: Paternoster, 2011.

———. *Listening to the Past: The Place of Tradition in Theology.* Grand Rapids: Baker Academic, 2003.

Howard, Thomas. *Evangelical Is Not Enough: Worship of God in Liturgy and Sacrament.* San Francisco: Ignatius, 1984.

———. *Lead, Kindly Light: My Journey to Rome.* San Francisco: Ignatius, 2004.

Hunsinger, George. "5 Picks: Essential Theology Books of the Past 25 Years." *Christian Century* 127/21 (October 19, 2010) 38.

Husbands, Mark, and Jeffrey P. Greenman, eds. *Ancient Faith for the Church's Future.* Downers Grove, IL: InterVarsity Academic, 2008.

Jones, Tony. *The Sacred Way: Spiritual Practices for Everyday Life.* Grand Rapids: Zondervan, 2005.

Kelly, J. N. D. *Early Christian Doctrines.* London: A. & C. Black, 1958.

Kerr, Fergus. *After Aquinas: Versions of Thomism.* Oxford: Blackwell, 2002.

———. *Twentieth-Century Catholic Theologians: From Neoscholasticism to Nuptial Mysticism.* Malden, MA: Blackwell, 2007.

Kilby, Karen. "Aquinas, the Trinity, and the Limits of Understanding." *International Journal of Systematic Theology* 7/4 (October 2005) 414–27.

Kimball, Dan. *The Emerging Church: Vintage Christianity for New Generations.* Grand Rapids: Zondervan, 2003.

King, Benjamin. *Newman and the Alexandrian Fathers: Shaping Doctrine in Nineteenth-Century England.* Oxford: Oxford University Press, 2009.

Lampe, G. W. H., eds. *A Patristic Greek Lexicon.* London: Oxford University Press, 1969.

Lane, Anthony N. S. *John Calvin: Student of Church Fathers.* London: T. & T. Clark, 1999.

Lossky, Vladimir. *The Mystical Theology of the Eastern Church.* Crestwood, NY: St. Vladimir's Seminary Press, 1976.

Louth, Andrew. *St. John Damascene: Tradition and Originality in Byzantine Theology.* Oxford: Oxford University Press, 2002.

MacIntyre, Alasdair. *After Virtue: A Study in Moral Theory.* Notre Dame: University of Notre Dame Press, 2007.

Mackintosh, H. R. *The Divine Initiative.* London: SCM, 1921.

———. *The Person of Jesus Christ.* Edinburgh: T. & T. Clark, 1912.

MacLean, Stanley S. *Resurrection, Apocalypse, and the Kingdom of Christ: The Eschatology of Thomas F. Torrance.* Eugene, OR: Wipf & Stock, 2012.

Makarios. *Early Fathers from the Philokalia: Together with Some Writings of St. Abba Dorotheus, St. Isaac of Syria, and St. Gregory Palamas.* Edited and translated by E. Kadloubovkys and G. E. H. Palmer. London: Faber & Faber, 1954.

McCormack, Bruce. "The End of Reformed Theology? The Voice of Karl Barth in the Doctrinal Chaos of the Present." In *Reformed Theology: Identity and Ecumenicity*, edited by Wallace M. Alston Jr. and Michael Welker, 46–64. Grand Rapids: Eerdmans, 2003.

———. "Grace and Being: The Role of God's Gracious Election in Karl Barth's Theological Ontology." In *The Cambridge Companion to Karl Barth*, edited by John Webster, 92–110. Cambridge: Cambridge University Press, 2000.

McGrath, Alister E. *Iustitia Dei: A History of the Christian Doctrine of Justification.* Cambridge: Cambridge University Press, 2005.

———. *T. F. Torrance: An Intellectual Biography.* Edinburgh: T. & T. Clark, 1999.

———. "Trinitarian Theology." In *Where Shall My Wond'ring Soul Begin? The Landscape of Evangelical Piety and Thought*, edited by Mark A. Noll and Ronald F. Thiemann, 51–60. Grand Rapids: Eerdmans, 2000.

McGuckin, John Anthony. *St. Cyril of Alexandria: The Christological Controversy Its History, Theology, and Texts.* Crestwood, NY: St. Vladimir's Seminary Press, 2004.

McKnight, Scot. "Five Streams of the Emerging Church: Key Elements of the Most Controversial and Misunderstood Movement in the Church Today." *Christianity Today*, January 19, 2007. http://www.christianitytoday.com/ct/2007/february/11.35.html.

McLaren, Brian D. *A Generous Orthodoxy: Why I Am a Missional, Evangelical, Post/Protestant, Liberal/Conservative, Mystical/Poetic, Biblical, Charismatic/Contemplative, Fundamentalist/Calvinist, Anabaptist/Anglican, Methodist, Catholic, Green, Incarnational, Depressed-Yet-Hopeful, Emergent, Unfinished Christian.* Grand Rapids: Zondervan, 2004.

———. *Why Did Jesus, Moses, the Buddha, and Mohammed Cross the Road? Christian Identity in a Multi-Faith World.* New York: Jericho, 2012.

Meijering, E. P. "The Fathers in Calvinist Orthodoxy: Systematic Theology." In *The Reception of the Church Fathers in the West: From the Carolingians to the Maurists*, edited by Irena Backus, 867–87. Leiden: Brill, 2001.

———. *God Being History: Studies in Patristic Philosophy.* New York: American Elsevier, 1975.

Metropolitan Philip. "Metropolitan Philip's Address to the 48th Archdiocesian Council." *The Word* 51/7 (September 2007) 36.

Meyendorff, Jean. *Byzantine Theology: Historical Trends and Doctrinal Themes.* London: Mowbrays, 1974.

———. *Christ in Eastern Christian Thought.* Crestwood, NY: St. Vladimir's Seminary Press, 1975.

———, ed. *Grégoire Palamas: Défense des saints hésychastes: Introducion, texte critique, traduction et notes.* Louvain: Spicilegium Sacrum Lovaniense, 1959.

———. "Introduction." In *Gregory Palamas: The Triads*, translated by Nicholas Grendle, 1–22. New York: Paulist, 1983.

———. *Introduction A l'étude de Grégoire Palamas.* Paris: Patristica Sorbonensia, 1959.

Migne, J. P. *Patrologia Cursus Completus Series Graeca.* 165 vols. Paris: 1857–1886.

———. *Patrologia Cursus Completus Series Latina.* 217 vols. Paris: 1844–1864.

Molnar, Paul. *Thomas F. Torrance: Theologian of the Trinity.* Farnham, UK: Ashgate, 2009.

Morrison, John D. Review of *The Trinitarian Faith: The Evangelical Theology of the Ancient Catholic Church*, by T. F. Torrance. *Journal of the Evangelical Theological Society* 35/1 (March 1, 1992) 117–19.

Murphy, Gannon. "Reformed *Theosis?*" *Theology Today* 65 (2008) 191–212.

Newman, John Henry. *Apologia Pro Vita Sua.* London: Catholic Book Club, 1946.

———. *The Arians of the Fourth Century.* London: E. Lumley, 1871.

———. *An Essay in Aid of a Grammar of Assent.* London: Burns, Oates, 1870.

———. *An Essay on the Development of Christian Doctrine.* London: Longman's, Green, 1909.

———. *Lectures on the Prophetical Office of the Church, Viewed Relatively to Romanism and Popular Protestantism.* Oxford: J. H. Parker Oxford, 1837.

Noble, T. A. *Holy Trinity: Holy People: The Theology of Christian Perfecting.* Eugene: Wipf & Stock, 2013.

———. "T. F. Torrance on the Centenary of His Birth: A Biological and Theological Synopsis With Some Personal Reminiscences." *Participatio: The Journal of the Thomas F. Torrance Theological Fellowship* 4 (2013) 8–29.

———. *Tyndale House and Fellowship: The First Sixty Years.* Nottingham: InterVarsity, 2006.

Oden, Thomas C. *Agenda for Theology.* Grand Rapids: Zondervan, 1992.

———. *Classic Christianity: A Systematic Theology.* 3 vols. New York: HarperCollins, 2009.

———, ed. *Justification Reader.* Grand Rapids: Eerdmans, 2002.

———. *Pastoral Theology: Essentials of Ministry.* New York: HarperCollins, 1983.

———. *The Rebirth of Orthodoxy: Signs of New Life in Christianity.* New York: HarperCollins, 2003.

———. *Requiem: A Lament in Three Movements.* Nashville: Abingdon, 1995.

Olson, Roger E., and Christopher A. Hall. *The Trinity.* Grand Rapids: Eerdmans, 2002.

Orr, James *The Progress of Dogma.* London: Hodder & Stoughton, 1901.

Oort, Johannes van. "John Calvin and the Church Fathers." In *The Reception of the Church Fathers in the West: From the Carolingians to the Maurists*, edited by Irena Backus, 661–700. Leiden: Brill, 2001.

Pagitt, Doug, and Tony Jones, eds. *An Emergent Manifesto of Hope.* Grand Rapids: Baker, 2007.

Palamas, Gregory. *Gregory Palamas: The Triads.* Edited by Jean Meyendorff. Translated by Nicholas Grendle. New York Paulist, 1983.

Palmer, G. E. H., Philip Sherrard, and Kallistos Ware, trans. *The Philokalia: The Complete Text Compiled by St. Nikodimos of the Holy Mountain and St. Markarios of Corinth.* 4 vols. London: Faber & Faber, 1983.

Papanikolaou, Aristotle, and George E. Demacopoulos. "Augustine and the Orthodox: The 'West' in the East." In *Orthodox Readings of Augustine*, edited by Aristotle Papanikolaou and George E. Demacopoulos, 11–40. Crestwood, NY: St. Vladimir's Seminary Press, 2008.

Parvis, Sara. *Marcellus of Ancyra and the Lost Years of the Arian Controversy, 325–345.* Oxford: Oxford University Press, 2006.

Prestige, G. L. *God in Patristic Thought.* London: SPCK, 1952.

Purves, Andrew. *Reconstructing Pastoral Theology: A Christological Foundation.* Louisville: Westminster/John Knox, 2004.

Quantin, Jean-Louis. "The Fathers in Seventeenth Century Anglican Theology." In *The Reception of the Church Fathers in the West: From the Carolingians to the Maurists,* edited by Irena Backus, 987–1008. Leiden: Brill, 2001.

———. "The Fathers in Seventeenth Century Roman Catholic Theology." In *The Reception of the Church Fathers in the West: From the Carolingians to the Maurists,* edited by Irena Backus, 951–86. Leiden: Brill, 2001.

Quasten, Johannes. *Patrology.* 5 vols. Notre Dame: Ave Maria, 2000.

Radcliff, Alexandra. "Sanctification: Words for the Weary." *Theology in Scotland* 20/2 (Autumn 2013) 45–52.

Radcliff, Jason. "A Reformed Asceticism." *Theology in Scotland* 20/1 (Spring 2013) 43–56.

———. Review of *Union with Christ: Reframing Theology and Ministry for the Church,* by J. Todd Billings. *Theology in Scotland* 19/2 (Autumn 2012) 81–83.

———. "T. F. Torrance and the Patristic Consensus on the Doctrine of the Trinity." In *The Doctrine of the Holy Trinity Revisited: Essays in Response to Stephen R. Holmes,* edited by T. A. Noble and J. S. Sexton. Milton Keynes, UK: Paternoster (forthcoming 2015).

———. "T. F. Torrance in Light of Stephen Holmes's Critique of Contemporary Trinitarian Thought." *Evangelical Quarterly* 86/1 (January 2014) 21–38.

———. "T. F. Torrance's Trinitarian Theology: Review of *T. F. Torrance: Theologian of the Trinity,* by Paul D. Molnar." *The Expository Times* 122/10 (June 22, 2011) 512–513.

———. "Thomas F. Torrance's Conception of the Consensus Patrum on the Doctrine of Pneumatology." In *Studia Patristica LXIX,* edited by Markus Vincent and Allen Brent, 417–33. Leuven: Peeters, 2013.

———. "The Vicarious Humanity of Christ as the Basis of Christian Spirituality." In *Evangelical Calvinism, Volume II,* edited by Myk Habets and Bobby Grow. Eugene, OR: Pickwick (forthcoming 2016).

Rahner, Karl. *The Trinity.* Danvers, MA: Crossroad, 1997.

Rankin, Duncan. "Carnal Union with Christ in the Theology of T. F. Torrance." PhD diss., University of Edinburgh, 1997.

Reid, J. K. S. "The Office of Christ in Predestination." *Scottish Journal of Theology* 1/1 (1948) 5–19.

Régnon, Théodore de. *Études de théologie positive sur la Sainte Trinité.* Paris: Retaux, 1898.

Rist, John M. *Augustine: Ancient Thought Baptized.* Cambridge: Cambridge University Press, 1994.

Roberts, Alexander, James Donaldson, and Philip Schaff, and Henry Wace, eds. *The Ante-Nicene Fathers.* Peabody, MA: Hendrickson, 1994.

———. *Nicene and Post-Nicene Fathers: Series I.* 14 vols. Peabody, MA: Hendrickson, 1994.

———. *Nicene and Post-Nicene Fathers: Series II.* 14 vols. Peabody, MA: Hendrickson, 1994.

Roldanus, Johannes. *Le Christ Et L'homme Dans La Théologie d'Athanase d'Alexandrie.* Leiden: Brill, 1968.

Romanides, John. *The Ancestral Sin.* Ridgewood, NJ: Zephyr, 2008.

————. *Franks, Romans, Feudalism, and Doctrine: An Interplay Between Theology and Society*. Patriarch Athenagoras Memorial Lectures. Brookline, MA: Holy Cross Orthodox Press, 1981.

————. *An Outline of Orthodox Patristic Dogmatics*. Rollinsford, NH: Orthodox Research Institute, 2004.

Rossum, Joost Van. "Creation-Theology in Gregory Palamas and Theophanes of Nicaea, Compatible or Incompatible?" In *Studia Patristica LXIX*, edited by Markus Vincent and Allen Brent, 373–78. Leuven: Peeters, 2013.

Sauve, Ross Joseph. "Georges V. Florovsky and Vladimir N. Lossky: An Exploration, Comparison and Demonstration of Their Unique Approaches to the Neopatristic Synthesis." PhD diss., University of Durham, 2010.

Scandrett, Joel. "The Robert E. Webber Center." *Seed and Harvest: Trinity School for Ministry* 35/3 (Summer 2012) 6–8.

Schaff, Philip. *History of the Church: Reformation A.D. 1517–1530*. Edinburgh: T. & T. Clark, 1888.

Schulze, Manfred. "Martin Luther and the Church Fathers." In *The Reception of the Church Fathers in the West: From the Carolingians to the Maurists,* edited by Irena Backus, 573–626. Leiden: Brill, 2001.

Scott, Melville. *Athanasius on the Atonement*. Stafford, UK: Mort, 1914.

Serafim, N. *A Conversation of Saint Seraphim of Sarov with N. A. Motovilov: A Wonderful Revelation to the World*. Jordanville, NY: Holy Trinity Monastery, 1962.

Shapland, C. R. B. "Introduction." In *The Letters of Saint Athanasius Concerning the Holy Spirit,* translated by C. R. B. Shapland, 11–47. New York: Philosophical Library, 1951.

————, trans. *The Letters of Saint Athanasius Concerning the Holy Spirit*. New York: Philosophical Library, 1951.

Shepherd, Victor. "Thomas F. Torrance and the Homoousion of the Holy Spirit." *Participatio: The Journal of the Thomas F. Torrance Theological Fellowship* 3 (2012) 108–24.

Shriver, George. *Philip Schaff: Christian Scholar and Ecumenical Prophet*. Macon, GA: Mercer University Press, 2003.

Siecienski, Edward. *The Filioque: History of a Doctrinal Controversy*. Oxford: Oxford University Press, 2010.

Sinkewicz, Robert E. *Saint Gregory Palamas: The One Hundred and Fifty Chapters*. Toronto: Pontifical Institute of Mediaeval Studies, 1988.

Stein, Jock. "Introduction." In *Thomas F. Torrance Collected Studies, Volume I: Gospel, Church, and Ministry,* edited by Jock Stein, 1–24. Eugene, OR: Wipf & Stock, 2012.

Stewart, K. J. "Evangelicalism and Patristic Christianity: 1517 to the Present." *Evangelical Quarterly* 80 (2008) 307–21.

Sutton, Jonathan, and William Peter van den Bercken. *Orthodox Christianity and Contemporary Europe: Selected Papers of the International Conference Held at the University of Leeds, England, in June 2001*. Leuven: Peeters, 2003.

Swete, Henry Barclay. *The Holy Spirit in the Ancient Church: A Study of Christian Teaching in the Age of the Fathers*. London: Macmillan, 1912.

The Thomas F. Torrance Manuscript Collection. Special Collections, Princeton Theological Seminary Library.

Tickle, Phyllis. *Emergence Christianity: What It Is, Where It Is Going, and Why It Matters*. Grand Rapids: Baker, 2012.

——. *The Great Emergence: How Christianity Is Changing and Why.* Grand Rapids: Baker, 2012.

Torrance, Alan. *Persons in Communion: An Essay on Trinitarian Description and Human Participation, with Special Reference to Volume One of Karl Barth's Church Dogmatics.* Edinburgh: T. & T. Clark, 1996.

——. "Towards Inclusive Ministry: The Logical Impossibility of Religious and Theological Inclusivism, Pluralism and Relativism." In *The Call to Serve: Essays on Ministry in Honour of Bishop Penny Jamieson,* edited by Douglas A. Campbell, 256–68. Sheffield: Sheffield Academic Press, 1996.

Torrance, David W. "Recollections and Reflections." *Participatio: The Journal of the Thomas F. Torrance Theological Fellowship* 1 (2009) 26–34.

Torrance, Iain R. *Christology After Chalcedon.* Norwich: Canterbury, 1988.

Torrance, James B. "Strengths and Weaknesses of Westminster Theology." In *The Westminster Confession in the Church Today,* edited by Alasdair I. C. Heron, 40–54. Edinburgh: Saint Andrew, 1982.

Torrance, Thomas F. *Atonement: The Person and Work of Christ.* Edited by Robert T. Walker. Milton Keynes, UK: Paternoster, 2009.

——. *Calvin's Doctrine of Man.* London: Lutterworth, 1957.

——. *The Christian Doctrine of God: One Being Three Persons.* Edinburgh: T. & T. Clark, 1996.

——. *The Christian Frame of Mind.* Edinburgh: Handsel, 1980.

——. *Conflict and Agreement in the Church.* Vol. 1, *Order and Disorder.* London: Lutterworth Press, 1959.

——. *Conflict and Agreement in the Church.* Vol. 2, *The Ministry and the Sacraments of the Gospel.* London: Lutterworth, 1960.

——. *Divine and Contingent Order.* Edinburgh: T. & T. Clark, 1981.

——. *Divine Meaning: Studies in Patristic Hermeneutics.* London: T. & T. Clark, 1995.

——. *The Doctrine of Grace in the Apostolic Fathers.* Grand Rapids: Eerdmans, 1959.

——. *The Doctrine of Jesus Christ.* Reprint. Eugene, OR: Wipf & Stock, 2001.

——. *God and Rationality.* London: Oxford University Press, 1971.

——. *Gospel, Church, and Ministry.* Edited by Jock Stein. Eugene, OR: Wipf & Stock, 2012.

——. *The Hermeneutics of John Calvin.* Edinburgh: Scottish Academic Press, 1988.

——. *Incarnation: The Person and Life of Christ.* Edited by Robert T. Walker. Milton Keynes, UK: Paternoster, 2008.

——, ed. *The Incarnation: Ecumenical Studies in the Nicene Constantinopolitan Creed A.D. 381.* Edinburgh: Handsel, 1981.

——. "Introduction." In *The Mystery of the Lord's Supper: Sermons on the Sacrament Preached in the Kirk of Edinburgh by Robert Bruce in AD 1589,* edited by Thomas F. Torrance, 13–36. London: James Clarke, 1958.

——. "Introduction." In *The School of Faith: The Catechisms of the Reformed Church,* edited by Thomas F. Torrance, xi–cxxvi. Eugene, OR: Wipf & Stock, 1996.

——. *Karl Barth: An Introduction to His Early Theology, 1910–1931.* London: SCM Press, 1962.

——. "Karl Barth and the Latin Heresy." *Scottish Journal of Theology* 39/4 (January 1, 1986) 461–82.

——. *Karl Barth: Biblical and Evangelical Theologian.* Edinburgh: T. & T. Clark, 1990.

——. *The Mediation of Christ.* Colorado Springs: Helmers & Howard, 1992.

————. *Preaching Christ Today: The Gospel and Scientific Thinking.* Grand Rapids: Eerdmans, 1994.

————. *Reality and Evangelical Theology: The Realism of Christian Revelation.* Eugene, OR: Wipf & Stock, 1999.

————. *Reality and Scientific Theology.* Eugene, OR: Wipf & Stock, 2001.

————. *Royal Priesthood: A Theology of Ordained Ministry.* Edinburgh: T. & T. Clark, 1993.

————. *The School of Faith: The Catechisms of the Reformed Church.* Edited by Thomas F. Torrance. Eugene, OR: Wipf & Stock, 1996.

————. *Scottish Theology: From John Knox to John McLeod Campbell.* London: T. & T. Clark, 1996.

————. *Space, Time and Incarnation.* London: Oxford University Press, 1969.

————. *Space, Time and Resurrection.* London: T. & T. Clark, 1976.

————. *Theological Dialogue Between Orthodox and Reformed Churches Volume I.* Edinburgh: Scottish Academic Press, 1985.

————. *Theological Dialogue Between Orthodox and Reformed Churches Volume II.* Edinburgh: Scottish Academic Press, 1993.

————. *Theological Science.* London: T. & T. Clark, 1996.

————. *Theology in Reconciliation: Essays Towards Evangelical and Catholic Unity in East and West.* Eugene, OR: Wipf & Stock, 1996.

————. *Theology in Reconstruction.* Eugene, OR: Wipf & Stock, 1996.

————. *The Trinitarian Faith: The Evangelical Theology of the Ancient Catholic Church.* Edinburgh: T. & T. Clark, 1988.

————. *Trinitarian Perspectives: Toward Doctrinal Agreement.* London: T. & T. Clark, 1994.

Turretin, Frances. *Institutes of Elenctic Theology.* Edited by James T. Dennisor Jr. Translated by George Musgrave Giger. 3 vols. Darlington, UK: Evangelial, 2004.

Walker, Andrew, and Luke Bretherton, eds. *Remembering Our Future (Deep Church).* Milton Keynes, UK: Paternoster, 2007.

Walker, Robert T. "Incarnation and Atonement: Their Relation and Inter-Relation in the Theology of T. F. Torrance." *Participatio: The Journal of the Thomas F. Torrance Theological Fellowship* 3 (2012) 1–63.

————. "Recollections and Reflections." *Participatio: The Journal of the Thomas F. Torrance Theological Fellowship* 1 (2009) 39–48.

Webber, Robert E. *Ancient-Future Faith: Rethinking Evangelicalism for a Postmodern World.* Grand Rapids: Baker Academic, 1999.

————. *Ancient-Future Worship: Proclaiming and Enacting God's Narrative.* Grand Rapids: Baker, 2008.

————. *Planning Blended Worship: The Creative Mixture of Old and New.* Nashville: Abingdon, 1998.

————. *Younger Evangelicals, The: Facing the Challenges of the New World.* Grand Rapids: Baker, 2002.

Webber, Robert, and Donald G Bloesch. *The Orthodox Evangelicals: Who They Are and What They Are Saying.* Nashville: Nelson, 1978.

Webster, John. "Theologies of Retrieval." In *The Oxford Handbook of Systematic Theology*, edited by John Webster, Kathryn Tanner, and Iain Torrance, 583–99. Oxford: Oxford University Press, 2007.

Weinandy, Thomas. *In the Likeness of Sinful Flesh.* London: T. & T. Clark, 2005.

Wendebourg, Dorothea. "From the Cappadocian Fathers to Gregory Palamas: The Defeat of Trinitarian Theology." *Studia Patristica* 17/1 (1982) 194–99.

Wiles, Maurice. *Archetypal Heresy: Arianism Through the Centuries*. Oxford: Oxford University Press, 1996.

———. *The Making of Christian Doctrine: A Study in the Principles of Early Doctrinal Development*. Cambridge: Cambridge University Press, 1967.

Wilken, Robert L. Review of *Divine Meaning: Studies in Patristic Hermeneutics*, by T. F. Torrance. *Theological Studies* 57/4 (December 1, 1996) 743–44.

Williams, D. H. *Evangelicals and Tradition: The Formative Influence of the Early Church*. Grand Rapids: Baker Academic, 2005.

———. *Retrieving the Tradition and Renewing Evangelicalism: A Primer for Suspicious Protestants*. Grand Rapids: Eerdmans, 1999.

Wilson, Jonathan R. *Living Faithfully in a Fragmented World: Lessons for the Church from MacIntyre's "After Virtue."* London: T. & T. Clark, 1998.

Yannaras, Christos. *Orthodoxy and the West: Hellenic Self-Identity in the Modern Age*. Brookline, MA: Holy Cross Orthodox Press, 2006.

Zizioulas, Jean. *Being as Communion: Studies in Personhood and the Church*. Crestwood, NY: St. Vladimir's Seminary Press, 1985.

———. *Communion and Otherness: Further Studies in Personhood and the Church*. London: T. & T. Clark, 2006.

———. *Eucharist, Bishop, Church: The Unity of the Church in the Divine Eucharist and the Bishop During the First Three Centuries*. Translated by Elizabeth Theokritoff. Brookline, MA: Holy Cross Orthodox Press, 2001.

Index of Patristic Writers